Advanced Tactics
for
Bass and Trout

In Memory of Art Justice
given by
Mr. & Mrs. William Muehring & Family

Advanced Tactics
for
Bass and Trout

Jerry Gibbs

DRAWINGS BY ROBERT RITTER

Published by Outdoor Life Books
Distributed to the trade by Stackpole Books

For Greg & Jon

Copyright © 1987 by Jerry Gibbs

Published by
  Outdoor Life Books
  Grolier Book Clubs Inc.
  380 Madison Avenue
  New York, NY 10017

Distributed to the trade by
  Stackpole Books
  Cameron and Kelker Sts.
  Harrisburg, PA 17105

Library of Congress Cataloging-in-Publication Data

Gibbs, Jerry.
  Advanced tactics for bass and trout.

  Includes index.
  1. Bass fishing.   2. Trout fishing.   1. Title.
SH681.G48   1987   799.1'755   87-1734
ISBN 0-943822-99-8

Manufactured in the United States of America

Contents

Preface

This is not a book you want to sit down and read through in one or even a couple of sessions. It is a book with a great many techniques to explore, a multitude of tricks to try. In the pages that follow you'll find specialized fishing tactics honed to perfection by innovative anglers at the top of their game. Despite your past success with bass and trout, I'm betting that once you've experimented with these techniques and have them working right for you, you'll find your fishing success improving markedly.

If you consider yourself an expert in a particular fishing discipline, the knowledge is here to help you hone your skills in another, or encourage you to expand the horizons of your chosen method. Deep trollers, for instance, could benefit from interesting ways to use their equipment for surface fishing. And bass anglers who like short casting rods had better make room for the super new long rod techniques that can put a lure right on the platter in the places where trophy bigmouths like to dine.

It is said that a videotape is a good teaching aid because you can keep going back and learning from it. I think it's easier still to keep coming back to key tactics as they're collected right here. In short, I know this is a book from which you will continue to learn. I hope you'll agree and use it as a favorite reference for years to come.

JERRY GIBBS

Acknowledgements

Attempting to list all who helped in a book like this would invariably result in someone being left out. Those who were most directly involved, though, and the good ways they catch fish, are already mentioned in the text. So they won't be mentioned here.

Still, you might be interested in hearing about the kinds of people who contributed their knowledge so generously. That's easy. First are fishermen—specialists on different species, techniques, or geographic areas from California to Florida; and outside the U.S. from Canada to Japan to the British Isles.

Some of the fishermen are tournament professionals, others are guides, and a few of them are simply unsung yet creative anglers who quietly go about being the finest innovators that we have in the sport today.

Thanks must also go to innumerable scientists whose ever-questing research triggered questions and opened new arenas of fishing to explore.

The tackle industry, of course, gets special recognition. Without new inventions and continued advancements in technology—both in primary equipment and intriguing accessories—there would be no new tactics and techniques to write about.

J.G.

Advanced Tactics
for
Bass and Trout

chapter 1

Fishing with the Long Bass Rod

"Well, suh," declared the old river fisherman, "after studyin' on it for sometime, I conclude that the first difference between this here twelve-foot cane pole and what you fancy fellers call a fishin' rod, could be as much as a hundred and fifty dollars. . ."

With the regularity of seasonal cycles, tackle trends roar into high fashion for a time, then bow out of favor like a whipped 1920s Hollywood villain. Typically, it's the extremes that do a thing in. Either that, or new materials and designs come along that make out-of-vogue equipment again acceptable, perhaps even more functional than something at the height of popularity.

To get a good perspective, we need to look at what was happening to bass tackle back around 1821. A refinement of the heavy brass or crude wooden single-action reel used primarily to store line was about to result in a breakthrough of American angling technique. The new reels permitted bait or lure to be cast directly from the spool. Before then, a bass angler had to present his offering as canepole fishermen still do today.

The years of the middle 1800s have rightly taken their place as the golden era of the Kentucky baitcasting reel. The period saw production of a number of advanced multiplying reels painstakingly handmade, mostly by watchmakers. Though the delicate and easy-turning spools of these reels permitted direct casting from the spindles, it took a while for rods to catch up in design proficiency. The typical bass rod of the day consisted of 10 feet of jointed cane. A few were even as long as the salmon fly rods of that period—up to 15 feet in length and weighing as much as 1½ pounds. Compare that to some of today's modern bass rods that tip the scales at a mere 4 ounces.

In the 1870s, Dr. James Henshall, the dedicated angler today lauded for his classic *The Book of the Black Bass*, introduced a fishing rod which, although intended for bass, used as its role model the weight and balance of the American trout fly rod of the period. Obviously, in order to cast a minnow rather than a fly, the rod was a good bit stiffer. To remain within the weight range of a 10-foot trout fly rod, the denser Henshall model had to be shorter. It measured 8 feet, 3 inches.

As the Henshall rod gained acceptance, it was soon followed by even shorter models made by others. The shortest of all was the so-called Chicago rod of just 6 feet. Some anglers, including Henshall, felt the sporting qualities of so short a design were nonexistent. The Chicago rods required a sharp forward-casting motion rather than the sidearm sweep used previously with the longer rods. The technique was more suited to man-made lures just being introduced, rather than delicate natural baits.

The short-rod vogue continued through the 1970s to the very end of the decade when "modern" bass anglers began to use a technique that originated before the fine Kentucky reels even existed. With only the heavy, metal, single-action English or domestic wooden reels available to him, the bass angler of the early nineteenth century presented his minnow along weed edges or pockets by stripping a little line from his reel, holding the coils in his hand or laying them in the bottom of his wood-planked boat, and flipping the bait out with an easy underhand or sidearm motion. Sound familiar? It should—today's stridently popular flipping technique is an extremely effective method of presenting a lure or natural bait quietly and precisely to a small target area.

Because the 5½-foot casting rods so popular throughout the late 1960s and 1970s are definitely not the ideal flipping tool, modern fiberglass, graphite, boron, or composite rods specifically suited to the technique were engineered. The preferred length was 7½ feet. Anglers who regularly used the flipping rods began to discover other advantages; they could, in fact, be used as casting instruments. Then, in 1982, when Paul Elias won the prestigeous B.A.S.S. Masters Classic tournament using a 7½-foot flipping rod, more fishermen began to take notice. Elias had not just been flipping jigs with his long rod. One trick he used was to cast a deep-diving crankplug, then thrust the rod deep into the water as he retrieved the lure. It caused the plug to run 4 or 5 feet lower—enough to reach bass that other fishermen were passing by.

Then, with Rick Clunn's unprecedented third-time win of the B.A.S.S. Classic on the Arkansas River out of Pine Bluff in 1984, recreational fishermen really began to take notice. Clunn used a 7-foot, two-handed rod with much more flexible parabolic action than the flippin' type stick. Rather than high-tech graphite or boron, it was simple fiberglass. The reason made sense: He was using the rods to pitch and retrieve billed crankbaits at high speeds. When a bass hit, the rod tip would bow under the strike, yet still maintain enough forward resistance to help set the hooks. With a faster, stiffer, high-content graphite rod, Clunn, and others like him, have found that they would rip the lure from a bass's mouth before the hooks were firmly set. Of course, the greater rod length also permits Rick to thrust the tip underwater to send his plug running deeper. The tournament pro still prefers graphite material for his shorter, stiffer worm rods.

Anglers who have begun using the longer blanks once again are realizing some other advantages. A longer blank will help you to quickly eliminate any slack line when you go to set the hook. You'll then gain increased leverage that will enable you to set the hook harder and easier. The result, naturally, is fewer missed fish. After hooking up, if you keep the pressure on, you'll find that it's also easier to slide a fish in one continuous movement away from heavy cover, and to steer it where you want it to go. When jigging, you'll be able to move a spoon or jig over a greater distance without cranking in or letting out line with the reel. A longer rod will also help you cast farther—especially with heavier lures—to reach schooling fish or to cover a greater bottom area on one retrieve. And that brings us to something else.

A generation of anglers has grown up thinking that all bass rods must be 5 to 5½ feet long and come equipped with handles that look like the grip of a .45 caliber revolver. The longer rods under discussion have a straight grip. Many of them have handles long enough to grip with both your hands, thus allowing you to make longer casts. Still, because the rods are made of modern synthetics, they are light enough for short to medium-length one-handed casts or for the various types of flipping.

There's also the strength factor to consider. Until recently, only better quality straight-grip rods employed the so-called blank-through-handle construction. This means the rod blank extends right under the reel seat and into the handle. With the advent of graphite-filled reel seats, you gain both increased strength and greater sensitivity. Light-tackle saltwater enthusiasts and steelhead/salmon drift fishermen have been using straight grip rods all along, but the majority of other freshwater anglers abandoned the design when the pistol grip handles became so popular.

Flipping rods are fairly stiff overall, and have plenty of butt strength. The design is excellent for handling leadhead jigs and spoons with various trailers or sweeteners, such as porkrind or plastic action tails, to be flipped into pockets or around close-range cover. The rods are necessarily stiff to move fish and keep them from the extremely thick cover that surrounds the target opening. Flipping type rods are also good for long casts and

certain other presentations which will be covered shortly. They are not the ultimate tool for high-speed crankbaits, as Rick Clunn so aptly proved with his "tippier" rods, nor are they best for casting lighter lures. Rodmakers are again producing longer rods in more flexible actions, however. No doubt they'll be available for some time. Despite all this praise for long rods, I favor shorter rods when using a baitcasting (revolving spool) reel, or at least a rod with a one-handed grip for spinner bait fishing and for "crawling" plastic worms by raising the rod tip. With spinning equipment I can go either way, but tend to favor a shorter stick.

Some of the current crop of longer one or two-handed grip rods are made with triggers. Gripped by the index finger on the underside of the handle, triggers were standard for years on so-called saltwater popping rods. They were and are used to fish for a variety of species with plugs or jigs. Flexible tip models can even be used for presenting delicate natural baits, mainly for red drum and spotted seatrout. Some anglers feel that triggers help greatly when hands are cold, wet, and slippery from handling fish in inclement weather.

As longer, straight-grip rods became popular again, the triggers seemed to go with them. Early on I kind of liked the triggers. I'm indifferent about them now, and become downright against them when I try packing a lot of rods in one rod case before a trip. Triggers may be of metal or graphite. If you find you dislike them, the metal ones are handily bent off with a pair of pliers, while the graphite variety can be sawed off, filed, and sanded smooth.

Those who feel they want or need triggers can easily fashion the devices, as does ardent West Coast angler Jim Hendricks. Jim obtains a piece of appropriately strong, preferably rust-resistant metal from a home building supply store, cuts it to size, and bends it into the proper configuration, making one arm longer to facilitate being fastened to the rod. The trigger is filed smooth and attached to the rod blank with heat-shrink tubing.

With or without triggers, the long rods with straight grips (especially the two-handed style) have other advantages. They easily fit into vertical or horizontal rod holders of all types, including stowage holders, trolling holders, and downrigger holders. In short, when you're not casting, the same rods can sometimes substitute as freshwater trolling tools.

Ray Easley, who has the second biggest largemouth on record, lands a bass with his long, two-handed rod while fishing with the author on California's Lake Casitas. Easely favors the long rod for casting large plugs long distances.

Long rods are effective in fishing live bait such as shiners, enabling the angler to work the bait into difficult spots and to cast with greater ease and accuracy.

With the longer straight-grip rods, you can toss bait or lure using the standard workhorse overhand cast. If you're using this method for a whole day's fishing, you'll be far less fatigued when evening rolls around if you cast with two hands. However, the rods also lend themselves well to achieving a quiet entry of your lure and pinpoint accuracy—the advantages of standard flipping. To obtain minimum entry noise, the lure's trajectory should be as low as possible to the water's surface. That effectively eliminates the overhand cast. The pinpoint accuracy achieved in standard flipping is a function of very close range. You control the line either by stripping out a specific length, or by disciplining the line that is shot out with your non-rod hand. More than anything, it most closely approaches flyfishing or simple canepole fishing—both of which are related to flipping and can claim accuracy and gentle presentation as just one of their many advantages.

The long rod presentations which will follow may be made with your baitcasting reel in freespool with line either stripped off, or cast out directly from the spool. With monofilament stripped off and laid at your feet or held in coils in your hand or your lips like fly line, you gain extreme lure speed with far less effort, plus low and flat trajectory. In most presentations, line stripped off the reel must be controlled by the non-rod hand both during the cast and as it shoots out. You therefore lose the ability to cast two-handed. You should practice both stripped line and off-the-reel methods to find which one is more comfortable. I suspect that you may settle on a combination as I have. Let me explain.

Whenever I'm drifting or slowly motoring my boat along a shoreline, I'm constantly hunting for and casting to a multitude of objects to which

Doug Hannon uses a long, straight-grip rod for flipping worms. By stripping off monofilament line and holding it in your hand or mouth (or laying it at your feet), you can gain lure speed with little effort and cast the lure in a low, flat trajectory.

Wading in heavy weeds, Rich Reinert flips spinnerbaits or worms into pockets with deadly accuracy using a long, straight-grip rod.

a fish may relate. I could be using the normal flipping method, having stripped enough line off my reel to achieve a desired distance or depth. As a right-hander, I hold the free monofilament in my left hand, just like a fly line. Using the long rod in my right hand, I swing the lure underhand and flip it the short distance to an open pocket while my left hand controls the line as it shoots out for a gentle landing on target. If I suddenly find some wonderful looking back-cut, stump, rock, or weedline break that is either deep under tree overhangs or farther away, I'll go into one of the other forms of lure presentation. The one to use at any particular time often depends on how much line is already stripped from my reel, or how quickly I need to make the presentation before the boat moves away (or how soon my partner can get there, if we're competing for fun). Being skillful in a variety of presentations and able to cast stripped line or line directly from the reel will give you the versatility to handle most situations as they come up. Not every time, of course; if you could perform with total perfection at all times, you would not be human.

Two-hand Side Circle Cast

This cast is one of the easiest to master, assuming you are already competent with baitcasting spool reels. (With the obvious changes in grip needed, this and other presentations can be adapted to spinning equipment.) You can either face the target head-on, or align it with your non-rod shoulder (your left shoulder if you're a right-hander). Hold your rod parallel to the water at waist level. The grip is similar to a golf club style grip, but not quite as choking as when holding a baseball bat. The lure should hang several inches below the tip. Now bring your rod back to the side, making a small circular motion with your rod tip. The power of this cast comes from the force generated by your wrists, which first causes rod flex, then creates a fulcrum against it. The lure is released in flight as the rod tip reaches the bottom of its circular travel. It is important to come out and up with your rod once the lure is on its way. This maneuver helps control the flight of the lure, keeping trajectory low, but allows for some lift to permit a soft entry.

In most cases you'll be casting the line directly from the spool. If so, proper thumbing is necessary to prevent overruns. However, for a quick, very straight firing of the lure beneath obstructions, you can use the stripped line technique. If you're right-handed, hold line on the spool with your right thumb. Put the reel into freespool, pull off a few inches of line, and pinch it with the middle finger of your right hand against the grip just behind the reel. At this point, the lure is hanging the proper distance

TWO-HAND SIDE CIRCLE CAST

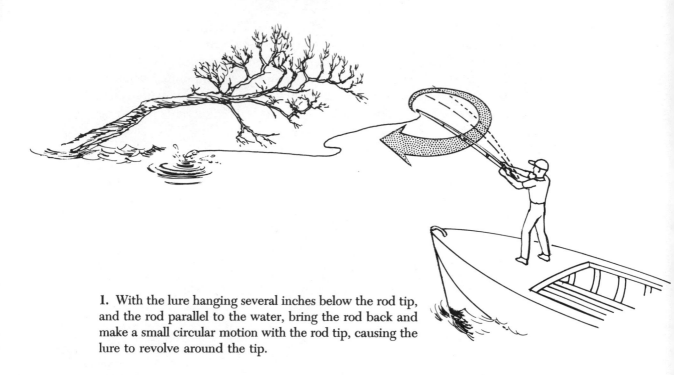

1. With the lure hanging several inches below the rod tip, and the rod parallel to the water, bring the rod back and make a small circular motion with the rod tip, causing the lure to revolve around the tip.

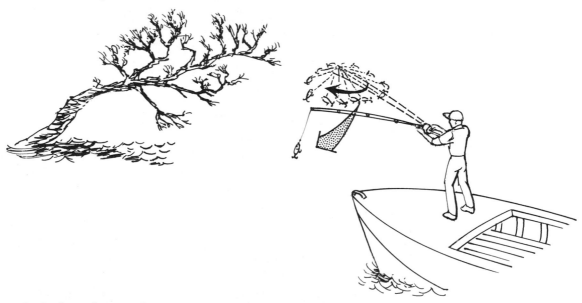

2. As the rod tip reaches the bottom of its circular travel, release the lure. Follow the lure's flight with your rod tip, raising the rod slightly.

below the rod tip. With line closest to the lure now locked against the grip, begin stripping off the desired length of line with your left hand, letting it fall to your feet or holding coils between your lips.

For the cast, you can use a two-handed grip, releasing the line from beneath your middle finger at the completion of the little circular motion with your rod tip. You can also make it a one-hand cast, taking the line from beneath your middle finger with the left hand and controlling its shooting flight with that hand, as in standard flipping. The most difficult thing in strip-line casting is learning to judge just how much line you need to strip from the reel. The best way is to estimate your distance to target, then establish some known distance against which to strip line. For example, the distance from your reel to the first guide on your rod may be 2 feet.

If you elect to try shooting the stripped line, then letting the momentum of the cast come up against the freespool to pull out more line, practice it in a non-fishing situation first. The lure will be traveling extremely fast with virtually no friction and, if you misjudge thumb pressure when the stripped line comes suddenly tight, you can encourage a nasty backlash rather quickly. Because this cast is powerful, your best bet is to make it either directly from the spool or to shoot just the amount of line you've initially stripped.

This cast is easily performed with the stiff flipping rod or a more flexible long rod with lighter line and lure. Anglers who first try this cast sometimes do not release early enough and find the lure shooting alarmingly up into the sky. It's like the straight, no-circle sidearm lob of a beginner who fails to release the lure early enough and finds it sailing off to the side instead of straight ahead—much to the disgust of the angler at the left who finds his neighbor's plug crashing down just where he'd planned to throw his own lure.

You don't need a lot of arm effort or rod waving to execute this cast. Wrists and rod do it all most efficiently. The cast can be used for getting the lure beneath some obstruction, far back beneath a dock, or the far underside of a bridge. You can also use it on open water. When properly done it's an efficient, effortless presentation.

Up-down Loop Cast

This cast is best performed with a fairly stiff rod—either the flipping type stick or one a little softer. After you've become competent, learn to use it with your more flexible rods and lighter lures. The idea behind this short-range cast, or flip, is to send the lure out beneath low-slung tree limbs, footbridges, boat houses, or piers. The lure will land lightly because it does not fall from as great a height as in the standard overhand cast. It's also handy if you've been making standard close-range flips and want to reach a target a little farther away without moving the boat closer for fear of spooking fish, then discover your fishing compadre is so near that the side circle cast would whack him.

Before you ever try this cast, turn down any anti-backlash controls on your reel. You want your reel as free-turning as possible. Face your target with your rod in front of you, reel in freespool mode. Let the lure hang between 2½ and 3 feet below the rod tip, or whichever distance is most comfortable for you. Now easily raise your rod tip so the lure begins a pendulum-like swing in toward you. As it does, lower the rod tip just slightly past waist level, and in one continuous movement come back up with the rod tip to just above waist level.

Here's what should happen as you do these things. As you drop your rod, the lure that was swinging in toward you and the rod now begins swinging down and out. As your rod tip comes up again, the lure is encouraged to continue around and out in a looping circle.

The finale is when you release the lure as it finishes making a complete circle and is attempting to climb on up and make another circle. Release too late, and you get another skybuster; too early, and the bait goes crashing to the water surface. Properly done, the lure sails out straight

UP-DOWN LOOP CAST

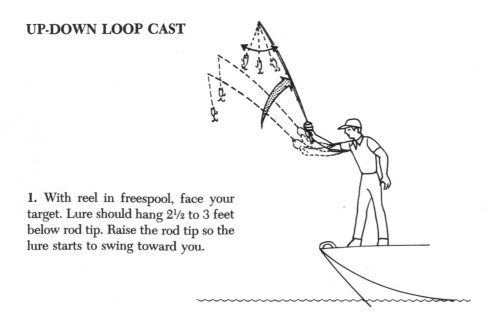

1. With reel in freespool, face your target. Lure should hang 2½ to 3 feet below rod tip. Raise the rod tip so the lure starts to swing toward you.

2. Lower rod to waist, angled slightly down so the lure swings out.

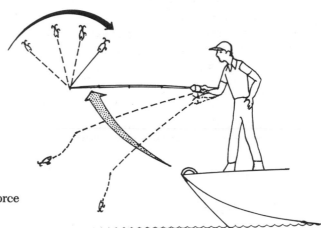

3. Raise the rod tip with some force so the lure describes a circle.

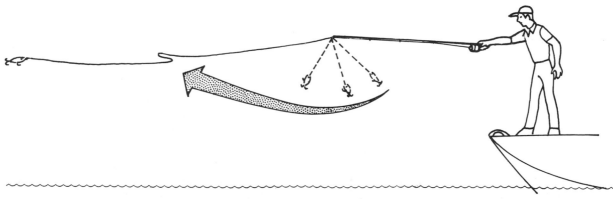

4. As the lure reaches the bottom of the circle, extend your casting arm and let the lure fly. Control the spool with your thumb, and raise the rod tip slightly while the lure is in flight.

and drops lightly as you carefully thumb the spool (remember, all cast controls are at zero). As in all casts where you want the lure to drop lightly, it helps to slightly raise your rod tip while the lure is in flight.

You can use the strip line technique here, too. Just pinch the line with the middle finger of your right hand while stripping off line. When you're ready to cast, take the line in your left hand, keeping it from shooting until you've made the circle. This cast lends itself to either one or two-handed technique from the reel, or one-handed when working with stripped line. Because you're not casting for distance with this presentation, one-handed style may be just as efficient.

The farther your lure hangs from the rod tip as you initiate the cast, the more momentum will be generated (for greater distance) as the lure circles. Be careful, though. Let too much line out, and your lure will smack the water's surface or crash into the side of the boat or bank as it comes around. With a short length of line out, you'll have to release the lure sooner.

The movements required for this cast are somewhat reminiscent of the up-down motion of the standard underhand cast using a stiff 5 to 5½-foot bass rod. That cast always began bothering my wrist if I did it long enough, but then I don't have wrists like Ted Williams or Wade Boggs. The longer rod makes underhand casting a lot easier, for sure.

Catapult Cast

This one is a takeoff from the old bow-and-arrow-cast, when you pull the lure back and bow the rod like a slingshot. In this case, however, it's an underhand presentation. Using it with a long rod lets you obtain all that stored energy in the tip and mid-section without having to turn the rod into an inverted U.

All you have to do to send your lure under low brush or up some culvert is face the target, letting the lure drop from the rod tip to the reel, with the reel in freespool. Lower your rod tip. Now grab either the hind hooks of the lure or the line just ahead of the lure. Raise your rod hand parallel to the water and extend it out toward the target. Point the tip toward the target, but then start pulling the lure back with the non-rod hand. Just get enough pullback so rod tip and middle are bending. Then release the lure with a quick, wide spreading of your fingers to avoid any chance of hooking yourself. The lure will shoot out on a low trajectory because the rod tip was down to begin with. Raise the rod slightly to follow through for a soft lure landing.

Obviously, this is a one-handed cast, but you can use it as an off-the-

CATAPULT CAST

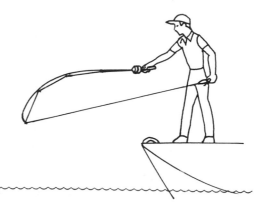

1. With the reel in freespool, pull the lure down to the handle and apply thumb pressure. Carefully grasping hook, pull lure back so rod tip is bowed. Keep rod arm straight.

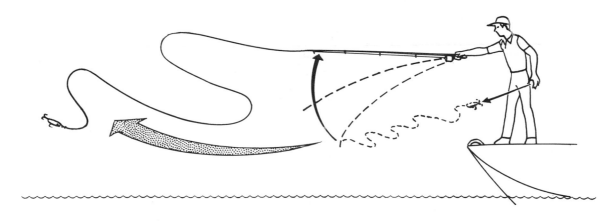

2. Release thumb pressure, pointing the rod tip toward the target. Raise the rod tip slightly to ensure a soft delivery.

spool, stripped-line presentation. If you choose the latter, use the same method for pinching the line to the grip. With this cast, though, you can get the kind of eye-popping backlash you never want to see again if you don't check the line with your thumb when the slack stripped line comes up tight. Casts are safer if the line comes directly from the spool, but overruns are still possible if you don't exercise thumb control.

Long Distance Flipping

Though you can use any of the longer rods, the stiffer flipping stick is best—especially if your lure is heavier than normal. The method will send your lure a long, long way, flying low and with super accuracy to land gently way back in those shallows where you'd spook fish by using an overhand cast or by trying to creep a boat in.

It's really standard flipping, but with all the monofilament you think you can handle stripped off. I like to start with my lure hanging almost to the lower rod grip. Put the reel into freespool and pinch off the line as you did before, using the middle finger of your rod hand just behind the reel on the grip. Now begin stripping off line. It helps to drop the first few strips to your feet, then take the next few between your lips. You can leave those coils there for the cast (they'll shoot free), or you can take the coils from your lips with your off-rod hand. Take the line with your free hand from its locked position beneath your rod-hand finger. Raise the rod, allowing the lure to swing back, then power down and forward with your rod, swinging the lure out low and straight. Release the line from your free hand as the lure begins shooting out. It's very simple and, if used faithfully, will put more fish on your hook.

The stress on these casts to tight cover is not meant to detract from the overhand cast. As mentioned earlier, the overhand is the workhorse presentation, very well suited to long rods and the two-handed grip when distance is important. There are also some very interesting retrieve techniques that are used with the overhand cast. They are especially effective, and sometimes a lot easier with longer or straight-grip, two-handed rods.

Instant Retrieve

This technique actually starts as the cast is in progress. I once called it the switch-hand technique, but the term is not completely descriptive because left-handed anglers never had to switch hands, and now more revolving spool reels are being offered with the handle on whichever side of the frame you desire. Previously, a right-handed angler had to make his cast, then place the rod in his left hand to crank because the reel handle was always on the right side of the reel frame.

As your lure is airborne toward a target, or simply reaching for distance, you must carefully track it to accurately judge its pending moment of impact with the water's surface. An instant before it lands, turn the handle to engage the reel gears. The result is that there is not a second's pause when the lure hits. Instead of a forceful landing, the lure skims the surface, continuing to move forward in one motion. It's a simple presentation but one that proves very effective when fish are not terribly aggressive. Instead of giving them time to get a good look at your lure, then trying to entice them with a fleeing retrieve, you're giving them a one-punch treatment—the illusion of terrified retreat. It's a presentation designed to trigger a response rather than to coax or convince. So are the others that follow.

Ripping

This method has been used off and on over the years, but each new generation of bass anglers has to discover its effectiveness through use. Sometimes even veteran anglers need to be reminded of the technique. Like some of the others to follow, the method can be tiring. As with other triggering techniques, ripping is most effective when fish are not falling for standard retrieves.

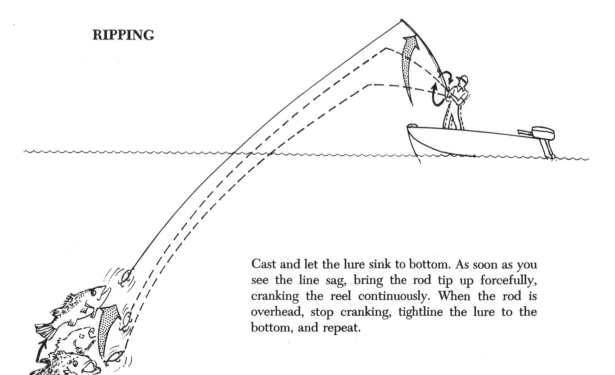

RIPPING

Cast and let the lure sink to bottom. As soon as you see the line sag, bring the rod tip up forcefully, cranking the reel continuously. When the rod is overhead, stop cranking, tightline the lure to the bottom, and repeat.

Ripping is best performed with a leadhead jig and plastic teaser action tail, tailspin type lure (leadhead and spinner blade), or jigging spoon. You can also use spinnerbaits or straight in-line shaft spinners. A few thin plugs have been specially designed for it. Some anglers prefer to use a big, striped bass-oriented spinning reel for ripping, in order to eke out a little extra lure speed. The long rod really helps.

The technique is a very good one whenever you're casting far, bringing the lure back a long distance. It's at its best in fairly deep water. What you do is cast and let the lure sink to the bottom. As soon as you see your line sag, take a turn or two with your reel handle to get out slack while lowering your rod tip toward the water. Now come back up hard and fast as though you were setting the hook into something with steel jaws. All the while you're doing this, crank your reel like a buzz saw. You'll be able to feel your lure vibrating madly as it leaps from the bottom. At the top of your rod movement—which can be just about overhead—stop reeling. Tightline the lure slowly down again, allowing no slack—unless, of course, a fish has grabbed on. Repeat these movements several times.

You'll have to learn not to raise your rod quite so high as the lure closes in on the boat, and also just when to stop this retrieve. It only takes a few times to judge when your lure has reached the point where the next rip will send it flying from the water high overhead to land on the backside of the boat.

Unlike many other retrieves, during which fish tend to hit the lure mainly as it's dropping, ripping can produce strikes both on the ascent or the drop.

Stroking

While ripping is generally performed in deep water, stroking is a technique for medium to shallow depths. It's also generally done with plugs—floater-divers or deeper diving crankbaits. Again, the longer rod permits you to move the lure faster and over more territory in one stroke. There are several variations on the stroking theme.

The first is faster, more violent and similar to ripping, but you use a sidearm movement. Cast a diving plug, take out slack, then pull the plug hard through the water with a side sweep of your arms and body, causing it to dig down and vibrate. As soon as you reach the limit of your sweep, move your rod tip back to the starting position, reeling fast all the while to allow no slack. Again, jerk the plug and return to the starting position. Try alternating long sweeps with shorter jerks.

The strike usually occurs as the crankbait is moving forward, but can

STROKING (I)

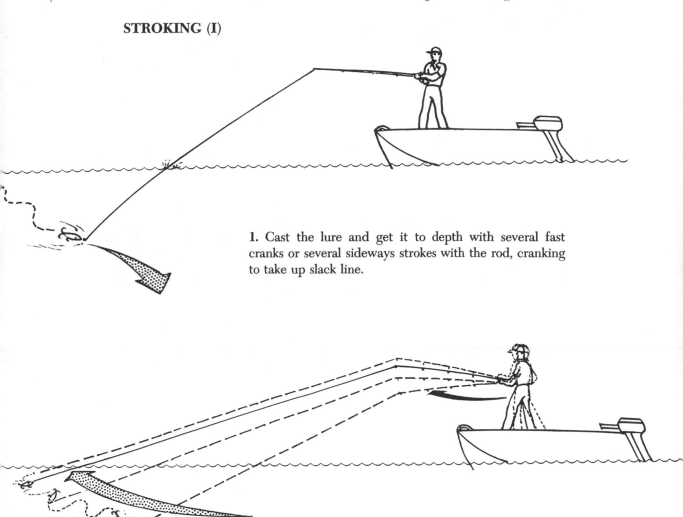

1. Cast the lure and get it to depth with several fast cranks or several sideways strokes with the rod, cranking to take up slack line.

2. Pivot body sideways, sweeping the rod to the side and causing the lure to dig down and vibrate. When you've reached the limit of your sweep, move rod tip back to starting position, reeling fast to take up slack.

come on the pauses. With a big-lipped diving plug, the lure tends to suspend in place once it reaches its maximum depth. The floater-diver plugs (like the original Rapala) try to rise at the end of each sweep unless you reel up fast enough so they never have the chance.

The second stroking version is more of a finesse technique. You get the

STROKING (II)

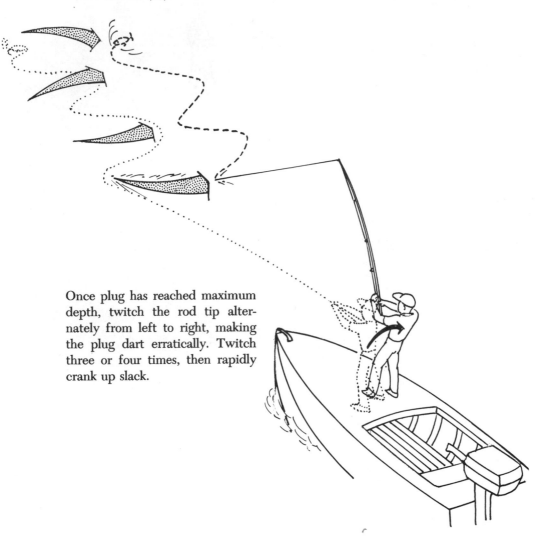

Once plug has reached maximum depth, twitch the rod tip alternately from left to right, making the plug dart erratically. Twitch three or four times, then rapidly crank up slack.

plug down to its maximum running depth with some fast cranks. Once the bait is down, commence a continual series of short, gentle twitches. Do not stop. You can twitch the rod tip continually in one direction—the direction in which you started the lure—or alternately twitch the rod tip to the right and then to the left. Make a series of three or four twitches before you instantly crank up slack. Alternate with one or two twitches while cranking the reel to keep out all slack.

You can also work the rod in an overhead position, popping it once the plug is at depth, then reeling in slack without a pause. It helps greatly to

SUBTLE STROKING (III)

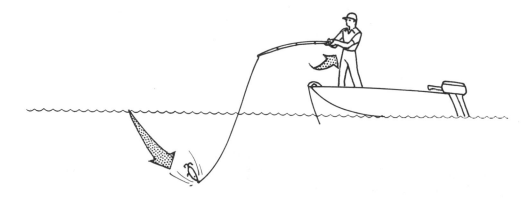

1. Bring plug to depth by cranking the reel handle rapidly.

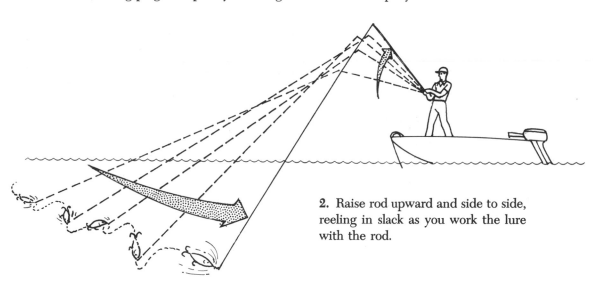

2. Raise rod upward and side to side, reeling in slack as you work the lure with the rod.

think of the lure as one being worked on the surface, even though it may be 5 to 10 feet deep. If you know how to work a Zara Spook or chugger-type lure on top, you're on your way. But stroking is a whole lot harder on your arms, wrists, and shoulders. Do it for a couple of hours and you'll know you've been working. Rebel Spoonbills and Rapala Shad Raps are just two of the good diving plugs that lend themselves to the technique.

Though stroking can be productive at any time of year, it's especially good during the pre-spawn period in early spring before bass have moved shallow. Try it on steep drops and off points. Work it later in summer along weedlines and near timber. When cool weather returns, again try the steeper dropping areas of your lake. The method brings up bass, walleyes, and other species from depths a lot greater than those at which the plug is working. And if wind has been blowing onto a point, chances are it has pushed baitfish there. Put your back to the breeze, cast your plug, and start stroking.

Twitch and Twist

Here's another retrieve that triggers fish into striking through sudden explosive movement of the lure. The method calls for a floater-diver plug or any of the popular surface baits—poppers, chuggers, stick baits, and propeller plugs. It's a sure bet to excite fish that have followed a lure without striking. There are a couple of good ways to perform this retrieve.

After casting to your target, let the plug sit a few seconds. Lower the rod tip to horizontal, pointing it at the plug. Now crank the reel handle until slack is out and the reel handle is at the top of its circular travel position. Now pop your rod tip up or slightly to the side and, at the same time, come down sharply on the reel handle. You make a 180° crank of the handle. The two movements will cause your lure to make a noisy power dive that often turns looking fish into biting fish. Repeated several times, it can call in more distant fish.

A variation on this method is to begin retrieving the lure in the normal fashion: twitching your rod tip and making the lure pop, gurgle, and sputter as it was designed to do. Then suddenly add the twitch and twist. The illusion is of a bait that finally realizes a predator is on its trail, with salvation lying in vacating the territory. You can also try making the plug take a direction change each time you add the twitch and twist. Sharp, sudden changes in direction often trigger strikes in commonly used retrieves as well.

The method is a good one whenever conditions warrant using surface lures. It can elicit strikes when the surface is a little rougher than you'd like for normal, less violent topwater retrieves. The extra rod length adds a little something to the dive when you pop a plug during the twitch and twist.

You can use the preceding retrieves with a shorter rod, but they're performed much more efficiently with longer models. I believe longer rods and the straight, two-handed grip with their many advantages will be with us for some time—unless radical extremes force their demise.

TWITCH AND TWIST

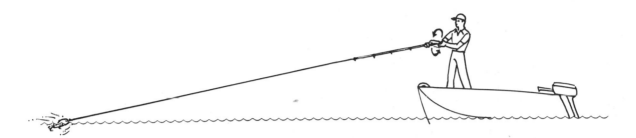

1. After casting to target, lower the rod tip and point it at the lure. Take up slack, stopping the reel handle at the top of its arc.

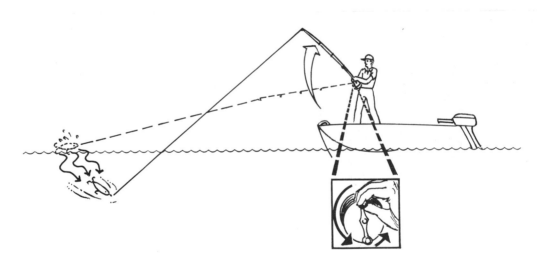

2. Pop rod tip up and turn reel handle down. This causes the lure to dive noisily. Repeat several times.

chapter 2

Fishing with
The Short Bass Rod

"Any bass rod over five-and-one-half feet must be compared with a vaulter's pole. Catapulting for the sky is not the object here; getting your lure to the fish, is. The only thing that impresses the bass is something they can eat."

—GILL JENNING, *former Yankee fly fisherman following an extended stay in the Southeast.*

Despite my mild passion for many long rod designs, I am quite happy that the short rod is not about to go away. In conventional casting and spinning styles, there's no question that one-handed rods are functional tools for specific assignments. In many cases the short stick serves very well for a fast, rather aggressive fishing style. It is an excellent design for tight quarters where medium-distance casts are the rule.

Before today's modern materials and design, short casting rods generally featured offset handles. The design was traditionally suspect in the area of strength, especially among muskie enthusiasts whose endless casting with huge plugs often was more than the design could take. Sometimes these rods would not collapse until a big muskellunge was being fought—which was even worse. Though stronger than the older, acutely offset design, even the one-hand pistol grip style handle was inherently weaker than a straight one-piece shaft because the rod blank ended just inside the handle ahead of the reel seat. Rod blanks needed to be beefed up.

Beginning in 1984, however, the results of work by a few custom builders began catching on with mass rod makers. The new design features a pistol grip through which the entire blank runs, just as it does in most long, two-handed rods. It not only increases strength, but also results in

Short rods are ideal for working up creeks and back into swamps where long rods would be ineffective except for flipping.

far less weight and improved sensitivity. There's no need to build up the rod blank where it enters the handle, and no need for chucks or other fittings to adapt the blank to the handle. No filler material is built up between rod blank and handle to deaden telltale strike vibrations. On some models, the handle is actually the rod blank itself, with an opening that holds the reel. The reel feet slide right into the blank.

One complaint I had with some pistol grip handles was that the flare at the butt end sometimes curved a little too sharply so that my little finger crammed up against my third finger. At the end of a hard day's casting, an irritation or a blister sometimes resulted. I solved the problem simply by sanding or grinding off the offending flare. The result may not look quite as racy as the flare, but I'm willing to trade it for a more rounded butt end for comfort.

Over the years I've come to prefer shorter casting rods for most spinnerbait fishing and some plastic worm fishing. I like short spinning rods for ultralight plugs and tiny jigs. Several aggressive cast-retrieve techniques that require basic competency with spinning and baitcasting equipment lend themselves well to short, fairly stiff rods and tight cover.

Two of the techniques call for mastery of a fast sidearm cast, which can be accomplished with the straight back-and-forth movement or the sidearm circle cast.

Bank Skimmer

The sidearm type cast is necessary in this situation in order to present your lure as close to the bank as possible. A standard overhand cast will not do the job if the bank has any overhang at all, or if any cover extends from the bank down toward the water. You can bet that bass will take advantage of the slightest underwater indentation in the bank formed by above-surface overhang.

The Bank Skimmer is used most commonly with a spinnerbait or jig type lure. First, fire the lure on a low, straight trajectory up under the cover or bank lip. If you've mastered the Instant Retrieve from the preceding chapter, you'll already have your reel engaged (bail closed if you're using spinning equipment) when the lure smacks the surface.

Just as soon as the lure gets wet, rear back with your rod and move the lure as fast as possible while still keeping it beneath the surface. At the end of your rod sweep, allow the lure to drop for just one second before retrieving as usual.

This presentation, as others, is aimed at triggering reflex strikes. The illusion is of a baitfish tearing madly from the bank, then slowing down in

BANK SKIMMER

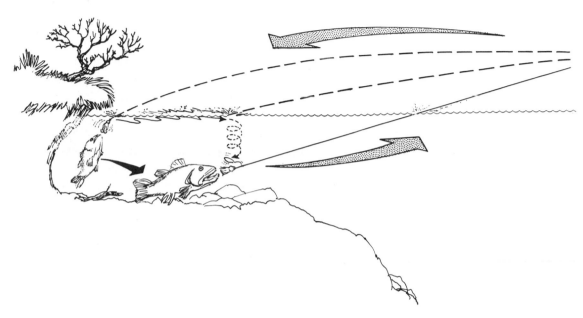

Cast the lure sidearm, low and straight, under an overhanging bank. As soon as the lure hits the water, engage your reel, rear back with your rod, and move the lure swiftly beneath the surface. At the end of your sweep, allow the lure to drop for a second and then retrieve.

the mistaken belief that it has somehow reached safety. The quick skim away from the bank is a sure bet to awaken any daydreaming largemouth. When the bass sees such easy pickings fluttering down toward the bottom, it generally finds the lure all but impossible to resist.

Skipping

This other short-rod technique also calls for a side type cast. A few top bass anglers prefer a longer rod for another form of skipping (which will be covered later), but most prefer to employ skipping as short-range technique. It's easier to learn the skip with spinning equipment because you do not run the risk of a monumental backlash. The rod should be stiff in any event. The method involves a Texas-rigged plastic worm with either a sliding or pegged sinker no heavier than $3/16$ ounce.

The whole point of skipping is to get the worm beneath objects such as trees with branches or roots that jut out, almost touching the water surface, and to put it there extra softly. Another prime cover type for skipping worms consists of near-shore jackstraws of fallen trees extending into the water. Skipping can also be used to reach in under docks or boathouses, but flipping sometimes works here, too, unless we're talking about a situation where the water surface is just a few inches beneath the dock, or the boathouse has some kind of door or canvas closure that leaves a low opening at the entranceway.

Here's how it works with the sliding sinker. Make your side cast, aiming so the slip sinker will hit exactly at the cover overhang. When the sinker clips the water surface, it will stop short and begin dropping. The worm will simultaneously skim across the water, pulling line through the sinker if you feed it out.

SKIPPING WITH SLIDING SINKER

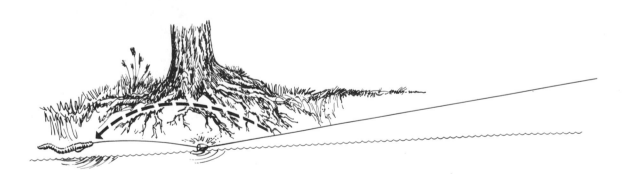

This cast gets a Texas-rigged worm beneath overhanging tree branches or roots. Cast sidearm so sinker hits exactly at edge of overhang. The sinker stops short, worm continues, pulling line through the sinker.

The technique is easier to learn with spinning tackle. With a casting reel, the worm will not skip far if there's too much resistance. On the other hand, too little thumb control will entertain a backlash.

The distance that the worm will travel depends on how much energy was in the cast. If the cast is made with a quick, wrist-snapping movement that quickly transmits that energy through your short, stiff rod, the worm should travel 6 to 8 feet. You can see the importance of a side cast in which the worm is moving on a parallel course to the surface. An overhand cast would only cause the lure to sink once the weight hits water. The shorter your cast, the farther the worm will skip because it has more momentum at the point at which the sinker hits the water. There is much less forward velocity at the end of a longer cast; thus the worm will slide only a few feet out past the sinker. Therefore, you should sneak your boat to within 15 to 20 feet of the cover beneath which you plan to skip. With no weight next to it, the skipped worm will descend slowly and enticingly—often to be grabbed before it hits the bottom.

Skipping with a sliding sinker also has its place for getting a plastic worm into clear, shallow water where a direct hit by a sinker would spook any bass holding there. Normally I'd prefer to use a long spinning rod and no weight for this purpose but, if I were working along with a normal rig and wasn't set up with the long rod, skipping could work.

Remember that after the worm is skipped and is some distance away from the sinker, it is in a free-fall state. Very little effort is required for a fish to inhale it. You need to concentrate on the slightest line twitch or faint tap that will indicate a strike. If no strike occurs on the drop, begin retrieving in the usual manner, using the rod to impart movement in the worm.

There's no time to play games once you stick a bass—especially a big one—back in or under all that cover. Don't strike by coming up high overhead with your arms. Remember how the worm went back in there? That's how you have to strike: sideways and parallel to the water; almost a reverse of the cast. The overhead hook set will merely slice your line up through the cover you were trying to avoid in the first place. Fairly heavy line and a tight drag will help keep the fish coming once it's hooked. If the fish does wrap around limbs or other obstructions, giving slack is usually a last resort that sometimes helps. But you're better off trying to bull the boat as close as you can to the fish. Remember that the bass will be tugging all the while, so stout line may make a difference between boating it and losing it.

The alternative form of this technique, using a pegged sinker, is best compared to skipping stones across the water. Remember how you did that as a kid? Maybe you still do when nobody's looking.

One angler who developed this technique to near perfection is Ron Shearer, Kentucky bass tournament angler and guide. Shearer, however, uses a long rod—a fast-taper, two-hand, 7-foot 2-inch, butt-tough spinning blank fitted with a medium-heavy-duty reel. The approach for a right-handed angler is to present the left shoulder to the target. A waist-high, two-hand, hard parallel cast is made. When properly done, your wrists turning over at the end of the cast, the rig will hit and skip several times, traveling 8 to 15 feet in the process. You use your forefinger to feather the line and stop the worm just where you want it. It's plain to see that casting reels are not very suited to this skipping form because of almost certain overrun problems.

A short-rod version of the stone-skipping technique with a pegged worm sinker is one of the favorite tactics of Richmond radiologist Dr.

SKIPPING WITH PEGGED SINKER

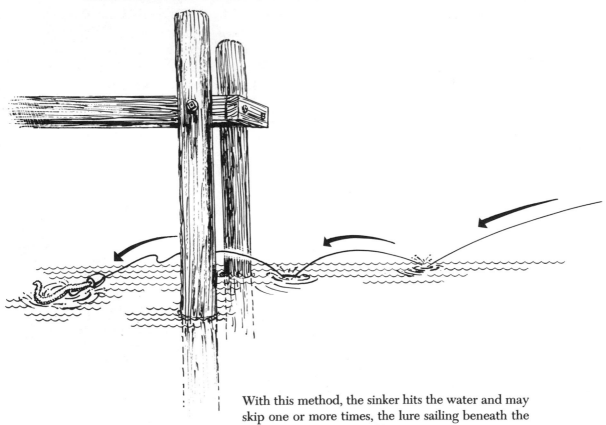

With this method, the sinker hits the water and may skip one or more times, the lure sailing beneath the obstacle and landing softly.

Dr. Greg South favors a stiff, short spinning rod to get under obstacles with the skipping technique. He can skip his worm, rigged with a pegged sinker, into a 2-inch slot.

Greg South. Greg has used it to score high in many bass tournaments, among them the prestigious B.A.S.S. Masters Classic on the Arkansas River in 1984. He uses a custom 5-foot 2-inch spinning rod made on one of the Skyline Rod Company's heaviest blanks normally used for casting rods. With it, Greg can skip a worm into the tightest nooks and crannies.

Greg favors this technique especially for fishing docks. He has fine-tuned the method so that he can skip a worm under docks that have just 2 inches of clearance between their undersides and the water surface—places most anglers never touch.

"To fish these docks, I get on my knees in the boat," Greg says. "Then I lean over the side and come back with my arm and rod nearly parallel to the water. The trick is to skip the worm back under there into the shady areas where the fish hide. The initial splashdown of the skip is just outside the dock, then the worm hops back in a couple of times before it goes down. I only use an eighth-ounce weight, but I also use twelve-pound line which lets the worm sink slowly. A slow sink is vital under shallow water docks."

Anglers can also benefit from Dr. South's observations about dock construction: "All over the country where I've fished, docks built into the water on wood posts hold fish far better than those plastic foam float docks. Even with wood docks, some are good and some are great. There are clues to the best ones. First, if there's some kind of outdoor light present, it usually means the owners like to night-fish for crappies. If you see a light, start searching for sunken brush piles placed to attract crappies. Those, plus a lot of wood cross-supports and wood ladder legs going down into the water, make the dock prime."

Skipping techniques can help you out during that tough time following the passage of cold fronts when bass are hugging cover tightly or hiding in places where normal presentations just won't reach. Use skipping where it's intended, avoid heavy grass beds (it won't work in them), and you're sure to pick up a number of fish that would never have responded to your bogus crawler otherwise.

Crashing

Factors other than weather cause bass to utilize very thick, stoutly constructed cover. They include fishermen, the filling over or rotting of more fragile cover types, and indiscriminate shoreline development. Angling pressure leaves fish that are not as aggressive or have utilized heavy cover to begin with. These are the fish remaining when the "easy" bass are kept instead of released. Change of habitat also forces bass to move into available heavy cover—typically timber, willow limbs, or heavier brush. In these situations there is often no space or overhang where the previously described bank skim or skipping method can be applied. Crashing is one method for reaching these fish.

Crashing is most easily done when dead limbs or branches extend down into the water. Where thick-growing, springy, live branches are concerned, a different method (to be discussed) is more practical. Crashing is

Author Jerry Gibbs uses a short rod to work spinnerbaits and weedless spoons through emergent weeds.

best done with a heavy—say, ½-ounce—solidly constructed spinnerbait. It is effective in both lakes and rivers.

Let's say you've approached a likely looking treetop with fingerlike branches thrusting deep below the surface. You've worked the perimeter edges and have made a few tentative casts past the outside twigs. Maybe you've caught a fish doing it, too. Good. Now it's time to go to work.

Move your boat in close—5 or 6 feet away from the limbs. Hold position with your electric motor directly out from the branches.

Now take your short baitcasting outfit, the reel equipped with 17 to 20-pound-test line, and look for what seems to be a thin spot in the branches. Fire the spinnerbait right in. If you're fishing in moving water, make your presentations up-current. You should be standing up, and your cast should be an overhand one that sends the lure *down* through the branches with all the force you can summon. If the lure hangs, just jerk it free and try again. Your spinnerbait will smash its way in through leaves and branches, often breaking dead twigs as it goes. Allow it to sink as deep as possible while lowering your rod tip.

Now draw the spinnerbait to the surface fast enough to make its blade spin. Chances are you won't be able to see it reach the surface, so you'll have to listen. As soon as you hear it—assuming a fish has not stuck at this point, which is very possible—lower the lure again. Keep this jigging going for as long as 2 minutes. If you draw a blank, move to the next main limb or weak-looking network of branches through which you think you can crash your lure. A good tree can be worked from 5 to 15 minutes and often produces several fish. South Carolinian Dog Odom, who probably originated this technique, reports having caught as many as 10 bass from one good tree.

Stout, stiff rods coupled with aggressive muscling often enable you to bull bass from the branch tangles. With larger fish, though, you'll have to push in there to get them, just as you may when skipping worms beneath overhangs.

Parachuting

Here's a method to use where the branches are just too thick to crash a lure through, yet have a few spaces back in at the very tops of the limbs. It's also very effective anywhere a lot of brush up to 4 feet high is growing right out of the water, or along the shoreline.

The openings in the cover this time are usually too small for spinner-baits. The preferred lure is a plastic worm with a cone sinker solidly pegged against its head. A short, stiff spinning outfit is the easiest tackle to use for this technique but, if you can flip with a baitcasting rig, that will work too. Strong line is a must. If the water is clear and the sky is bright, so much the better—the fish will be holding even tighter to the main limbs or brush stalk. Heavy line won't spook fish in the clear water because you'll be planting the worm virtually on a bass' nose and very little line will be in the water anyway.

Cast or flip your worm up high over the top of the cover. Stop the lure short so it falls straight down through any little opening it can eel its way through. Hitting twigs will slow its fall so little disturbance is created when the bait hits the water surface. Let the worm settle down through the roots or branches as deeply as it will go. Your line may be draped over the cover at this point.

Jiggle the worm up slowly and gently, then let it swim back down. Repeat over and over. Do not expect the usual tap that generally indicates a fish taking a plastic worm. In fact, if you do feel a tap, it's most likely the fish expelling your artificial. If you strike at that point you'll come up empty-handed more times than not. Instead, feel for a slight heaviness or resistance on the line. Concentrate on the limbs or brush, and on your line as well. Be alert to the slightest movement of either, or to the fact that your worm did not sink as deeply, say, the second time it began swimming down. A bass may well have it.

You don't feel the normal tap because the fish is not grabbing the worm and turning. It doesn't need to. When you get the plastic wiggler to float past its nose, all a bass has to do is flare its gills while opening its mouth, and the worm will swing right in. Some anglers report they've actually raised and lowered their worm a couple of times until they finally brought it all the way to the surface and discovered that there was a bass holding onto it. They had felt a slight heaviness, but assumed they had simply picked up some debris, and hadn't even set the hook. It can happen easily when you're first learning to parachute.

The best covers on which to concentrate your parachuting have some kind of structural bottom variation or visible difference about them. For example, the target bush could be growing on a hump on the bottom. There could be a depression near it, or a boulder could be protecting its roots. Bass are attracted to these things, but they have to be ferreted out through actual fishing or possibly when boating close to the cover and looking down through the water after you've finished working the spot. Easily seen objects that make some bushes better fish magnets include an adjacent stump, log, fenceline, rock, or simply a cluster of several bushes that together form a kind of super-cover sanctuary.

Canny anglers who discover bushes that consistently yield fish because of underwater irregularities will frequently mark the shoreline by piling up several rocks, or tying a snip of fishing line nearby. If you try this ploy, don't make the marks too obvious. But some parachuting spots that produce well once probably will do so again, depending on seasonal or weather influences. If you try an old faithful place and it gives up not a fish, return to it several times during the fishing day. It's possible the bass have moved off but will return again.

Calling

Let's say you now must deal with tree branches, timber jackstraws, or brushy tangles that are simply too thick to parachute and too limber or twisted to crash. You still have an option that's seemingly so bizarre you will not believe it can work until you see it produce for others or give it a fair shake yourself—and catch fish.

You can use either a spinning or a casting outfit. You can also get away with a bit lighter line, although you'll probably already be rigged with the heavier outfit with which you were crashing.

Here's the scenario. You locate a prime-looking live willow tree, its branches reaching down into the water like a skeleton's ribcage. Vines are growing over the branches, weaving a tight mesh that's impossible to slam a spinnerbait through. You first cast and retrieve in the normal way all around the edge of the cover, then move in close. If there is current, head for the downstream side of the trees. Make sure you've got a spinnerbait equipped with big blades, preferably wide Colorados. Now you can begin.

Let out a little line and, with a hard overhand pinwheel movement, slam the lure down on the surface near the boat. Repeat about four times. Then cast the spinnerbait up tight to the cover. Let it sink, then start it back with a stop-go retrieve for a couple of feet. After it has traveled a short way, start cranking it like crazy, just burning it back toward the boat. You can also use a sideways sweeping movement of the rod to accomplish the high-speed flight of the lure. Try alternating this retrieve with a slow and steady crank back. Now slam the lure again. If you're fishing with a friend, have him slam a spinnerbait near the boat once or twice while you're casting and retrieving. Then switch jobs.

Sometimes you'll have to let a little more line out and slam the lure down next to the trees near where you're holding the boat instead of right near the boat itself. The slapping noise really can call bass from deep water under all that cover. It brings them—first, because they're curious creatures; and second, because I believe the sound may simulate spawning baitfish such as shad that usually perform the reproductive function near some solid obstruction or cover. The crashing technique described earlier can also play to this phenomenon. It may be why late spring and early summer are good times to use the crashing and calling techniques.

Also try calling against weedline edges of coontail, milfoil, hydrilla, and other vegetation that is too matted to penetrate with any other method. I can almost guarantee that bass are holding up under those weedmats, their backs not far from the surface. They don't have to be in an aggressive mood to be lured out by the sound effects. Non-feeding largemouths may be attracted too.

You're going to get the old sidelong walleye look from your fishing companion the first time he sees you calling, but stick with it and keep it in your bag of tricks to use for those truly jungle-like places. You can bet that these are the spots where the bass populations are pretty well undisturbed.

Although spinnerbaits and plastic worms—two of our more weedless attractors—are the prime lures for the foregoing timber techniques, there are times when light floater-diver minnow plugs would be even more effective, especially when spawning baitfish are present. You can't, of course, get these lures into all that thick cover. However, there are some modifications that can be made on these lures that permit them to be worked through and over less dense branches and brush. Frequently, bass that have been aroused by calling and crashing techniques but have not taken the spinnerbait will take one of the carefully worked minnow plugs swimming and limping past the edge of their hideout.

Rapalas, Bang-O-Lures, Rebels, Bomber Long-A Minnows, and Lindy Baitfish lures are all prime examples of the plugs in question. The shallowest swimmers are best. These plugs come equipped with two or three sets of treble hooks. The first and easiest modification is to take a pair of pliers and slightly bend in the forward hook on each set of trebles toward the shank. This is the hook that usually snags. In moderate cover, just bend the hook in a little. Close it up completely if you want to work a little closer into the branches. You're left with two hooks on each treble now, and these are plenty to catch a fish. In fact, some anglers switch to double or even single weedless hooks for these plugs. That's just a little more bother, and you also have to be careful: Altering the weight of the hooks just a little too much can ruin the action on these delicate baits.

Another hook trick is regularly employed by Florida bass researcher and angler Doug Hannon. To try it, get some small rubber bands and snug the hook shanks on your floater-diver up against the plug body so just one point of each treble sticks downward. The hook shanks will face the tail of the lure. Swing the rear or tail hook up on the lure's back and slip a rubber band around the plug and hook shank as you did with the first two hooks. The arrangement allows the plugs to slip through timber and brush that would normally foul them. When a bass hits, the rubber bands will slip from the shanks or simply break.

Doug has modified the fat, muskie-size Jitterbugs used by anglers who hunt trophy bass at night. He takes off all the hooks and arranges them so they ride on the back or upper side of the lure.

"The fish don't mind a bit," confides Hannon. "The only thing is, with some plugs you have to counterweight the bottom side so the lure won't roll over."

The third modification is quite interesting. It's fairly easy to do on any of the balsa wood plugs. You need your pliers again. Pretend you're a dentist and extract the little plastic bill that makes the plug dive a few inches to a foot or so beneath the surface. Just trimming the bill down isn't good enough; pull it all the way out. The result will be a plug with a totally different action from the original. It kind of wiggles in one direction, then the other when you twitch it with your rod tip. It will not dive. What you have is a beautiful little surface minnow you can zigzag over brush that rises to just within an inch or so of the surface. You can hop the lure over a few emerging branches, too. If you've been using the calling technique next to weed beds that reach to just beneath the surface, you can now try these doctored plugs right over the weeds. They'll skim over that small space of water between the surface and the weed heads. And very often, the bass will explode right up through those weeds to eat them.

A short and stiff spinning rod is the right tool for working the light modified floater-divers. If you like the result, fill the gap where you made the bill extraction on balsa plugs with waterproof white glue so those plugs won't become waterlogged.

My case rests. Although longer rods are suited to a lot of my bass fishing needs these days, it should be clear that the short one-handed stick is very much alive and catching fish as well as ever—when used in the right places.

chapter 3

Unbeatable Plastic Worm Systems

I like the lad, who when his
father thought
To clip his morning nap by
hack-
neyed phrase
Of vagrant worm by early song-
ster caught,
Cried, "Served him right! It's not
at all surprising;
The worm was punished, Sir, for
early rising!"

—JOHN SAXE, *poet.*

"The first tap you feel at the end of your line is the fish; the next one
is me tapping you on the shoulder to tell you you're too late."

—JOHN POWELL, *fisherman.*

We've come a long way in plastic worm design—and fishing—since the late Nick Creme began putting his imitation crawlers on the market in the closing years of the 1940s. Creme worked for an Akron, Ohio, tool and die company back then, and decided to make his own worms when he grew tired of being unable to find or buy real crawlers whenever he needed them.

Those first manufactured wigglers were made of rubber and gave off a repugnant odor that fish just didn't like. Fourteen months of experimenting later, Creme had most of the early problems whipped. The artificials really worked. But it took him another 4 years for fishermen to begin using the things. Once they started, though, word spread fast. At last count, the Creme plastic worm company was making some one hundred seventy different worm patterns and selling between ten and twelve million worms a year.

A lot of other worm makers have come along since then, too. Some of them are major firms and are members of the American Fishing Tackle Manufacturers Association. Others are basement or garage workshop operations producing complex custom patterns in limited quantity. All of this is rather conclusive evidence that plastic worms catch a lot of fish—mostly bass. One U.S. Fish and Wildlife Service survey states that at least a third of all the largemouth bass annually caught in the nation were nailed by plastic crawlers. B.A.S.S. president Ray Scott claims that 80 to 85 percent of the fish taken in his tournaments are caught on worms.

It follows that, if so many anglers are fishing artificial worms, a lot of experimentation involving the lures has been going on. It has and, because of it, you can now choose from half-a-dozen varied techniques to use with this most productive artificial. There are worms whose size and shape are geared to special fishing methods. There are floating, semi-floating, sinking, fairly hard-skinned, and super soft models. Many come with built-in scents. And the selection of colors and finishes now available is mind-boggling. Some very effective worm specialists maintain that if an angler has confidence in a particular color or finish, he'll catch bass with it no matter where or how he fishes. This statement is probably true, *if* he works at it hard and long enough. I've fished enough places, however, to know that certain colors and patterns seem to be more effective in particular locales. The determining factors seem to be water clarity, color, depth, and the forage on which the bass are feeding at the moment. The color chart in this chapter will help you narrow down your worm color/ finish choices to match conditions. First, though, let's look at some special hooks and rigging methods for use with the advanced worming techniques.

Hooks

Time was when the plastic-worm fisherman's best worm hook was a straight sproat design with a couple of barbs on the shank near the eye to better hold the worm in place. Today, there are a number of good hook models. Each hook works and has its own advantages. One central mail-

SEVEN TYPES OF HOOKS FOR RIGGING PLASTIC WORMS

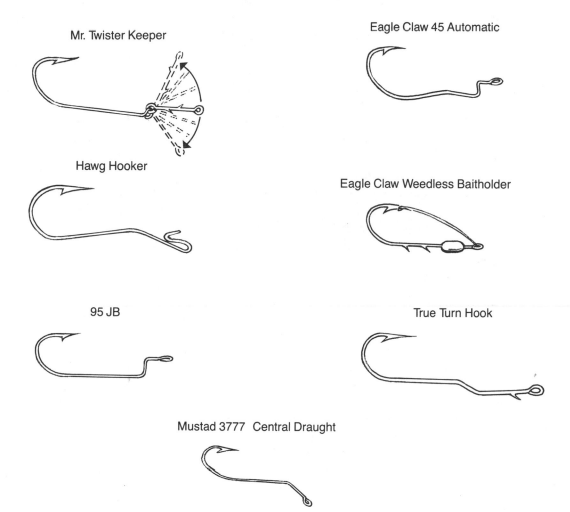

Mr. Twister Keeper

Eagle Claw 45 Automatic

Hawg Hooker

Eagle Claw Weedless Baitholder

95 JB

True Turn Hook

Mustad 3777 Central Draught

order source for each model that follows is Bass Pro Shops, Box 4046, Springfield, MO 65808 (1-800-BASS PRO; outside the U.S. call 417-883-4960).

The Mr. Twister Keeper hook is good for fast rigging when you don't want to be bothered with aligning the worm precisely when inserting the hook. You also don't need to bring the point out at exactly the right spot just aft of the head, so the worm won't bunch up on the hook when rigged

Texas style. The Keeper has a little free-swinging barbed shaft attached to the eye. You simply insert the worm head over this barbed keeper section as far as it will go, then insert the hook point into the worm body. That's it. The worm is now weedless and you can use it with any sinker you choose.

The Hawg Hooker model has a little curled device on the eye to hold the worm from slipping down the hook. The eye of the hook enters the worm head without ripping it. Once the head is over the eye, you pull it slightly back (as though you were going to try to slide the worm down the shank). The little hook grabs into the plastic and holds the worm. Other features of this hook include a slight bend-back shank shape and special barb angle for good worm penetration.

The 95 JB and the extra sharp, stainless Clincher hook both have devices at the eye to keep the worm from slipping down the shank. Two short 90° bends just aft of the eye create an elbow effect. The shank itself is straight. Some people call this a kinked-shaft. It, too, is effective. The hook bend is southern sproat style.

The Eagle Claw 45 Automatic has the same little elbow as the above models. It also has a unique compound curve hook shank that causes the hook to rotate automatically after a bass chomps down on it and you set. The result is superior hook setting and fewer missed strikes.

Eagle Claw Weedless Baitholder Hooks, both weighted and un-weighted, are not new but worth mentioning because a lot of anglers exposed to all the new models forget about them. They're handy when you need a weedless rig but bass are either letting go quickly or being missed with the usual weedless, Texas-style rigging. The worm head may become cut from the wire arm that makes these hooks weedless, but you can live with it. The weighted version has a series of cone-like ridges on the lower hook shank that help hold the worm in place. The unweighted version has two shank barbs for the same purpose.

The Tru Turn hook, currently my favorite, has two compound bends. When you strike, the design of the bends permits the point to rotate up to 360° to assure positive hook setting. In very few cases will the hook fail to find purchase. In fact, the United States Air Force Survival School reports a minimum of 20 percent more boated fish when using this model. It's available in popular Carlisle bend, nickel plated, or Aberdeen design in smaller sizes and lighter gold-finish wire. New saltwater models that are now available may be good when fishing for larger-than-usual large-mouths.

The Mustad 3777 Central-Draught hook, size 28, is the only one not carried by Bass Pro Shops. It features a single bend of about 50°; a more severe bend-back than the Hawg Hooker earlier described. The hook bend and point are angled upwards. Don't let the No. 28 size designation fool you—it has nothing to do with a miniscule No. 28 dry fly hook. The hook is more comparable to a No. 2 bend in a Mustad sproat style. The hook is fine wire, and the bend gives a quick raking penetration. It is a style that is well suited to small diameter, 4-inch worms as will be explained later.

Rigging Methods

A couple of rigging methods are specifically suited to some specialized presentations. First is a variation of the Carolina rig. It's called the Eufaula rig and was engineered by bass veteran Tom Mann. If you don't do a whole lot of worm fishing and want to perfect your touch while gaining confidence in the plastics, this is the rig to use. Instead of the barrel sinker commonly used in the Carolina rig, the Eufaula uses a ⅛-ounce cone-shaped slip lead. After the sinker is slid over your line, tie in a barrel swivel (no snap). Now tie on a piece of 9-inch leader. (The standard Carolina rig employs a leader of up to 3 feet.) The hook goes on the end, which is embedded in the worm Texas-style.

With the simple changes from the Carolina, the Eufaula is easier to cast and fish. To retrieve, just cast, let the worm settle, and start slowly cranking. No fancy rodwork is required. "If you feel something tugging," says Tom, "you'd better strike because it's surely going to be a fish."

The original Carolina rig is often used with a heavy sinker for sus-

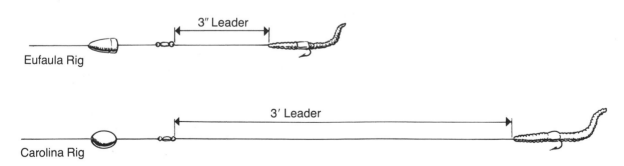

Eufaula rig (top), a variation of the Carolina rig, is easier to cast. The Eufaula has a cone-shaped slip sinker instead of a barrel sinker and a shorter leader.

pended bass in deep water. The worm most often used with the rigging was a Super Floater—a model that acts as though it's trying to rise to the surface. With the Eufaula rig, you can use a high floating worm, a neutral density model, or any other worm you choose. You can work it in fairly shallow water and medium depths as well. The conical sinker goes through cover easier, too.

The Gaumer Ultralight rig was cooked up by friend Dick Gaumer of La Crecenta, California, the state which may be the hotbed of plastic worm innovation. Dick is one of the pioneers in using mini-worms and developing lightweight spinning tackle for bass. He was the one who discovered

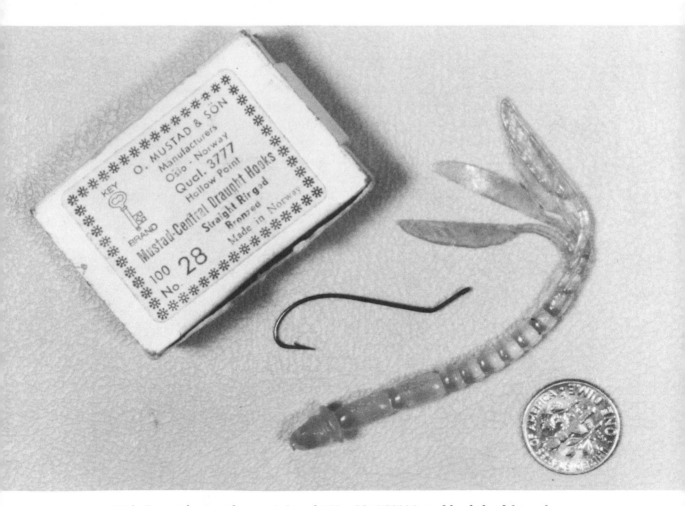

Dick Gaumer's special central draught No. 28, 3777 Mustad hook for fishing the Haddock multi-tail worm on ultralight tackle.

Dick Gaumer lands a bass on his favorite Haddock multi-tail worm rig.

the Mustad 3777 Central Draught hook—at the time, the only ultralight hook of the proper shape to permit weedless Texas rigging, give quick setting, and not overpower a small-diameter worm. The whole point in ultralight worming is to work a tiny lure with light sinkers and lines in super-clear water for spooky bass.

Dick's method was designed to be used with the Haddock multitail worm, a mini-diameter wiggler with a little collar at its head. The collar causes the worm to tip up when it hits an obstruction. That motion just serves to enhance the wiggling of the tentacle-like finned tails.

Dick also needed quick penetration of both bass jaw and worm plastic but, with lines of 6 and even 4-pound test, he needed everything in his corner that he could get. Gaumer devised the method of inserting the point of his fine hook so it just nicked into the side "skin" of the worm rather than imbedding it directly into the center. His technique requires less force to tear the point free of the plastic and impale the fish. The texture of the Haddock worm is tough enough to hold the hook so implanted without it ripping free on the cast.

Other parts of the system are equally important for consistent success. Besides the light lines, a light cone sinker is needed. You can use $1/16$, $1/8$, or $1/4$-ounce weights, but the $1/8$-ounce is best. The rod action is also vital. A medium-flexible $6^1/2$ or 7-foot spinning model permits casting the light rig good distances, which is especially important in clear water where there's not a lot of overhead cover. The more flexible action rods are also important to keep from breaking the light lines or opening up the thin wire hook. The Fenwick Company built their models GFS 64 and GFS 70 specifically for this technique.

A lot of early skeptics who were used to hammering bass with pool-cue-stiff rods and heavy lines insisted that Gaumer's system would not hold up under the strain. It did. After nailing largemouth bass of over 7 pounds on the rig, he went on to use the same outfit on stripers up to 20 pounds!

Bass that grab the mini-worms on light line tend to engulf them and not go away. They do not tap hard; sometimes all you experience is a feeling of increased weight. To set the hook, allow slack line for a moment, then come back. You use a slow rod lift when working this rig, and you can use the setup in deep water—25 to 30 feet. Many anglers said the lightweight worms and sinkers would sink too slowly. They forgot about the light line causing less resistance.

Though many anglers are now custom making their own multitailed worms, the original Haddock worm is still available from Bob Suekawa, Haddock Fishing Supplies, 2321 W. 230th Place, Torrance, CA 90501.

No technique is an absolute. Bits and pieces of one method can be applied to another in most fishing, which applies to the following worming methods. Though each can work as an entity, you'll doubtlessly find yourself combing methods here and there after mastering the basics of each technique. It helps to define terms, though, especially when you're visiting a new fishing ground and trying to learn how the bass are being caught.

Split-Shotting

Remember when rigging a plastic worm only consisted of clamping a split shot on the line ahead of it? Well, here we go again. Despite a variety of sliding weights, pegged weights, and swivels, the split shot is still the best sinker in various situations by virtue of the small sizes in which it is available.

A relatively recent variation in mini-weights is the split sleeve. Available in copper or lead, the sleeve is lightly crimped to line or leader with pliers. Sleeves are available in a variety of small sizes and can be found in fly fishing specialty shops. Their more streamlined shape helps to keep them from snagging in underwater cover. If you use regular round split shot for worming, choose soft lead without those little tabs that enable the shot to be easily opened for reuse. They only tend to hang up in cover.

An excellent worm to use for split-shotting is a 4-inch curly tail. Hook it as you would for a normal Texas weedless rig. When you reinsert the point of the hook in the worm to make it weedless, do so in the worm seam so the tail rides up. Align the rig perfectly so the worm will swim straight with only the curly tail wiggling. Crimp your split shot about 18 inches ahead of the worm on the line.

Don't worry about the shot injuring the line. Tests show that unless you really mash the shot down hard with pliers, it will not injure monofilament. After you snag a few times, though, check the line around the shot as you would any part of your terminal tackle. It's possible that some nicks or frays will have developed.

The split shot rig's first use is in clear, shallow water. A weight just light enough to sink the worm brings the artificial crawler down to the bottom almost as slowly as cold molasses drips off a spoon. To super-fussy bass that are holding just off the bottom, the effect must be of a helpless natural descending into the depths. The effect is further enhanced by

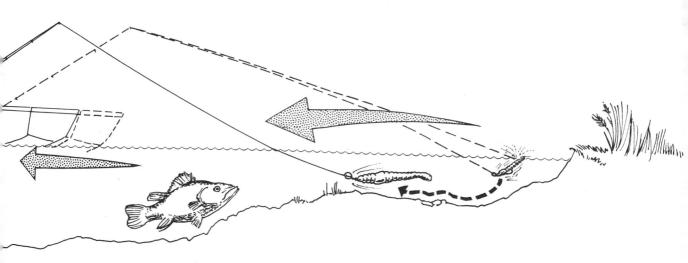

Fishing a plastic worm rigged with a split shot in clear, shallow water. Allow worm to sink slowly, then retrieve with very slow cranking.

comparatively light 6 to 8-pound-test lines that are typically used on spinning tackle and now on the newer ultralight bait-casting rods and reels as well.

Once the worm reaches bottom, you don't lift it up with the rod, as is normally done with the Texas rig. Instead, you begin a painfully slow crank of the reel handle. The worm will be more or less suspended behind the split shot. In heavily fished waters, the preferred worm is not over 5 inches long.

Some of the most successful split-shot anglers don't even crank at all. Instead, they put their reels in gear or close their bails if they're using spinning equipment, then start an electric trolling motor. After casting out the worm, the lure is allowed to rest on the bottom. Then the boat is slowly eased along in a teasing stop-and-go rhythm. The target areas are usually points that continue out underwater, bars, and shallow reefs.

I don't know if this method would be considered trolling if used in a bass tournament, but it sure attracts bass. An alternative to this technique is to work over sunken islands or rock piles using the wind and electric motor for controlled drift. No other action is imparted. This technique begins to cross the boundaries of the following method, the name of which sounds self-explanatory but actually isn't.

Do-Nothing

This technique covers a couple of different worming approaches. Tennessee native Charlie Brewer coined it first, I believe, as used in his slider fishing approach. It was followed by another variation of the system made popular by tournament angler Jack Chancellor. The term is also a misnomer because you are really doing something. You're just not giving much action to your worm. Today's most commonly practiced version employs a jig or slider head. Many of these heads are thin, light, and disk-shaped so they fall slowly with a wobble movement. The disk-shaped heads may be trimmed with cutting pliers for an even slower drop or shallower presentation to suspended fish. Depending on the cover and jig head design, you can leave the hook exposed for easier setting, or rig weedless by inserting the hook point back in the worm.

Charlie Brewer bases his method on the swimming action of small minnows that seem to slowly slide through the water with barely a flick of their tails. He uses 4-inch plastic worms without any fancy action tails. The worm is rigged perfectly straight, to avoid twisting or spinning on the $\frac{1}{8}$-ounce slider type jig head with thin wire hook. Depending on drop rate or depth desired, the head is left as is or trimmed evenly in front and on both sides to lighten it. A short and stiff spinning rod with 6-pound-test line is standard.

Let's assume you want to fish 10 feet deep with the untrimmed ⅛-ounce head. First, cast lure to the target area. Engage your reel when the worm hits water, crank quickly a few times to take up slack, and raise your rod tip to the two o'clock position. Then begin an extremely slow retrieve: 3 full seconds for one complete revolution of the reel handle. All the while you do nothing with your rod—just hold it at the prescribed angle and slowly reel. If you're in a calm, controlled state, you'll handle this fine. If not, don't try it.

If you want to reach depths of 15 to 18 feet with the above rig, crank at the rate of 4 or 5 seconds per one complete revolution of the handle. If you want to fish shallower, trim the head and crank a *little* faster. Try to hold your rod as still as possible. The slight nervous tremor of your body and the gentle wave action or boat movement will impart extremely subtle motion to the little lure.

It's important to maintain this retrieve steadily. No sudden speed-up, slow-down, or twitch should be made. This technique is extremely effective on normally hard-to-interest suspended fish.

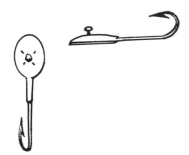

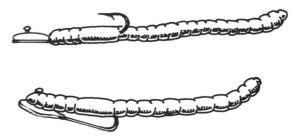

Sliderhead jig used for Brewer's Do-Nothing Technique (left) and two methods of rigging it (above).

If you want to fish the bottom, you can do so almost as though you were fishing a normal Texas-rigged worm very slowly. Once the do-nothing slider head and worm are on bottom, raise your rod tip slightly to crawl-swim the lure. Now stop. Let the worm settle until you see your line sag again, indicating that the lure is on the bottom. Take up slack by cranking, lower the rod tip slightly, and swim the lure again.

This rig gets a lot of attention from small panfish as it eases its way through the water. You'll recognize them by short, rapid tap-tap-taps. Their interest will keep you alert, but don't try to set the hook. Just keep the lure coming slow and steady. When a bass takes, you'll feel the difference. Because the lure is moving so slowly, a bass will just suck it in and begin moving off. You may get a subtle tap first, from the fish holding onto the light rig for a long time. Don't rush and, above all, don't rear back hard to set the hook. The striking procedure here requires some finesse.

When you feel a tap, slowly lower your rod and extend it by stretching out your arms while slowly cranking slack from the line. When you've reached the end of your stretch and all slack is out, come back either straight up or up and sideways in a slow sweeping movement with your rod. No wham-bam strike. From the time the rod is positioned just above the water surface to the end of your sweeping set, it should take you 3 or 4 seconds! Pretend you have a rod in your hand and try it. You'll see how slow it is. With lines of 2, 4, or 6-pound-test, you could easily break off using the standard hook set. But with the sweep, you're going to lose few fish. Don't stop in the middle of that sweeping movement because you feel the fish. Keep on going. The extremely sharp and thin wire hook, coupled with the bass's swimming-away movements, will aid point penetration.

Those are the basics. As you experiment, no doubt you'll come up with a number of variations on the primary technique. The key, though, is to go slow—slower than you believe you should.

Jack Chancellor's system is different. The Chancellor Do-Nothing worms don't look like anything that would catch bass, but they do. They are little stick-like sections of plastic worms—no fancy paddle, split, or curly action tails. In fact, they have no tails at all. They look like limp cigarettes, except that they're more colorful. They are also equipped with tandem snelled hooks. The snell loop emerges from the nose of the worm. The hook points emerge near the tail end of the worm and about a third of the way back from the head. They're obviously not weedless.

The Chancellor worm is fished on the Carolina rig in deep, fairly open water. The heavy—1 ounce or more—cone or barrel sinker takes the worm to the bottom and you just let it sit there. After awhile you bump

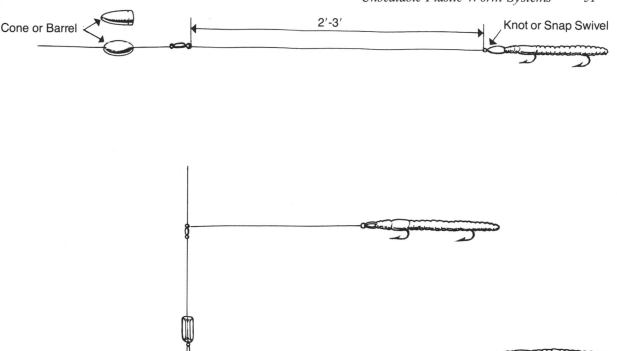

Chancellor's Do-Nothing Worms can be rigged in two ways: for fishing deep, open water it is rigged Carolina style (top); for dead drifting or fishing in a slight current, two worms are rigged on droppers.

the sinker a little, or try the electric motor trick and ease your boat into a different position.

You can fish the Do-Nothing stick worms on a conventional Carolina rig with a 2½ to 3-foot leader coming through the sinker hole, but stopped from going back by a good ball bearing swivel. In this case, rig one worm at the end of your leader. For dead drifting or slight current fishing for suspended bass, you can try a double setup. Tie a swivel on the end of your line, add a 6-inch leader to its end eye, and thread on the barrel sinker. Now tie on another swivel so the sinker remains between the two swivels. Now you can tie droppers with the Do-Nothing worms attached to the swivel eyes away from the sinker, so the lead will never hit against the knots. You just ease around or drift, as mentioned, and the suspended bass eat the worms—when they want to, of course.

Remember, a good ball-bearing swivel like the Sampo is strongest with continuous rather than split rings.

The Swimmer

This set-up is a combination of the Do-Nothing and split-shot worm techniques. Tie 8 inches of leader with a hook at the end to a ball-bearing swivel. Tie your main line to the swivel and clamp a split shot just ahead of the swivel. Thread the hook point into the worm nose but do not let it exit the worm until you've reached its simulated breeding band. You are not going to reinsert the point as you would with the weedless Texas rig. If it's properly threaded, the worm will lie straight along the hook shank, with just a little of the body beginning to curve on the hook bend. You don't want a humpbacked appearance.

After casting, begin retrieving your worm with a slow crank, punctuated occasionally by a twitch of the rod tip. Your rod should be of medium flex, not the ultra-stiff poles used in many regular worming

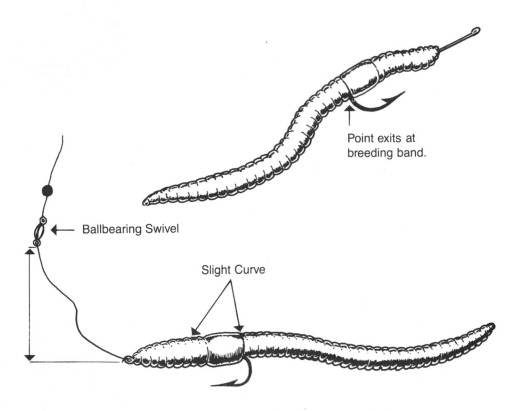

Swimmer rig consists of a plastic worm threaded on a straight-shank hook with its barb emerging at the breeding band. Leader is attached to a swivel; split shot is crimped to line.

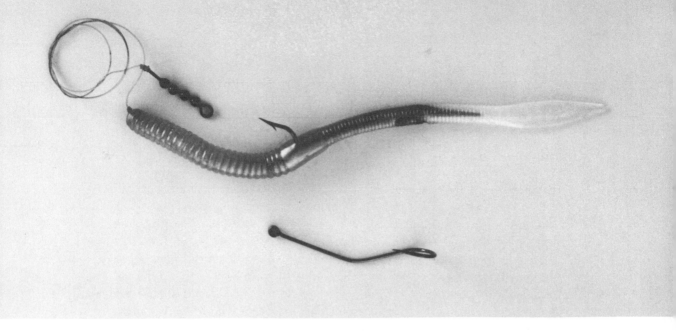

Burke Swimmin' Worm, designed by Doug Hannon, is rigged on a crooked-shank hook which produces a bend in the worm, giving it a snakelike swimming action.

techniques. The worm will zip up and to either side, then down in an erratic swim. The method is more like working a light floater-diver plug than worm fishing, which is helpful when you remember that there is no weed guard on the hook.

Another swimming worm is built around the rig designed by bass researcher Doug Hannon of Odessa, Florida. It is sold commercially by Burke Fishing Lures, Traverse City, MI 49684. The rig is built around Hannon's special compound bend No. 3/0 hook tied to 12 inches of camouflage 20-pound-test leader material, which is attached to a black bead-chain swivel. To obtain the correct swimming action, the worm must be correctly threaded on the Hannon hook. You can use any straight-tailed worm. The Burke Swimmin' Worms have an X on the body at the spot where the hook point exits. The hook is inserted into the head in the usual way.

When retrieved at a slow and steady pace, the body of the Swimmin' Worm undulates like a water snake. Its head remains pointing in the direction of travel, just as does the head of a real snake. Hannon uses the rig unweighted along docks, piers, and some shallow shorelines. He also fishes the swimmer with a weight in deeper water. The hook is exposed on the original rig, but a weedless version is now available.

The rig is easy to use. It is simply cast and cranked slowly—about the speed that a snake swims. The heavy leader tends to stabilize the worm's undulation, and allows the catching of several fish with no need to re-rig. It also tends to catch bigger bass—6 pounds and up.

Shake 'n Bake for Bass

If you think that the term is too corny, call it doodling with an artificial, but the guy who made it famous uses the first description. Bass guide and tournament contender Don Iovino of Burbank, California, perfected one version of the method that proved deadly on hard-pressured fish. The story goes that the technique was further advanced when Bill Beckum of the Bait Barge in Orange, California, showed Iovino how he sliced the tail of a straight-tailed worm into four sections with a long-bladed fillet knife. You can try cutting the tails yourself (it's a little tricky and requires a few of the lures for practice) or you can buy one of the worms that already comes with tails like Iovino's own make paddle-tail Doodle King or the Haddock worm earlier mentioned. For the record, Beckum caught an 18-pound, 11-ounce largemouth from Lake Casitas on one of his cut-tail worms. It was the lake record until Ray Easley took his 21-pound, 3.5-ounce monster, which is the second biggest largemouth on record as of this writing.

The shake 'n bake method for bass is best combined with a slow crank as employed with the split-shot technique. Together, the two coax and convince a bass to strike, while giving it a long time to make up its mind.

Once your worm has landed on target, let it settle. Then begin to shake your rod horizontally over the water. This calls for hand, wrist, and forearm effort with a very stiff rod. Shake the rod for 10 seconds or so, then pause awhile—the "baking" period—before shaking again. Take up slack now and again by slowly cranking the reel.

The vigorous shaking is slightly dampened by the effect of line stretch and the water, resulting in a very provocative motion under the surface. The worm shimmies, jiggles, and writhes. You might want to reserve the method for those especially reluctant fish, though, because after you do it long enough your arm will let you know about it.

Iovino uses his method in shallow water and medium depths. It can be employed for deep suspended bass as well. The technique is also effective on spotted bass and on smallmouths. Although multi-tail worms are overall best for this method, on some days the straight single-tails do better. It's smart to carry both varieties with you.

Several hybrid plastics that resemble crosses between worms and grubs lend themselves perfectly to the shake 'n bake technique. One such is the

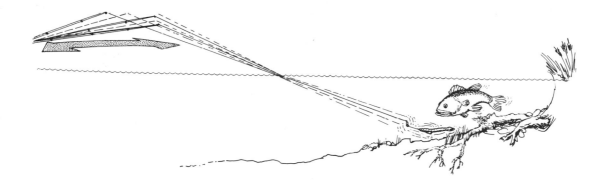

Shake 'n bake method of fishing plastic worm rigged with split shot. Shake wrist horizontally back and forth for about 10 seconds; pause awhile; then shake again. Take up slack slowly.

Fat Gitzit, created by Utah angler Bobby Garland. Bob was Western Bass Angler of the Year for 1984, and the 1983 Grand National winner.

This Gitzit is a hollow-headed creation with lots of tiny tentacles sticking out back. It is most frequently used with special jig heads that Garland manufacturers. The heads can be rigged to ride outside and in front of the Gitzit, like a worm with a pegged sinker. They can also be inserted into the Gitzit so the line-tie eye sticks through the top of the plastic head. This internal rigging is generally employed when vertical jigging shake 'n bake methods are to be used. The Gitzit rides in a naturally appearing horizontal position when in the water if it is rigged in this fashion.

Ron Bargan of Bodfish, California, employs another rigging method. In 1984, Ron collected what at that time proved to be the largest total weight limit of largemouths from Lake Isabella, California: five fish weighing 51 pounds, 6 ounces. He jigged those fish with some of the shaking methods, but Ron reserves this specialty rig for the very toughest conditions—suspended bass in cold and clear water.

Ron uses a long Aberdeen hook. He fastens a bit of cork scrap to the hook shank. The corked hook goes inside a blue-smoke Gitzit. Now a split shot is clamped to the line ahead of the Gitzit. Ron may put the shot on the line as much as 9 *feet* ahead of the lure. The shot goes to the bottom, and the cork-rigged Gitzit floats up to reach the suspended bass. The rig

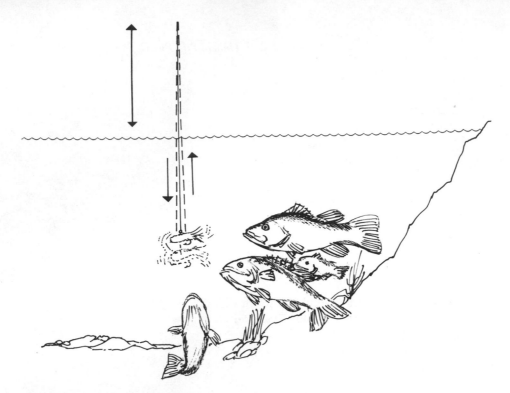

Shake 'n bake with Fat Gitzit rigged with jighead inside hollow plastic body.

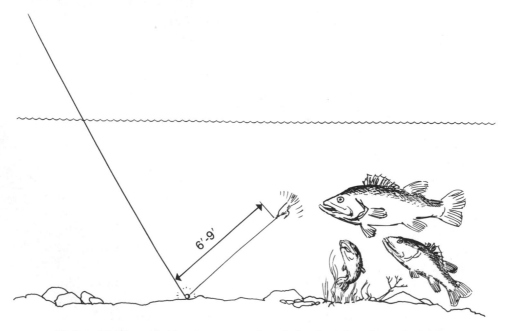

6'-9'

Shake n' bake with Fat Gitsit rigged with hook and cork inside body and split shot 6 to 9 feet up the line.

cannot be cast with a split shot that far ahead of the lure; it is simply dropped to the bottom on target. The rig is then shaken with a long rod over and over again—until a fish hits, of course.

Fly-Lining

Here's another descriptive but somewhat inaccurate term for an important phase of worming. You don't use a fly line, but your line is "fly light," so to speak, because no weight is involved. You need a good bass class spinning rod. Rig the worm weedless with the hook point going back into the worm body, and combine any of the previously described techniques. Crawl the thing through vegetation, pull it over logs, or treat it like a surface plug. Just make sure the hook is lined up straight so you don't end up with a twisted line.

Maybe the most interesting version of the no-weight worm is the dead drift, which is best accomplished with a high-floating plastic like the Super Floater. Work it in areas where some current is present, caused by wind, spring, or river. Cast up tight to vegetation and simply let the worm drift along the weed edge. Bass, if they're in the mood, will come out after it. You may want to give the worm just a hint of a twitch once in awhile as it drifts. And don't forget to try a fly-lined sinking worm of the proper color when bass are eating forage fish. Who said that a worm has to simulate a worm in the first place?

Color

Before diving into the subject of worm color selection, let me make the observation for Easterners, Midwesterners, and Southerners that, in hard-fished water on the West Coast, anglers are having terrific success with multi-colored worms. As a result, new and wild color patterns have evolved. Anglers elsewhere are beginning to use the multi-finish crawlers, but seem more inclined to switch between an endless variety of single hues and various degrees of translucency. All catch fish.

As mentioned before, I tend to base my worm finish decisions on water depth, color, and clarity, and the primary forage on which the bass are keying. The forage is especially important if you're presenting the worm using any of the swimming or dropping techniques.

Some of the really hot multi-finish worms as of this writing are crayfish color combinations: primarily orange/black/green; translucent cinnamon with a black bloodline; translucent cinnamon with a blue line (especially in clear water); brown/black/white/smoke stripe; brown/green/black stripe; and purple and blue with blue metal flake.

The most popular worms today are translucent. Light passing through makes them appear to be generating the light themselves. Opaque worms are generally best in extreme low light conditions, such as at night or in dingy water. When selecting opaque worms, I prefer them dull, like the brown and black-striped Topay worm by DeLong. In general, the brighter the day and the clearer the water, the lighter worm finish you should use.

Here, then, is my rule-of-thumb guide for matching worm color to fishing conditions:

COLOR	USE
Black	This was one of the first really popular worm finishes. Black is really the end result of the absorption of all light waves. I like black at night and in deep dingy water conditions—any time you want the best contrast. (Rarely is there "total" darkness; other colors turn grey under dark conditions while black will stand out.) It's good on the bottom, or on the surface when fish observe it from below.
Blue	This is one of my favorite clear water colors. Many shades of blue worms are available. The lighter ones should be used in clearer water. Consider using a blue worm with a higher contrast tail just for a different effect.
Brown	Another good high-contrast worm for nearly all conditions. As mentioned, the Topay worm gets the nod in most dingy water conditions, especially when stained green. If the water is very muddy, go to black.
Chartreuse	This is a super high-visibility color, especially good in shallow and medium depths. Try this finish for spotted bass and small mouths in clear water, too.

COLOR	USE
Green	This is my favorite color smallmouths and spotted bass. Try it for largemouths in clearer water—especially where they're eating crayfish in rocky areas.
Ice Worms (Bloodline Worms)	These include the multi-colored worms previously mentioned. They are excellent in shallow water and clear water at mid-depths. A clear worm with a single high-contrast bloodline gives the illusion of a very slim creature eeling through the water, which proves interesting to bass in hard-fished lakes.
Metalflake	Metal flakes are glittery specks added to the plastic when the worms are poured. They are best used in clear or fairly bright conditions where the flash helps attract fish. One of the hot new finishes is purple fire—purple with red metalflake.
Motor Oil	This is the best all-around color for prospecting in most waters. There are a very few places where it is seemingly not very productive. It is a combination of green, red, amber, yellow, and whatever else the particular manufacturer elects to pour in. Because of its multicolor aspect, it contrasts nicely with virtually any background when viewed from the side, top, or bottom.
Purple	Another old, all-time favorite color. It's a good high-contrast finish. I like it for working the bottom. Try firetail worms with purple bodies and white or fluorescent colors on the tail.
Red	A translucent red is excellent in clear or muddy shallow water. The red color begins fading out soon when fished deeper.

COLOR	USE
Smoke	I like the grayish hue when bass are eating various forage fish. In bright conditions, consider smoke with metalflake. Also try smoke with black stripes.
Violet	A good shade in clear shallow water and in greenish water.

Don't fail to experiment if fish are snubbing your lure when you're sure they should be eating. Finally, although most worming techniques call for a slow or medium-speed retrieve. Try speeding things up once in awhile. You might be pleasantly surprised.

chapter 4

Spoon Jigging

"A spinner is one thing, but a spoon. . .why, you can make it swim and wobble, or drop to the bottom with more wiggle than a Main Street lady before the rent is due."

—JUNIOR VILLAS, *spoon fisherman.*

We can trace fishing spoons back to primitive Pacific Islanders who used iridescent sea shells to which they attached bone hooks. The spoons were jigged rather than being retrieved horizontally. The first use of a spoon in the U.S. is attributed to a young furrier, Julio Buel, whose story of discovery was widely told—by Buel himself.

Luncheons were a bit more gracious back in 1847. There were no hamburgers available from the house of the golden arches; no handy grinder counter close to the water. Buel was taking his lunch afloat on a Vermont lake that he had been fishing. He accidentally dropped overboard the silver tablespoon with which he was eating and, watching it flash and wobble into the depths of the clear water, saw it suddenly attacked briefly by a fish; no doubt a lake trout or big squaretail as natives call the brook trout. Some doubted Julio's story, but the fact remains that he soon thereafter fastened a hook to another spoon whose handle he had removed. He drilled a line hole at the narrower end, and caught fish with the device. Shortly, Buel was experimenting with different finishes, adding feathers and other attractors. In 1848 he began producing his spoons commercially. After receiving a glowing review in print by Frank Forester (Henry William Herbert), a well-known writer on outdoor subjects at the time, Julio found it difficult to keep up with orders and still find time for his own fishing.

These early spoons, and others like the Skinner that shortly followed, were mainly used for trolling. This eventually led to cast-and-retrieve methods for a variety of game fish as is widely practiced today.

Two distinct forms of spoon presentation revolve around jigging. Though less utilized among freshwater anglers, saltwater fishermen have used the methods for years with great success. The techniques include cast-jigging and vertical jigging for bass.

The versatility of spoons for these two methods has been overlooked by many otherwise experienced anglers. Sometimes early-season fishermen who troll spoons for trout in lakes pick up occasional bass. Experienced bassmen who refuse to put away their tackle when the weather grows sharp and tough late in the year sometimes vertically jig steep banks and timber for bass. Beyond these two extremes, there is much more.

After the spawn, from late spring through early fall, bass in 10 to 20 feet of water are prime targets for cast-jigging. So are bass in 6 to 10-foot water, but these fish will pounce all over light trolling spoons normally used for trout. As colder weather moves in, vertical jigging is the ticket for working the fish in water from 18 feet to as deep as you care to fish. Concentrations of deep-holding bass in clear water lakes in the middle of summer can also be jigged vertically.

Spoons are to "drop" fishing what crankplugs are to horizontal fishing. There are five spoon types that serve well for cast-jigging. Consider these styles first, then we'll look at how to manipulate them.

Spoon Types

Concave Spoons. Various makes of concave spoons—the Dardevle is the classic—come in different thicknesses; a short model may be heavier than a longer one. The concave bends of this type spoon vary, too, and cause a variety of actions when cast-jigging. Besides the overall concave shape, there is the bend at the bottom of the spoon where the hook is attached. The more pronounced this bend, the harder and better the spoon will work when trolled, cranked, or jigged at slow speed. The less bend, the faster the speed needed to produce a flutter. These bends are subtle, however. Don't look for extremes. Often there is a bend near the line-tie ring at the narrow end of the spoon. This bend, if it occurs, is in the reverse direction of the bottom bend. The top bend gives a trolled spoon its erratic, darting action to one side or the other. The effect comes through during a jig retrieve also. This erratic dart can trigger active fish.

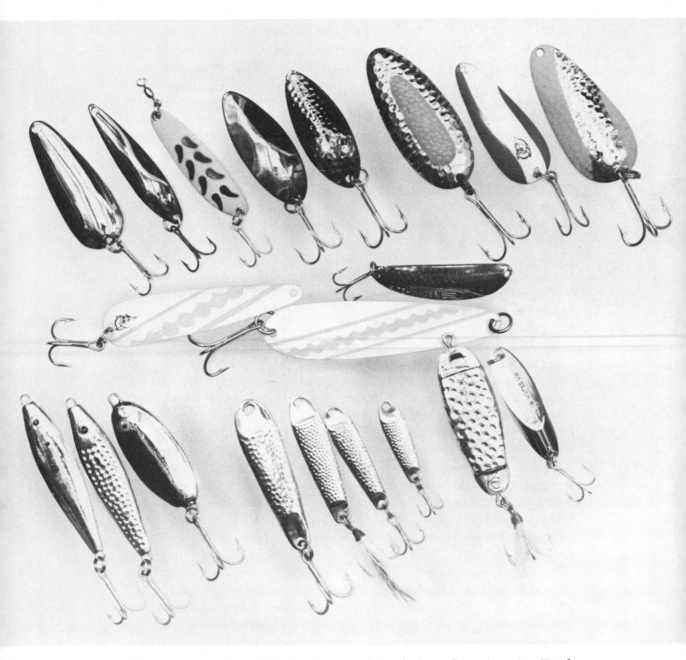

Concave spoons for cast-jigging (top row, l. to r.): Acme Lone Star, Ace Fiord, Krocodile, Little Cleo, Little Jewel, Pixie, Daredevle, Tor-P-Do.
Trolling spoons (center): Seneca Sidewinder, Flutter Chuck, Westport Wobbler.
Lead-body spoons (bottom row, l. to r.): Man-O-Lures (2), Bomber Slab Spoon, Hopkins (4), CC Spoon, Acme Kastmaster.

It does little on fish that are basically inactive because they have no interest in chasing their food, but want it to come to them like an hors d'oeuvre served by a pretty cocktail waitress. Besides the Dardevle, the Little Jewel, Little Cleo, Krocodile, and Tor-P-Do are spoons in this category.

Lead Body Spoons. These are inexpensive spoons and good to use in areas where snags result in more lost lures. The larger ones are also easier than some to shake free of hangups. The bigger ones produce thudding type vibrations when snapped or jigged.

Lead body spoons drop quickly. They can also be bent to alter their dropping speed and action. Wrap them in a rag to preserve their painted finish, then put them in a vise and bend them. When working rocky areas, the paint finish on a lead spoon will chip off in a couple of hours of hard fishing, but plain lead finish is often better. I like to scratch it up with a sharp tool or wire brush to make it shiny. Tom Mann's Man-O-Lure, the Cordell Stinger, and the Bomber Striper Slab spoon fall into this category.

Vertical Jigging Spoons. These are the thin, rounded, elongated, and tail-heavy spoons so popular for vertical jigging. The Hopkins is the classic. It is made of stainless steel in hammered chrome plate or gold plate finish. The ¾-ounce Model 75 is the most popular for bass jigging. Less expensive models like the Cordell CC Spoon made of lead in the same configuration, have also become very popular. These spoons are great for long casts and fast drops. They have a strong vibration when jigged hard. The tail-heavy balance of these spoons allow them to be easily shaken free of snags. The fast drop can be an additional strike stimulator at times, and is also the reason these lures have become the standard for vertical jigging. For cast-jigging you must practice to obtain a sense of the proper movements in order to bring out the right action. Incorrectly worked, this design lure will go into a spiral drop—acceptable when probing vertically but not what you're trying to achieve with the cast-jig technique.

Trolling Spoons. Many spoons designed for trolling can be effectively used for cast-jigging. The Northport Nailer, Eppinger Flutter Chuck and Wing Bat, Seneca Side-Winder, Arbogast Doctor Spoon, and many of the trolling models by Luhr-Jensen and other companies fall into this category. Some of these spoons are designed for trolling up big salmon and are available in long lengths. If shorter models are available, they are usually better for cast-jigging. However, the 5-inch spoons sometimes work very well.

Ultralight Trolling Spoons. These almost paper-thin spoons are best for cast-jigging and flipping in water less than 10 feet deep. Examples of this type spoon include the Badger and Looter spoons from Acme, Miller and Andy Reeker spoons from Lazy Ike Grizzly Division of Dura-Pak Corporation, the variety of flutter and other lightweight models from Luhr-Jensen, the Evil Eye from Red Eye Lures, and the Mepps No. 1 and No. 2 spoons from Sheldon's Inc.

Besides shallows around cover, these spoons work well near man-made structures like docks, boathouses, and boat moorings. They also produce well along rock rip-rap, near standing dead trees, and in rock rubble areas. I like these spoons in sizes from slightly under 3 inches to about 3½ inches.

The equipment I'm going to recommend for cast-jigging won't work for these ultralight spoons. You'll need a spinning outfit with a fairly flexible tip. Even then, the lightest of the flutter spoons will require a split shot on your line near the spoon. In extreme shallows or even slightly deeper

Ultralight spoons that can be flipped in shallow water for bass.

water when you want a slow sink, use a casting bobber, one of those tear-drop-shaped clear floats you can weight with water. Some of them are already weighted with ballast.

The other technique for presenting these spoons is flipping. I find the lightest of the flutter spoons work beautifully when flipped into pockets or around target objects using a bass model fly rod. When you get into serious vegetation, though, you'll probably want to switch to stouter tackle.

The standard 7½-foot flipping rod with levelwind reel and heavy mono-filament works very well with the ultralights for fairly close-in flipping, as long as there's not a strong breeze that can knock the gossamer spoons off course and target. If I'm going to use the ultralights around fairly thick cover, I make sure all treble hooks are removed and a single No. 2, 1/0, or 2/0 hook is in its place. You can use a weed-guard type hook, but the slow drop of the flutter spoons is easily controllable, allowing you to stop its descent before hanging up.

The fluttering, dying-minnow simulation that is the heart of cast-jigging is accentuated with the ultralight spoon. Pocket flipping is more akin to vertical jigging, and only a small part of using the ultralights. In spring, when bass are preparing to spawn or guarding nests, they do not want anything resembling another fish near them. The ultralights score well then, as they do any time you can locate largemouths in the shallows. Another excellent time for these lures is autumn, when thick inshore weedbeds begin dying and the bass move to the less dense weeds slightly out from shore. These places are easily worked with the light spoons.

Among the various shapes in the light trolling lures, you'll find that the widest tend to sink slowest (weight and density being equal) and the narrower configurations slightly faster. A thin cut of party balloon or latex doctor's examination gloves (available in drugstores) can be used as a teaser dressing on the hook. I generally use silver finishes or silver with stripes or spots of color.

The best method of testing these spoon actions is to take a sample of all the categories of spoons just listed and head for a swimming pool, or a lake that is extremely clear in the shallows. Here, you'll be able to see how each spoon falls and responds to the various cast-jigging movements.

Cast-Jigging Techniques

After casting your spoon to the target area, you can let it drop in three ways: freespooling, backcranking, or tightlining. The first method is good when you need the spoon to drop nearly straight down over a target, a small holding cover, or concentration of suspended fish. As you feed out line, be ready to clamp down on your spool—revolving or spinning—because bass often hit on the initial cast and drop. A slight variation on the controlled freespool method is to check the outward flow of line just momentarily from time to time as the lure sinks. Simply thumb your baitcasting spool or hold the line to your spinning reel spool. This will cause the descending spoon to falter a second and often change its action.

Backcranking is just that. Most modern levelwind reels have a control that takes the reel out of the anti-reverse mode. So do spinning reels. As the spoon descends, you follow it down by reeling backwards, thus letting out line. Because the descent is not as unrestricted as in the freespool technique, the spoon will describe a long, very gradual arc from its point of entry to the bottom. Backcranking maintains a bit more tension on the spoon as it drops, which tends to cause a slight variation in action.

When tightlining, the reel is in the anti-reverse mode. No line is paid out as the lure drops. You watch the line, keeping out slack by raising your rod as needed. Determine when the spoon hits bottom by noting a sag in the line. Depending on wind or boat drift, you may need to reel—taking *in* line—to keep slack from developing while the lure drops.

Those are the basics, although there are many variations on the themes. For example, you often don't want the spoon to drop all the way to the bottom. Perhaps the bottom is full of snags, so that a spoon hitting it becomes a lost lure 80 percent of the time. Perhaps you're working on suspended bass, or bass feeding on some forage fish just beneath the surface. Naturally, in cases where it is undesirable to reach bottom, you count the spoon down to the desired depth. As you gain familiarity with different makes and weights of spoons, you'll acquire a sense of just how fast a particular model drops, thus avoiding the need to count on each cast.

Each of the previously mentioned spoon types has its particular drop characteristics, but you must initiate the action. Left to its own devices, a spoon that plunks through the surface may or may not begin a good drop. This is especially true with the tail-heavy Hopkins type spoons. To get a spoon started you need to pop it with an authoritative snap of your rod tip. (Obviously, an extremely limber tip won't work.) The snap starts the spoon up and forward from the vertical attitude. This accomplished, the lure will fall in a more horizontal attitude, wobbling, vibrating, and sliding from side to side, depending on its design.

Except for the freespool drop (which is often checked, as mentioned), good cast-jigging requires that you enhance the falling action all the way down to the spoon's intended stop point. This is accomplished through controlled line tension with your rod tip, alternately lifting or simply retarding the spoon drop. You virtually "feel" the spoon down with alternating pressure and slack, without developing true loose line.

As this is done, the spoon will perform two basic actions. It will wobble either fore and aft or from side to side, and it will slide or skid from the vertical fall line. These slides will be erratic—both short darts and longer side movements. Imagine an autumn leaf dropping from a tree and caught in puffs of wind that come and go. These erratic movements beautifully simulate an injured baitfish and frequently encourage even inactive fish to strike if the spoon comes close to them. Usually spoons with less violent action work best for inactive fish, while those with wilder slides trigger aggressive fish, giving them no time to examine the spoon closely. They must feel the spoon has to be grabbed immediately before it escapes. Some experienced anglers liken this controlled line pressure to the movements used in working a plastic worm. There is a similarity in rhythm, although the spoon falls faster and the worm lacks the side-slide movements.

The dropping, back-pressure lift in cast-jigging enables you to work your spoons through different layers, searching for fish. For instance, your first cast may work the spoon through the 10 to 12-foot level, the next through the 15 to 20-foot level, and so on. For the retrieve, if you elect to work water layers all the way to the bottom, utilize the ripping method. Bouncing the spoon once quickly on the bottom and then ripping it as high as possible with a longer rod covers a great deal of the lower water column.

When working a dropping point, rip-rap, rubble, or ledges, make your cast-jigging retrieve downslope. The spoon will hang up far less often this way, even though it is more difficult to maintain bottom contact as you work out from the structure and toward your boat. If you do hang up, don't immediately go over the spot with your boat. Try to snap the spoon free. If you do, be ready for a possible strike because fish often pop a snagged lure that they've been watching struggle the moment it breaks free. If you're fishing with a friend and you can't work your lure free, have him cast near the spot where you're fouled. Fish examining the snagged lure will often hit a free one swimming close by. As your spoon leaves the target area and nears the boat, work it faster. Get it traveling in a steady twitch with no drops. This often convinces following fish to strike and also sometimes triggers fish that have been hanging, unknown to you, close to the boat.

Besides working all the usual shore-oriented fish-attractive areas, don't fail to work offshore for suspended fish, fish surface-schooling on bait, and wind- or current-oriented fish. Remember that an onshore wind often pushes bait toward the windward shore, then boils the forage out again.

Bass can relate quite closely to the wind-lashed shore or that area just off it, because waves that roll in cause a curling downcurrent that moves outward along the bottom. You'll need to experiment working with and into the wind as well as at a right angle to it. Suspended fish are often easy to locate with good depth sounders, but not always.

In time, you'll develop your tackle preferences for cast-jigging spoons. Some anglers like using fairly heavy line—up to 20-pound-test. It enables them to free snagged spoons more successfully. My usual choice is 12-pound line for good distance and for less resistance when the spoon is dropping underwater. I also like a two-handed casting rod with hefty butt and medium-stiff tip. Your rod should be able to handle ¾ to ⅞-ounce spoons, which are the most commonly used spoon weights. A good quality levelwind reel completes the outfit.

There is a problem with spoons, but one that can be reduced to a good degree with some modifications. The problem is one of bass throwing the hooks. You have only one single or one set of trebles on a spoon. The rest (except for the flutter spoons) is heavy weight that slaps around underwater but even more so when a fish jumps. Couple this with the fact that the fish often swipe a spoon quickly, trying to keep the thing from getting away, or hit it just as it makes one of its sideways slides. The result is that they're frequently hooked lightly. Naturally, hook sharpening with a fast-cutting file or stone is a must. You may even want to consider changing hooks. The original equipment hooks on many spoons leave much to be desired. At the least, you need to file through the plating to get a sharp point on them. Often they're too heavy for quick setting. If you change hooks, go to normal strength, non-hollow-point wire in bronzed finish. And don't go too small. Some anglers even like a finer wire than normal because it can be slightly bent under rod pressure, and that little bend is often all it takes to free a snagged spoon, just as it is with fine-wire jig hooks.

How the hooks are attached to the spoon can also affect the lure's action. Original equipment rings that attach hooks to spoon are often too small. They can be responsible for a hook tangling on the spoon body, catching on line or line ring, or getting stuck in other oddball positions. A rule of thumb is to use a No. 5 ring on ¾ to ⅞-ounce spoons, and No. 6 or No. 7 rings for bigger spoons. Rings of good size should also be used in the line-tie hole. Not only do they help prevent line twist, but they also keep line from sawing and fraying through. The line-tie eyes of some spoons are not too smoothly finished. A swivel is usually not required for cast-jigging, although you might want a good quality ball-bearing swivel on your line ring for vertical jigging, which tends to cause most twists.

Welded rings are strongest of all, but top-quality split rings suffice. Just

A variety of plastic action tails that can be affixed to either single or treble spoon hooks. Some work only on singles.

remember, split rings can be rated for strength. The Sampo Company, which sells its fine ball-bearing swivels with both solid and split rings, is one firm that rates the units for strength on the packaging.

Plastic action tails and pork trailers can both sweeten a spoon's appeal and change its action because of the lifting affect on the hook. Generally, they tend to dampen a spoon's wobble and slow its sink rate. Some anglers slip a piece of plastic grub over the hook shank before putting the hook on a split ring. Sheldon's is one company that was marketing one of the Mepps spoons with plastic action tail already on.

Many of the preceding cast-jigging techniques apply equally to trout or salmon in lakes. I've had great days tossing some of my favorite trout spoons—many of which were designed for trolling—and catching fish both on the drift and anchored at hot intercept points such as river-mouths, along old underwater river beds, and near docks and points. Many times, traditional trollers motoring by were drawing blanks. But a slow troll or controlled drift using an electric motor is a fine way to work an area using these spoon tactics whether for trout or bass.

Overall, the cast-jigging method works best by day, especially bright ones. The action tends to fall off toward dusk or on overcast days.

Vertical Jigging Techniques

Longer ago than I care to think about, I dropped a diamond jig over the side of a boat. It was a heavy jig, and I let it plummet considerably deep. It bounced on the bottom and I caught a fish. The bass weighed somewhere between 18 and 20 pounds. It wasn't a largemouth bass; it was a striper and the scene was the ocean of our mid-Atlantic coast. There soon followed subsequent trips for bluefish, cod, pollock, sharks, and then a host of southern species such as groupers, jacks, and mackerel. All of them hit a vertical jig of one kind or another.

Anglers in saltwater have been using vertical jigging techniques from the earliest days of sportfishing. Their use in freshwater has been a relatively recent development, but one whose time has definitely arrived—for good reason. Vertical jigging takes largemouth, smallmouth, striped, and white bass, plus a lot of other fish, too. The technique in freshwater developed around tightly concentrated cold-weather bass or those holding deep in clear reservoirs. Usually the fish held around dead standing timber, pilings, steep bluffs, or other drop-offs.

The development of landlocked striped bass fisheries also advanced vertical jigging methods for bigmouths. The stripers were chumps for dropping and bouncing jigs—especially those of the tail-heavy Hopkins type brought inland by experienced saltwater fishermen. Naturally, largemouth bass anglers thought they'd try the sport for their favorite species. The rest is history.

Vertical jigging in freshwater is essentially a pinpoint technique to be used when you need to drop a lure on the small target area in which the fish are confined, and keep the lure working there long enough to trigger fish to eat. Everyone who jigs vertically develops his own particular method of working the slab spoon. I have seen all manner of twitching, high-arm raises, and snapping, but never a very effective saltwater technique known as stemming the tide. Yes, it surely does work on deep holding largemouths, and on landlocked stripers too, for that matter.

The method is a good one when you are working in a wind or on a controlled drift. We don't have real tides in freshwater, but there are some underwater currents, especially in large lakes. Largemouths normally don't hang in the more serious currents unless they're on a school of bait; stripers often do. In any event, you still frequently have to contend with wind pushing the boat.

To stem, you drop your spoon alongside the boat or at the stern, downwind. Don't flip it upwind. The spoon must drop as freely and quickly as possible. Turn down the mechanical brake on revolving spool reels, almost to the point of causing side-to-side spool slip. Control the line with your thumb. The moment the spoon hits, snap your reel into gear. The spoon must hit hard and make a clean bounce if the bottom is hard. Do not let it drag a moment if your boat is moving. That drag will turn off fish. If the bottom is semi-soft, snap your rod to jump the spoon up.

After the spoon bounces or snaps up from the bottom, you have some options. First, a fish may have grabbed the lure; in which case you know what to do. If not, you can simply let the spoon hang there while your drift and line bow causes it to begin rising. Or you can try cranking the reel five times—slowly. Another alternative is to crank fast about ten revolutions. Following each of these movements, allow the spoon to hang several seconds. Then go for another drop, and add a bounce or snap.

Repeat any of the movements after the second drop. Try for a third. Depending on the speed of your drift, you may still get another bounce. As you stream out more and more line, however, you'll come to a point where you'll lose feel of the bottom when the spoon hits. When that happens, crank in fast and go again. Try a controlled cross-wind drift using your electric, if that will still allow you to work the target area to which you believe the fish are relating.

An additional twist to this stemming technique is also borrowed from saltwater, although in modified fashion. In certain coastal areas, anglers couple trolling with metal lines (primarily single-strand Monel, today) with a type of jigging in swift, powerful rips. This is rugged business, requiring non-stop jigging effort that leaves your arms feeling like those of a gorilla—if you still have feeling left in them. Things aren't quite so rough in sweet-water situations. Still, there are times you'd like to fish when the wind is beyond the coping ability of an electric motor and/or you're forced to deal with a fairly stiff underwater current. Metal line can help control your jigging spoon and give better feel of what's happening below under such difficult conditions. Without wind and current, metal line can be an effective tool when you're fishing extreme depths, say from 35 to 70 feet—levels at which bass are taken by skilled anglers.

We're not dealing with big trolling reels filled with wire line—the kind of rig you might use for lake trout, for instance. This spoon-jigging method calls for segments of wire line. I believe it was angler Ron Uyeda of California who first came up with the idea.

"Why not use short sections of metal between a mono leader and

STEMMING THE TIDE

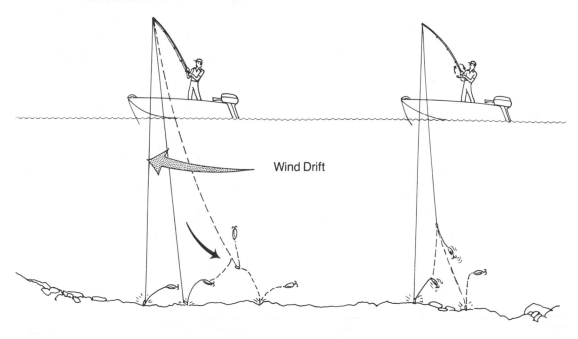

Wind Drift

Method 1: Engage reel the moment spoon hits bottom and bounces. Then allow boat drift and line bow to raise lure slightly; free spool and let spoon drop again to bounce off bottom.

Method 2: After lure has hit bottom and bounced, crank reel slowly about five times, then fast about ten times. Then allow lure to drop and bounce again, and repeat.

Dacron or monofilament main line?" Ron asked. Why not indeed?

Experiments were shortly forthcoming.

Various lengths of wire or leadcore lines were tried. The most effective length proved to be 25 feet. Of course, conventional revolving spool reels are called for; spinning has no place with wire. Reels as small as the popular bass casting reels can be used. The junctures of main line to the metal segment and the metal to the mono leaders can be made using a small Bead Chain swivel. These swivels will fit through the levelwind mechanisms of the older baitcasting reels, not the newer ones with smaller eyes integral in the levelwind. If the newer reels are used, you can make the various line junctions with specific, easily-learned knots.

For the main line (Dacron or monofilament) to leadcore connection, you use a modified nail knot. After the first three turns of the main line

Jon Gibbs caught this nice largemouth on a light spoon usually used for trolling for trout. Even light spoons can be flipped in shallow water for bass.

are made around the leadcore, the tag end of the leadcore is lifted up and away from the wrappings and from whatever nail knot tool—nail, tube, etc.—you're using. Then one turn of main line is made in the normal way, and the leadcore tag end laid back in again. The same knot works for the monofilament leader and leadcore connection.

To connect the mono leader or mono main line to Monel single-strand wire, first form a loop in the wire using the haywire twist. Then squeeze the loop into an elongated shape. If you're using fairly light mono—say 10-pound-test—now attach a short piece of heavier mono—25 or 30-pound-test—to the lighter line. A 15-inch section of this heavier mono is more than enough to work with. You then insert this heavier mono into the wire loop and pull it through so the heavy and light mono connection is near the wire loop. Then proceed to tie the standard Albright knot.

If you use a Dacron main line, join the single Monel segment to it by first making a loop in the Dacron main line using a Double Surgeon's Knot, Spider Hitch, or Bimini Twist. Insert the end of the wire line through the loop in the Dacron, and wind it five times over both parts up the loop. Next, wind back down the loop. When you reach the end of the Dacron loop, stick the wire end through it, then continue by twisting the wire end around the standing wire about three more turns.

Unless your reel has an extremely small levelwind eye, all these connections should pass through. If you have a problem, consider a reel without a levelwind. Many small reels designed for light saltwater fishing are being manufactured today without levelwinds. Although they may be a bit heavier than your favorite bass fishing baitcaster, they're a far cry from a big trolling reel. Companies such as Daiwa, Newell, Penn, and Shimano all produce good reels for this purpose.

Keep in mind the following tips when using the short wire segments for vertical jigging. Your leader should be short—4 feet is fine. Let your line out fast, carefully controlling it with your thumb as it shoots down. This is especially critical with monel. If you have never used wire before, be forewarned that monel (and braided wire) can spring up in the most disastrous backlash you've ever experienced. Unlike monofilament, you can't always pick it free. The real damage comes from kinks that form in the wire when you're trying to straighten even a few sprung coils of the stuff. There is a wire straightener made by the DuBro Company of Wauconda, Illinois, which can straighten kinks in single strand wire line. If you do develop a kink and cannot straighten it, cut the wire, or its strength will be vastly reduced.

In practice, I've found that a relatively stiff, two-handed, 7-foot rod suits me best for vertical jigging with wire line sections. By using both hands and arms, I'm able to ease the burden of long jigging sessions, which can be tiresome to say the least. The extra length enables me to raise the lure through a wider water column and achieve a longer spoon drop than is possible with a shorter rod. Stiffness is important when you're trying to put some movement into your spoon at greater depths. If you're planning to jig fairly deep water regularly, or work in strong wind and current, I'd recommend using Dacron as the main line rather than monofilament. Do keep the mono leader, however.

I have fond memories of gray windswept days, the inland lake gulls sliding down the sky or coasting far on air currents—days that, in the past, I'd have been relegated to picking straggler fish in protected places, if I could fish at all. My good memories were made possible by the short metal line segment coupled with a fairly heavy spoon that proved their worth on largemouths, landlocked stripers, and, yes, even smallmouths.

chapter 5

Landlocked Striped Bass

"Men cannot become fish, nor can fish transform themselves into men. But over the centuries, men have learned to appreciate in creatures, qualities that are also recognizable in humans. Men who know the striper know it to be a creature of strength and sinew, endowed with a unique determination to survive."

—John N. Cole, from *"Striper."*

Back in 1969, Stu Tinney left the New Jersey seashore and the big ocean-going striped bass he'd been catching for the hill and lake country of central Tennessee. In the huge TVA impoundments of his newly adopted home were healthy populations of a relatively new species for inland anglers: striped bass. The fish had already grown to good size—larger, for example, than the popular black bass everybody normally sought. But there was a problem. Virtually no one had figured out how to catch the stripers.

Why, reasoned Tinney, should these fish not respond to methods used in saltwater? There was no reason at all, and the rest is history. Tinney's pioneering work on landlocked stripers mushroomed into a full-time guide service with ten regular guides on the payroll. Next, the energetic angler launched an informative newsletter, and finally formed the national fishing and conservation organization called Striper, based in Lavergne, Tennessee.

During the ensuing years, Mr. Striper, as Tinney is today affectionately and accurately known, is responsible for the development of some of the most effective angling techniques now regularly used on inland waters.

Two of them in particular are different shallow water methods for spring and winter; the latter a season that is virtually ignored by most inland striper fishermen. First, consider the early-season method that was responsible for helping to build the man's reputation in those early days during Tennessee's developing striper fishery. That the technique is now being used by top guides and anglers throughout the U.S. is ample testimony to its effectiveness. Many anglers have tried spinoff approaches that, although sometimes are effective, lack a subtle element of the original. Here's how it all began.

Saltwater stripers like to eat herring. In spring, herring of various species run up small tributary creeks of bays and estuaries. In many areas it is a time when families traditionally make a holiday of dipping the small fish with nets, buckets, or whatever is at hand. The herring are then pickled, salted, or smoked.

As the herring gather in saltwater before the run, they congregate in the currents at the mouths of the creeks. They hold there, head to the flow, gently wiggling. This is where the stripers find them and eat them. For the stripers it is a tradition, too. In southern New Jersey, anglers began using floating minnow plugs with bucktail trim on the tail end to vibrate in the current, as did the herring. Tinney figured that the same kind of thing might work in freshwater in spring, when the striped bass come shallow. He began looking around the tackle shops for a topwater plug that might work. He tried quite a few, then hit upon Cordell's Red Fin.

The plug is a true topwater minnow imitation. It has an air chamber in the head that keeps the front section right up on the surface, even when water is being forced against the lure's small bill. The Red Fin can be retrieved cold-molasses slow without losing its wiggle. When worked that way, the head and front part of the back will break the surface, resulting in a kind of waking effect across the water. Some anglers say it looks like herring, others insist the action is of shad. Stripers eat both types of forage in various impoundments but, in the end, it does not matter because the big stripe-sided bass clobber the waking Red Fins beautifully. They like the 7-inch size in spring.

Many other plugs have been tried successfully, but none so consistently as the Red Fin. Some of them dig a little too deeply, or lose their wiggle when worked too slowly. Sometimes, of course, the stripers won't hit a bait on top, and that is when other lures come into their own. Some of the more popular plugs for fishing the surface or just under it include the CD Rapala, Storm's Little Mack, and Bomber's Model A Long Minnow. Favorite colors include rainbow trout finishes, red and white, and blue and white.

A live skipjack herring and the Red Fin that attempts to imitate it and is the most successful striper lure.

The waking technique is best done very early in the morning. In spring on many reservoirs in the Southeast and Southwest, local experts will tell you to be fishing by 4:00 A.M. By 5:30 A.M., the action can be over. You fish the points that come out from main shorelines—especially those that extend near deep water. The technique works up major tributaries and into creeks where the stripers run. You can use it below locks and dams, too. Any major feeding flat used by the fish offers potential. Some flats will have dead willows or brush on them; others may have dips or saddle contours on the bottom. In the spring, the stripers literally explode on these plugs, often smashing them clear of the water.

The waking Red Fin technique usually lasts until the bass are changing from their springtime patterns, although Tinney has taken fish using the method in June, when everyone else in Tennessee has switched to warm-weather techniques. But the surface method is not done for the year. It works again in winter.

Stu Tinney (rear) pioneered fishing for striped bass in TVA impoundments. Here he's shown with Ralph Dallas (left) and Herbert Odum after a morning's fishing in Tennessee's Old Hickory Lake.

Winter Stripers

Winter is the time when most anglers think the fish move deep, hanging suspended near sheer bluffs or in wide holes in the old river channel of a reservoir. Sometimes they do, usually by day. And usually there are birds in the vicinity hoping for some action. You can jig or troll for the fish then but, if you want some unusual excitement, you'll wait until the bass move shallow. They go up river or creek arms, and back up long shallow coves. The water will be as shallow as 2½ or 4 feet. The river and creek arms, and sometimes even the coves, often have another feature present: current. In the coves, current often is caused by runoff, seep springs, or springs in surrounding bluffs and banks. Current results in the backwaters clearing quickly after a muddying rain. Current also helps attract bait. So does the shallow water.

Just a little sun can warm the shallows. On cloudy days, even the infrared rays alone can be enough to raise the temperature of the backwaters and coax the baitfish in. The extra warmth can mean survival to some baitfish. In many reservoirs, great numbers of shad begin dying late in the year when the water temperature drops, yet not all of a lake's shad die each winter—if they did, enormous (and improbable) stocking programs would be required to maintain forage for the striped bass. Those surviving shad enter the warmer water areas of the reservoirs. From Christmas into February, the stripers come after them. They come at night.

The bass move from the deeper water at the mouths of long coves and river arms, swim quickly far up into the shallows, and begin to feed. Striped bass are extremely photosensitive fish and, although they go on surface feeding binges in the bright sunlight both in freshwater and saltwater, it is normally in the open water where they have only to sound into the depths for safety. Far into the backwaters they lack the safety of deep water and are skittish because of it, which is why they choose the hours of darkness. Sudden careless flashing of vehicle headlights or portable lights can put them off their feed or even move them out. So can heavy footfalls on the hard-frozen banks from which most of this fishing is done.

During the winter, smaller Red Fins of 5¼ inches are more productive. You cast and slowly wake them across the surface just as in spring. If you've taken fish from an area for awhile and the action dies, rest the place for fifteen minutes or more. Also try moving a little ways away and using one of the deeper running plugs before going back to surface lures. The subsurface lures are also better when mist covers the water surface.

Many lakes across the country offer winter fishing of this sort in the shallow backwaters. Examples include Maumelle and Beaver in Arkansas; Whitney in Texas; Herrington and Cumberland in Kentucky; Percy

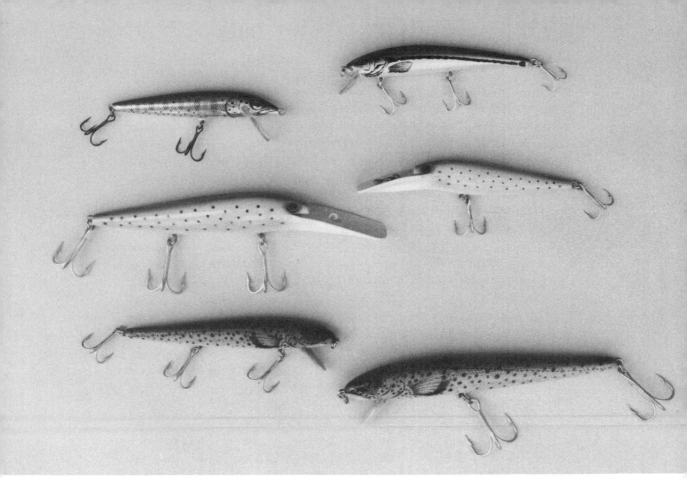

Some popular striper plugs (left row, from top): Rapala CD11 in rainbow trout finish; Storm's Big Mac Diver in rainbow trout finish; Cordell Red Fin C–0993 L4. (Right row, from top): Bomber Long A in Shad Finish; Storm's Little Mac Floater-Deep Diver; Cordell Red Fin C–1093 E5.

Priest, Tims Ford, and Norris in Tennessee. The western Colorado River canyon lakes also offer potential, but bank access is a problem and boat fishing will be necessary.

In lakes where ice forms, the fishing is over the same kinds of areas that are productive in the unfrozen reservoirs. Kansas' Lake Wilson is one example. Icefishing for stripers is normally effective with small spoons and even crappie jigs. It is all slow jigging, and the bass must be brought in gently on the light hooks.

Besides the arms and coves with natural current, winter striper fishing is also productive near areas of thermal discharge, such as from nuclear plants or other power generating facilities. And the forage is not always shad.

Once, during a record freeze on Tennessee's Old Hickory lake, veteran striper anglers Ralph Dallas and Herbert Odum showed me their dedication to the sport. Using a construction hoe and a two-by-four, the pair smashed over 75 yards of 2-inch-thick ice to make a boat path to open water. In the sub-zero weather we inched through the narrow passage, occasionally grinding the fiberglass boat hull like a Coast Guard ice breaker. We ran through the cutting air and pre-dawn mist, tears whipping from our eyes and freezing to our cheeks.

Our destination was a nearby (I was glad for that) nuclear plant and a "magic" point that the end of a plume of 60° water washed past before spreading into a big bay leading to the open lake. Here the stripers ambushed skipjack herring from 5½ to 15 inches long. The bass would feed at the point, work along the bank upcurrent, and finally move all the way up near the plant where boils of water marked the strong outflow. You could fish here with natural bait—both live and dead herring, or cut steaks and fillets—but the surface plugging was most exciting, which was what Dallas and Odum planned to do. They had limited out on their last ten trips and, despite the weather, did not plan to strike out now.

Ralph told me what had happened two trips ago.

"We had worked the point, then moved up into the boils when a huge herring jumped clear of the surface," he said. "It was as long as your forearm. A huge striper was after it. The skipjack went down, then exploded into the air right next to the boat with the bass after him like a shark. I'm a taxidermist and I think I'm a pretty good judge of fish size, and that striper was five inches across at the eyes! He was our new state record. The herring made for the outflow mouth, and skittered just once more over the surface before the bass nailed him and disappeared."

That frigid day we did not find the new state record, but we did find other fish. The Red Fins were devoured greedily, even after the dawn broke and the sky turned pink. They were fish from 10 to 15 pounds, some of them firm and lean, others fat and already approaching spawning condition—perhaps because of the warm-water environment. Like all winter stripers, they were in prime condition, healed from the stress of summer.

There are some equipment cautionary notes for winter striper fishing. Conditions are not normally severe throughout open water areas in the landlocked striper's range, but still there are times when icy guides and lines are a real possibility. The line may become abraided where a sheath of ice forms around it—especially the section that moves through the rod guides. You must check this line section constantly. Also, it's necessary to hold the line between your thumb and first finger when retrieving, to shuck the ice off before it spools on the reel. If you don't, whether you're

Herbert Odum of Tennessee smiles over winter striper that hit a surface-running Red Fin in shallow water.

using spinning or revolving spool equipment, strands of line will freeze together and fluff up eventually when you cast. Backlashes are miserable by day in warm weather; in the cold and in the dark they are worse. After each fish or solid strike, it will pay to retie the knot that holds your lure on. And, of course, sticking the rod into the water from time to time to clear ice from the guides is par for the course. It's most important if you're using revolving spool equipment. Continued slow cranking will cause the cold-stiffened line to coil loosely on the spool. Therefore, a long cast followed by a rather brisk retrieve is recommended from time to time to eliminate slack coils that may build up.

An important factor to consider for this winter fishing is access. If you keep fish, a long hike back with the extra and often quite substantial weight is to be avoided in the cold over rough terrain, or through snow or mud. Careful reconnaissance using a good map of the area is important. Finally, take a small flashlight along, but use it judiciously with your back turned to the water, for things like unhooking fish or tying knots. Don't try to reline a rod the way a friend of mine did when the temperature was way below freezing. He used his tongue to feel the end of the line through, and his tongue froze to a guide.

Summer Stripers

Then, there is summer. Warm-weather fishing for landlocked striped bass can bounce between the predictable and unpredictable. It can be extremely fast, or so slow as to be virtually nonexistent. It can be tough, even for veterans, and can be pure frustration for first-timers trying it on their own. Still, some of the year's largest bass are caught during summer, and sometimes the fishing can catapult from the doldrums, ripping so wide open both underwater and even on top, that you can only shake your head in wonder. Because summer is the time when so many vacationing anglers have the opportunity to fish for the landlocks, it is certainly worth exploring the factors that affect the bass, and therefore determine how you must fish.

Temperature and oxygen are strict governing factors for the stripers. Once the water has warmed to about 75°, the bass will have moved. In some cases that movement can be far offshore, but in most it's a combination of going deep as well as moving out. Aging lakes, or those that are forced to absorb increased nutrients, have developed oxygen problems in deeper, cooler depths. The bass have to compromise between temperature and oxygen preferences in such situations. Because of it they will be in a stress condition, often lethargic and not very disposed toward eating.

In some lakes the stripers can find the proper temperatures and enough oxygen, but frequently these sanctuaries are small areas formed by seep springs. Huge numbers of bass crowd them, often being unable to move elsewhere in the lake. If there's not enough forage to feed the numbers of stripers present, the fish become emaciated. Some may die.

In many lakes, though, life for striped bass is a lot easier. They are able to find the right combinations of temperature and oxygen with plentiful forage near by. Summer grounds for landlocks can be 25 to 30 feet deep in some lakes or rivers; 50 to 60 feet in others. A good depth sounder (a chart recorder or an LCD display unit is best) is vital for locating the bass schools in the big lakes. But besides depth, there is so much territory that

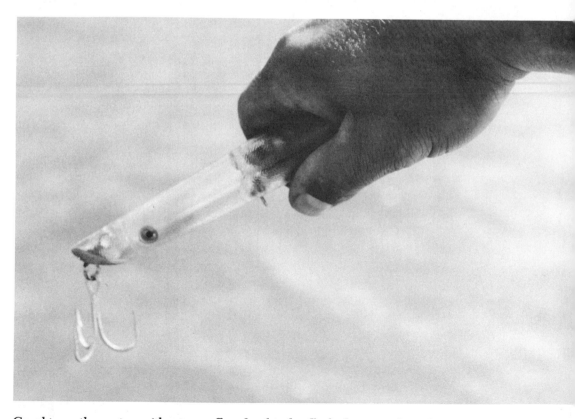

Caught on the water without a gaff and a big landlocked striper brought to boatside? Try this method of Joe Hughes to make an instant gaff. Reverse hooks—put trebles on line tie eye—of big striper plug. Remove all other hooks. Jam plug into striper's mouth.

can seem to offer potential, you must know the types of physical terrain or configurations that attract the fish in a big reservoir or river system. Check river, creek, or cove mouths, especially areas where two or more nearby tributaries enter the lake; large points of land that extend from the mainland to deep spots, such as holes or an old river channel; large rivers with deep underwater ledges; holes at river mouths; and feeding flats with an edge that drops off into deep water. Concentration points on the flats can include dead trees or brush. The same holds true for the ridge of the old, now-underwater river channel.

Before they move over the flats to feed, the stripers are usually suspended, but probably not over an even bottom. They prefer bottom areas where there are humps, saddles, or hollows—anything irregular.

Major river systems hold the summering stripers in specific areas. Look for the fish below dams and locks, as well as in the deeper holes and along deep ledges. When electrical generation causes current, the fish usually will eat. Without current, the stripers will act as if they're fasting.

Once on their summer grounds—which they may have traveled miles to reach—the stripers could adopt a couple of different routines. They may begin a routine of travel within the area, following forage schools and feeding on them from time to time. The bass usually hit the bait when the schools of smaller fish compress while going through narrows, over a bottom rise, or over the remains of some buildings, bridges, or railroad beds on the bottom.

Another summer routine for some schools of bass is suspension over irregular bottom, as mentioned, with quick forays at regular intervals onto flats or over points where there's forage. Sometimes those forays necessitate the bass leaving temperature/oxygen comfort zones. They may move from areas where the dissolved oxygen is 5 parts per million (usually the lowest that the bass will tolerate) or more, to places where it is 3 or even 2 ppm. Concurrently, they may move into 80°-plus water, when they normally don't want it higher than the middle 70° range. Smaller bass are more likely to remain in the warmer water than larger stripers.

Once schools of stripers or forage are located on your depth sounder (they're easy to spot) it's time to go to work. If the bass are beginning to move on the baitfish, they'll be most likely to hit your offering. But even when they're in a neutral state, suspended somewhere near the forage, they may take a bait presented in such a manner that they don't have to move to get it. Artificials and live or dead bait all work. Natural bait is often best at this time of year, especially by day.

Whole preserved anchovies are the most popular offering in many Western inland striper lakes. Elsewhere in the nation, steaked pieces of larger baitfish (called cut bait), fillets, or other whole dead forage are effective. But if it's available, I'll pick live bait in summer. It's logical to use the forage on which the stripers are normally feeding this time of year. In many river systems or big reservoirs, that means gizzard or sometimes threadfin shad. These may be the toughest baits to keep alive. You need cool water, plenty of aeration, and an uncrowded tank.

Skipjack or blueback herring are also tough to keep alive, but make an excellent bait wherever they are a normal part of the striper's diet. Easier to keep are shiners. The other assorted minnows in creeks that flow into the striper reservoir you fish are often hardiest of all. Many anglers use various sunfish—bluegills, warmouths, or pumpkinseeds—with great success in areas where doing so is legal.

You obviously cannot use too large a hook on a small baitfish and expect it to remain alive. Many striped bass anglers mistakenly believe that only huge hooks are suitable for their quarry. Big stripers have been taken on little crappie jigs with thin wire hooks. You just have to play them more carefully. Angler J.B. Bennett fishes such light fare in the lower Illinois River, from Tenkiller Dam 10 miles downstream to the confluence with the Arkansas River. Here the water stays a comfortable 56° in summer, about 50° in winter. Bennett uses tiny ⅛-ounce blue jigs on 4-pound-test monofilament to catch stripers in the 10 to 15-pound range. His largest to date weighed 17 pounds. Even for the very largest stripers that haunt some of our impoundments, a No. 1/0 to 4/0 hook will do the job every time. The smaller live baits should be hooked through the lips from the bottom up. The larger herring can be hooked just behind the dorsal fin.

After you locate the striper schools, the best way to present your bait may be through a controlled drift. You use the wind in conjunction with an electric motor to keep on course for a series of passes through the school. To mark that school I often rely on a free-drifting buoy. This type of buoy is used frequently by anglers in the Great Lakes to mark schools of salmon or steelhead. It does not employ an anchor lead and line to hold it in place, such as the buoys used in largemouth bass or walleye fishing to indicate specific cover or structure below. The drifter free-floats and must be retrieved periodically. Cannon, S&K Products (1732 Glade Street, Muskegon, MI 49441) manufactures an excellent model with telescopic flag staff.

The simplest way to rig for drift fishing is with a hook and enough weight 18 to 24 inches up your line to keep the rig at a level just above the stripers. Simply lower your bait down alongside your boat and drift. The line should have enough weight on it so it maintains a near vertical attitude as you drift. If it angles out, you cannot be sure exactly how deep your bait is. Should the stripers be holding in water that lacks enough oxygen or is too cold for a fragile bait to survive, you can lower the

Ralph Dallas caught this 30-pounder in a deep hole on live bait. Dallas will fish on top, at medium depths or deep, depending on the season and where the fish are. Note downriggers for deep trolling on stern of boat in background.

offering into the striper zone for a moment, then retrieve it to a safe level. The bass will usually rise for it.

Should repeated passes through a school not produce a strike, it could be because the bass are not pointed in the direction that you think. You could be bringing your bait or lure over their backs crossways, or from their tails toward their noses. Careful checking with your depth sounder may reveal something that resembles a little elbow turn in a point that you first thought thrust out straight from shore, and to which the fish are relating. They can also be affected by underwater currents, heading nose-first into a flow that results from a spring, a creek, or possibly the lake being drawn down. Such a flow can be very slow and subtle, affecting primarily the deeper levels. Making your passes in different directions may very well change your luck drastically.

Stripers can take your bait with the softness of settling thistledown, especially deep-holding summer fish. It is vital to keep your concentration focused. When a fish does hit, let it take out more line than you would at other times of year—perhaps 20 feet—before setting the hook.

It's a well-known fact that striped bass can be among the most boat-shy fish at times, for no apparent reason. Without even the sound of an electric motor, bass holding at 15 to 20 feet can become so agitated by a boat drifting overhead that they will not eat. Sometimes they'll move or descend. On such days you can try moving away from the marked school and casting the bait past the fish. Put your reel into gear or close the bail on a spinning reel, and allow the offering to descend on a tight line. The bait will describe an arc on its descent, curving slowly back toward you as it drops. You can alter the drop, causing the bait to fall vertically at any time by kicking your reel back into freespool or opening the bail.

When you've counted down your offering to where the fish should be, begin a slow retrieve. When fish are too deep for enjoyable continued casting, trolling can be extremely productive and will not spook the bass. Deep trolling with downriggers is sometimes the most consistent means of taking summer stripers. Lacking downriggers, you can use side-planer trolling boards and weights. You can also employ planing devices, or the simple three-way swivel with a sinker attached to one eye, a leader and lure or bait from the other swivel, and the main line tied to the third eye. Adjust your sinker weights for the desired depth.

Naturally, the live bait must be trolled quite slowly or it will soon die. You may have more speed leeway with cut bait or lures. In situations where current is present, downriggers can be used as control devices to stream bait or vibrating plugs at any depth and at virtually any distance behind your boat.

One favorite and most productive method at this time of year is vertical

jigging. The lures to use are vertical jigging spoons, or leadhead jigs with a variety of trim including hair, plastic, and pork. The Hopkins model Shorty 75 is the standard spoon. The technique is the same as you'd use for largemouth or smallmouth bass. Perhaps even more than those fish, stripers seem to prefer to hit a spoon on the drop. Once in awhile, though, and just often enough to keep your guard up, they'll pull a reversal and nab the lure as you jig it up.

Keep just a bit of slack out of the line as the spoon is dropping. If not, you'll miss the soft strike for which the bigger bass are notorious. When it's necessary to get deep fast, the leadhead jigs will do the job. They're especially effective when you need to bump bottom and get the lure coming up again—times when fish are holding very close to the bottom or some other object. The spoons sink slower and flutter nicely through suspended fish.

Because they may be under stress or simply not in a feeding mode, the suspended stripers you find just will not hit. Some extremely skilled anglers I know fished a school of stripers that were suspended around a steeple-like pinnacle thrusting from the bottom. They worked the bass for several days without a strike. Finally, nearly a week later, a heavy electrical storm hit the area. When it was over, with moisture still heavy in the air and a flush of new water in the lake, the bass began to feed. They ate well, then disappeared for parts unknown. Of course, most of us don't have a week to wait around until some natural phenomenon triggers the bass from the doldrums. But if you've located schools of stripers that refuse to feed by day, suspect that they may be feeding at night.

Night-feeding stripers will respond to the same natural offerings you presented in daylight, but are especially susceptible to artificials. They are more confident after dark, and are far more likely in summer to gulp a plug or other lure. And if the water temperature is a bit cooler, as often occurs just before dawn, they'll be more apt to remain in the shallow feeding areas—the submerged points, the expansive flats—for a longer period. You stand your best chance to take a trophy striper on an artificial after dark in summer.

Then, after the bass have trained you into believing that you must use painstaking techniques in order to catch them during hot weather, there

Joe Hughes rigs a variety of Spoonbill Minnows which can be used not only for stroking (see Chapter 1) but for trolling for stripers.

are times when they become almost suicidal. Every once in awhile, usually on the very largest lakes, the stripers will go on a surface feeding rampage. Any topwater plug, jig, spoon, or narrow vibrating rattle plug that somewhat simulates the forage in size or color will probably be taken. The action never lasts long, which is why most anglers have one or two extra rods rigged to cast for these breaking bass when flocks of gulls indicate that the fish are up. When you see the birds wheeling and diving, haul in whatever other tackle you have out, and get to them as fast as possible.

These surface-feeding binges are excellent times for flyfishing enthusiasts to get in on the action, but it's not the only time. Fly anglers normally don't find their best sport in the summer when the bass are suspended deep, even though fast-sink lines can put a fly to the proper depth. The fish are just too moody then. But at night in summer, when the stripers prowl the flats, flyrodders often score. Flyfishing is often successful, especially in spring, when the bass are concentrated up rivers or creek arms that feed major reservoirs. If the conditions are not too cold, the night-time, shallow-water movements of winter stripers can give fly enthusiasts a chance. Try a topwater slider (not a popper) eased across the surface in slow strips.

All manner of fairly large saltwater or salmon streamer flies are successful for the landlocks, and some anglers have built effective streamers primarily with the "living" rubber leg material used on jigs and various poppers.

We've come a long way since the early days of freshwater striped bass fishing, when the principal technique was to cast a piece of cut bait on a weighted line with a sliding float out near the edge of a channel drop, and just sit and wait. But, with all our modern sophistication, it's nice to think that that simple method can still work too, if you ever have the inclination to lean back, sip a long cooling drink, and just tell fish stories.

゙゙゙゙゙゙゙゙゙゙゙゙゙゙゙゙゙゙゙゙゙゙゙゙゙゙゙゙゙゙゙゙゙

chapter 6

Tactics for Trout in Lakes

"A pond never hurries."

—John Merwin, *fishing accomplice.*

Perhaps sportfishing's greatest fascination lies in solving that ever-changing, three-part enigma: where the fish are, what they want to eat, how to present it to them so they will. Each year, just when you think you have all the factors figured, you know as well as I do what happens. The fish will relocate to take advantage of another forage that demands a different presentation. Changing water temperature is a prime cause of such shifts. It's all part of a predictable cycle, though, and you can deal with it if you're willing to become proficient in a variety of techniques and move as the fish do.

For many anglers, once the inshore spring flurry of stocked, holdover, or wild trout is over, so is the year's trout fishing. That's too bad, because the rest of the open-water period can continue to produce wonderful near-shore and offshore sport, both near the surface and deeper. Learning what happens in your favorite lake or one you fish for the first time is vital for consistent success. Trout key mainly on insects in some waters, while in others they eat forage fish as their mainstay. Basically, though, fish are opportunists, consuming what is available for the least expenditure of energy. To gain a thorough knowledge of what is possible in a season of open water fishing, let's work with a hypothetical body of water.

Our lake has three species of trout: brown, brook, and rainbow. There are rivers into which the fish can run; ample insect life and forage fish species exist. It's good-sized, with a generous number of flats, bays, smaller coves, steep dropoffs, weedbeds, boulders, and both inshore and offshore reefs and shoals. The water is subject to stiff winds and winter freezes. In short, almost anything is possible.

In early spring the fish are near shore. They cruise windswept points and enter bays and harbors early and late in the day to swim around docks and piers. Many of the rainbows are spawning far up tributary rivers, although some will attempt to spawn near river inlets or outlets if the right kind of bottom gravel is there. Newly stocked hatchery fish swim about in aimless schools until pounced upon by stripers or largemouth bass. When that happens, you can sometimes see the stocklings shooting across the surface like flying fish. The brook trout in this lake will be on near-shore reefs, shoals, and rocky pinnacles. Sometimes they'll relate to stone jetties and piers. Browns will do that also, as well as cruise bays, big harbors, the water off rivermouths, and along sandy beaches.

The reasons why these trout are inshore are obvious to most anglers. For one thing, the water is not quite as frigid in the protected shallows as it is farther out. Of course, exceptions occur on other lakes where currents or power plants affect deeper areas or water farther offshore. The inshore waters is also where key forage fish will be.

Trout will be feeding on various minnows, followed by smelt or a combination of alewives and smelt, depending on availability in the lake. In our model lake, browns sometimes avail themselves of drifting eggs from rainbows spawning near rivermouths. This is truly the easy-pickings time of year. You can catch fish on all kinds of natural or unnatural bait from a pier or while trolling spoons, plugs, or streamers. Wind, temperature, and rain are the keys to when this early fishing shuts off.

A long, cool spring results in extended spawning both for rainbows and forage fish, which keeps the other trout around. Normally, with some rain and a gradual warming trend, trout finish spawning upriver and begin to move down. As they do, live minnows cast into rivers and at rivermouths can be deadly bait. Cool-water baitfish are affected by warming water sooner than trout. Once spawning is done or they're roaming inshore, they begin to move on. It doesn't take the gamefish long to realize that they better move if they want to eat.

A very dry spring can have another effect on rainbows far upriver. If the water level has dropped down quickly, they may hold upstream in pools until a good rain finally raises it again. Only then will they run downstream. In a dry year, when most trout have left the harbors and bays, try fishing around rivermouths following a heavy rain. You might hit a second contingent of fish just returning to the lake. The same rain can bring pods of bait through bottlenecks at cove or bay mouths, even

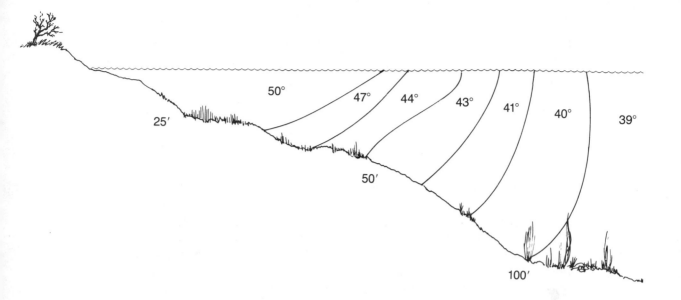

These two diagrams show the difference in water temperature in lakes with a gently dropping and a steeply dropping shore. From early to mid-spring, in a lake with a gently dropping shore (above), the water gets cooler very gradually, so fish have to swim farther out in the lake to find a comfortable temperature zone. In a lake with a steeply dropping shore (below), the temperature change is more rapid, and fish do not have to swim as far to find cooler water.

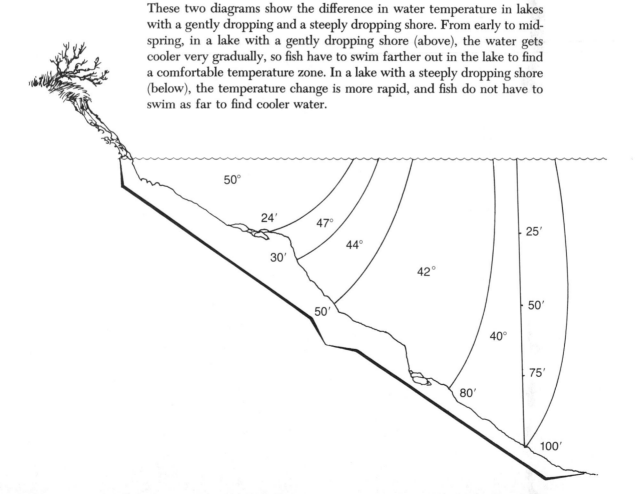

though the majority of forage and trout has already left. Often you'll have this final flurry of inshore fishing virtually to yourself. Once it's over, though, the new behavioral patterns begin.

During the mid-spring, trout are on the move. They're still far from summer patterns and still not deep, but the warming water of flats or other shallow, lake-basin areas is forcing them to look elsewhere. Depending on the lake, what they find may not be far from shore.

Besides the seasonal warming trend, two other factors govern water temperatures which affect trout and their forage. The first consists of bottom and shoreline configurations. The second is wind. Contrary to popular belief, water temperature is not so neatly stratified in mid-spring as it is in mid-summer. In spring, different size and temperature bands of water move offshore or over steeply dropping bottom. The band of warmer water grows thinner as you move offshore or over a steep drop. In other words, a fish seeking slightly cooler water at this time of year need not go deeper—it can go a little farther offshore, or seek areas of good dropoffs around points and steep cliffs. Now what about the wind?

An onshore wind can cause warmer water to build up on that shore. An offshore wind can cause the warmer water band to be pushed from that shore and replaced by colder water. The different trout are affected in various ways. Brook trout, for example, tend to move to boulders and reefs farther out in the lake, unless a steady offshore wind keeps cooler water handy on shoals closer to the shoreline. Brown trout, which can be unbelievably tight to shore at ice-out, tend to seek areas of sharply changing temperatures during this mid-spring period. They continue this affinity for areas of sharp temperature change on into summer, when lakes stratify more vertically and a sharp thermocline forms. Look for them in the mid-spring period near rock rubble, sharp bottom humps, or pinnacles close to a steep, near-shore drop. Later, browns will be within 10 feet of the thermocline and many of them will hover in areas where the bottom and thermocline intersect. Basically, like the brook trout in lakes, they prefer not to wander too far offshore.

Rainbows are another story. Migrating rainbows—steelhead if you prefer—begin moving from the shallow, warm water bands, then just continue following the cooler water plumes farther and farther offshore. The lake's coldest—and densest—water can reach to the surface if you go far enough offshore. Wherever different water densities meet, distinct edges form. These edges tend to collect wind-blown debris on the surface or, lacking debris, are sometimes visible through a difference in water color or a subtle smoothing of the surface. These are signposts for offshore rainbow fishermen who know that big trout follow such edges.

In huge waters like our Great Lakes, trout tend to feed on plentiful

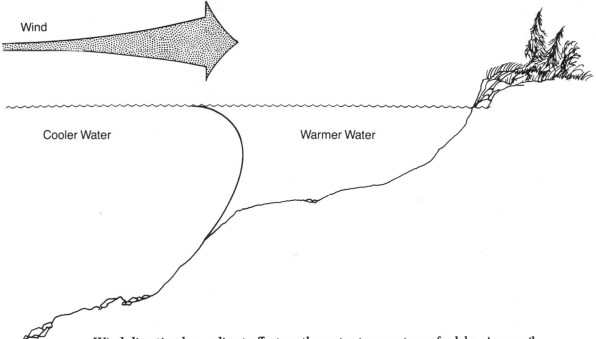

Wind

Cooler Water   Warmer Water

Wind direction has a direct effect on the water temperature of a lake. A prevailing inshore wind keeps warm water near shore (above). This is water that had warmed earlier in the shallows. A prevailing offshore wind pushes a band of warm water out (below), which is replaced by cooler water near shore.

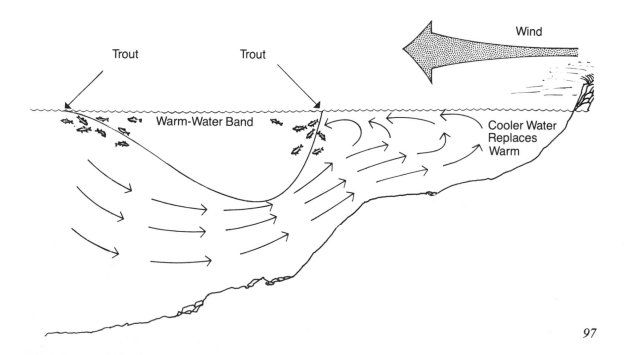

Wind

Trout   Trout

Warm-Water Band   Cooler Water Replaces Warm

alewives and smelt while following these patterns. In countless other large and small lakes across the nation, the progression is similar, although forage fish are utilized only part of the time. Insects fill the bill otherwise in these lakes. Mayflies, caddis, midges, and damselflies later on will produce some of the heaviest feeding and most exciting sport of all. During the mid-spring period when trout have moved from the extreme shallows, key spots to search for them are the quiet main lake shorelines, off bay mouths, offshore island shores, ends of long points, and a little way off tributary mouths. In these spots the fish can hold in the cooler water and move only a short distance to intercept maturing insects in adjacent, somewhat shallower areas.

Until you learn the areas in your lake that regularly hold trout that feed on insects, you'll have to wait until the rise. There'll be no doubt when it happens. You will see the gentle head-and-tail rises of trout sipping midges, mayfly spentwings, or flying ants. Splashier action indicates the trout are chasing escaping caddis or mayfly duns.

Of course you can catch some trout on dry flies during the hatch, but usually more productive is to fish an unweighted nymph of matching size and color on a leader about 15 feet long, the last 3 or 4 feet of which consists of fine tippet.

Long, commercially tied leaders once were hard to come by, but these days you can buy knotless tapered leaders to 12 feet, then add desired length tippet to them. Now, even 16-foot leaders are available. For example, Kaufmann's Streamborn (Box 23032, Portland, OR 97223) offers 16-foot Climax leaders from 4x to 7x, and Buchner Fly Designs (Box 1022, Jackson, WY 83001) offers braided butt leader tie kits with instructions to tie leaders to 16 feet.

The trick here is to grease all but the last couple of feet of the leader. Then touch the nymph with a quick-sink preparation. The way it's *supposed* to work is for you to establish an individual trout's direction of travel by watching its rises, cast several feet ahead of where you think it ought to be, then make your presentation. Let the nymph sink a little, then begin a series of short pulls of the line to simulate the nymph working toward the surface. When the trout hits, gently lift your rod. The fish should be on. This sounds simple, but it's not.

The big problem is getting your nymph to finish settling just a little way in front of where the trout will be, if it decides to continue on its last heading. It's a little like leading a bird with a shotgun, without being able to see the bird. Sometimes the fish will continue on course, the nymph's sinking will intersect with the fish's forward movement, and you'll hook up. With light tippets and violent reactions by the fish, you'll break off if you can't slip out line fast. At times, during massive hatches, it's nearly impossible to believe that a trout will single out your artificial among so many naturals. Precise presentation and timing can make it work. Sometimes a nymph or true dry fly slightly larger than the natural is the key. In these situations, I usually dress the entire leader and tie on an undressed nymph that will float just beneath the surface.

A typical example of frustrating, fascinating, and awesome hatches occurs on Hebgen Lake near West Yellowstone, Montana, although it's a summer rather than spring event. Between 9:00 A.M. and noon, the insect life swirling about the water or on the surface is so thick you almost dare not open your mouth. Trout cruise like sharks, breaking the surface film with their snouts, opening their maws and devouring huge numbers of

A fly fisherman casts to gulpers on Lake Hebgen, Montana. These are trout that cruise the lake during a hatch and devour huge numbers of tiny insects in a gulp.

bugs in a gulp. They duck under, move ahead, and do it again and again. They have aptly earned the nickname "gulpers." To make matters worse, you frequently can't tell if the fish are on *Tricorythodes* or *Callibaetis* flies. It's quite a sight to witness skilled anglers in float tubes dotting the water, scratching their heads, testing different patterns, trying to make the presentation just right. It's an even nicer sight when someone does everything correctly, is graced with a little luck, and his rod suddenly bends in that vibrating living arc that is what we live for.

This kind of fishing can't stand more than a gentle breeze. A wind will destroy it. So will some idiot who sees rising fish and tries trolling through them. However, trollers often take trout in slightly deeper water, out from the area where the hatch is taking place. Perhaps the activities surrounding the insect emergence are communicated to nearby deeper-holding trout, exciting them enough to feed. Perhaps it's just that being opportunists, the trout that are holding on an edge of water temperature band, outside the insect activity, simply react to a baitfish-like lure that happens by.

Once you learn the key areas where trout feed on insects, you don't have to wait for the hatch. If the insects on which your trout are currently feeding hatch in the late afternoon or evening, you can work the morning segment of the maturing insect cycle with sunken nymphs.

Let's assume you've located some insect-supportive deep weedlines, or channels in weed beds where fish will cruise from the cooler water edges. Let's say the insects involved are mayflies that normally hatch late in the day. In the morning, the nymphs of these flies will be starting to grow active, rising 7 or 8 inches above the vegetation, then settling back. Trout have no trouble cruising the weeds and picking off these nymphs. An ideal technique is to use a leader about 20 feet long with a weighted nymph.

If you choose to make up such long leaders from scratch, the butt, middle, and tippet section should be about equal in length. Forget the 60-20-20 formula. The heavier butt section can be of level material, or you can use the butt section of a commercial knotless tapered leader. Just cut the leader a little below the obvious start of the taper. Then make up the middle section of several lengths of material in decreasing diameters. It's difficult to list exact diameters, because so many new materials with different characteristics are now available. A rule of thumb has been to not connect any two sections that vary more than .003 inches. But by doubling the finer material, using a triple surgeon's knot (overhand knot) or improved blood knot, materials of surprising difference in diameter can be joined. The single length of fine diameter tippet of up to 5 feet forms the final section. The new braided butt materials (especially the tapered variety) turn over extremely long tippets. Using leaders already tied with the tapered butts, I've increased total length by extending the mono taper part just slightly, then tying on very long tippets.

In any event, you should use a strike indicator—a tiny cork, a bit of foam colored bright red-orange, or a 2-inch section of bright red-orange No. 9 or 10 fly line that you can thread over your leader butt by removing the core. Scientific Anglers sells the latter specifically for this purpose. Trout take these deep nymphs gently, and you'll need all the help you can get via the indicator to see the slight leader twitch that indicates a strike. Bass fishermen who fish the plastic worm a lot should be good at this. Imitate the action of the naturals by moving your deeply sunken nymph in slow pulls to make it rise slightly. Let it settle and repeat erratically.

Later in the day, the mayfly nymphs will be more active, rising higher from the weeds. Later still, a few duns will have begun hatching. The trout will still be on the nymphs, though. Now you should use an artificial with less weight and a slightly shorter leader. Bring your artificial higher

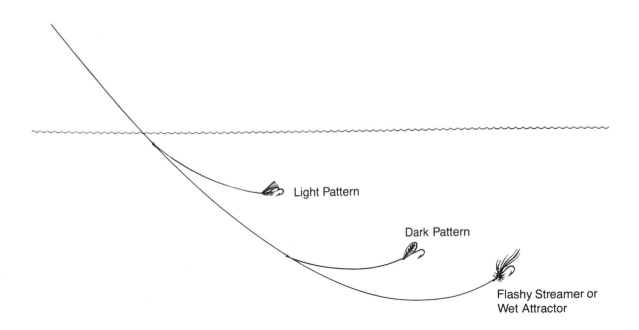

Typical tandem fly rig for lake fishing.

off the weeds with a somewhat faster action. Work the fly in short pulls, pause momentarily, then move it again.

There's another technique that can be extremely effective during this period, if you're willing to stick with it. The method involves multiple fly rigs or "casts" of two, three, or four flies, depending on local fish regulations. Unfortunately, multiple fly use fell from fashion in the U.S. sometime in the 1930's. Despite the less efficient casting and increased tangles that you must accept, multiple fly casts are one of the more effective trout fishing methods for flyfishing and spinning enthusiasts alike.

Multiple fly setups continue to be the rigs to fish in lakes throughout the United Kingdom. I've used them successfully in both Ireland and Scotland, and have increasingly put them to use in lakes close to home. They are extremely productive just before mayflies and caddisflies begin to break the surface, and also after spinner falls are over. Multiple flies can simulate stillborn or drowned insects, or rising nymphs. They can also look like little fry or minnows. If you use a nymph ahead of a flashy wet fly, the illusion can be that of a little fish chasing the bug—which brings out the competitive instinct of any trout.

Both nymphs and the venerable wet fly are productive on multiple-fly casts. Certainly you should begin by matching color and shape of the predominant insect at the moment, but experiment from there. Alternating somber with flashy patterns is smart. My frequent choices include flies in black, gray, brown, and cream. Old-time standard patterns continue to work. Among the best in subdued hues are the Dark Cahill, Light Cahill, Black Gnat, Leadwing Coachman, Teeny Nymph, and Gold Ribbed Hare's Ear. Flashier steelhead patterns and old-time wet flies that were originally tied for brook trout are excellent attractors. Three of the more popular wet fly attractor patterns in the United Kingdom are the Black Pennel, Peter Ross, and the garish Bloody Butcher. They work in the U.S. as well.

I've had days when I've fished three flies and trout would single out just one, no matter where on the cast it was located. On other days, the fly in a particular position is the one that catches the trout.

If you're used to flycasting with a hard, sharp, power stroke and extremely tight line loop for maximum efficiency when fishing a single fly, you'll need to modify your approach with the multiple setup. A looser, gentler approach is needed. A slightly softer rod can sometimes help. With spinning equipment, the more flies you use, the longer the line will be hanging below the rod tip before you make your throw. You'll need to make a sweeping or lobbing cast for your presentation. Whether you use fly or spinning equipment, though, a fairly long rod is a help.

If you're spinning, a flexible rod to handle light lines is necessary. You rig a multi-fly spinning setup with either a small sinker or a clear, tear-drop-shaped casting bobber at line's end. Try placing the casting weight above the flies, too.

One key to more tangle-free fishing with multiple fly rigs is in the type of monofilament you use for leaders and the droppers (from main line or leader) to which the flies are tied. The droppers should be of stiffer mono, so they'll better stand away from the leader or main line. There are several ways to rig droppers. For flyfishing, if you are tying up knotted compound leaders using blood knots for each section of monofilament, leave one of the two tag ends of mono about 8 inches long after completing the knot. Use this longer end as the dropper. If you're going to be serious about fishing multi-fly rigs, tie up several leaders and attach the flies. Tie a loop in the end of the leader, plus a loop in the end of the leader butt section that's permanently affixed to your flyline. If you're spinning, tie a loop or snap to the end of your line. Now you'll be able to quickly change leaders and their attached flies by means of interlocking loops.

If you change flies a lot, the droppers will soon become too short. There are several knots with which you can tie on new droppers. One of the easiest is to cut a dropper from stiff mono, tie a fly on one end, and knot a loop on the other. Then bend the loop around the leader just above the old knot. Slip the fly through the loop and snug up tight. If you use stiff mono leader to begin with, you can make droppers simply by pinching a good-size loop in your standing leader, then tying it off with a double surgeon's loop. Now cut one leg of the loop close to the main leader. A dropper will unfold before your eyes.

If you want to fasten droppers of stiffer mono to a knotless tapered leader, you can use the preceding technique. Or, pinch a section of your leader to form a loop or double section. Now, handling the double section as though it were a single strand, lay it across the length of stiff dropper material and tie a blood knot.

For flyrodders, the maximum leader length is about 16 feet, consisting of 6 to 7 feet of butt, made of knotless tapered, or level mono; the tippet; and the dropper(s). Anglers using a leader of this length often space their flies 2 to 3 feet apart, although I prefer my flies somewhat closer together. The leader I use most frequently stretches to just 12 feet. I tie the flies 16 to 18 inches apart. I'm not comfortable fishing with more than three flies, and use just two in windy weather. Four or more flies are frequently used in the United Kingdom.

A handy 4-inch wheel for coiling pre-tied leaders with the flies on them

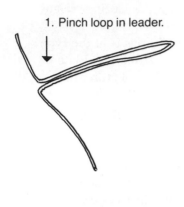

1. Pinch loop in leader.

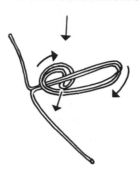

2. Tie two overhand knots.

3. Cut top or bottom leg of loop.

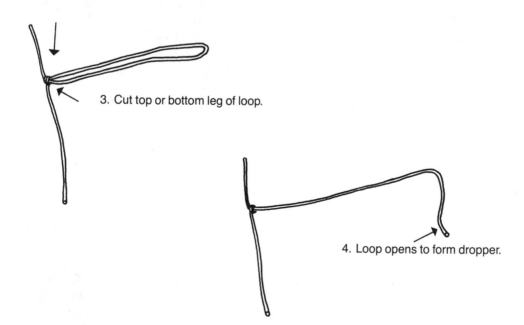

4. Loop opens to form dropper.

Forming a dropper at any point along a knotless leader.

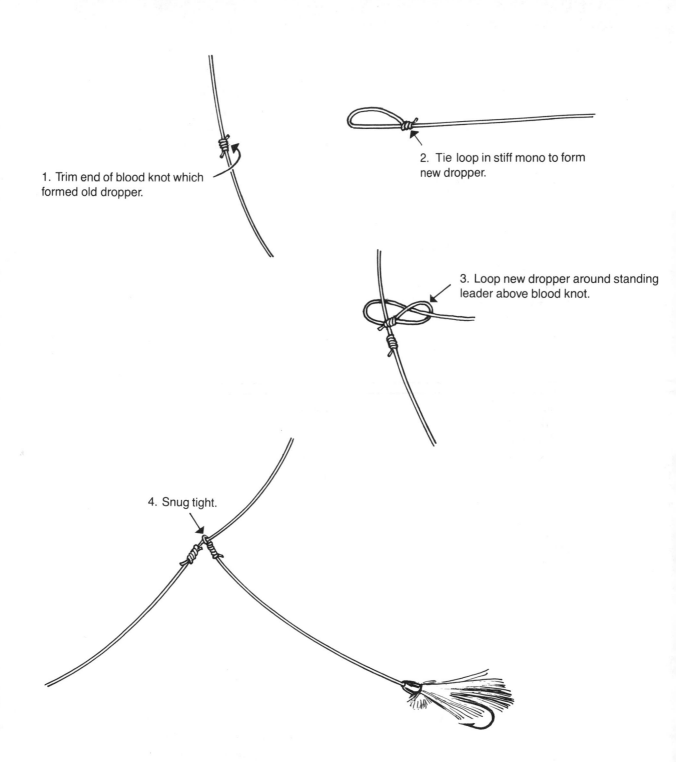

1. Trim end of blood knot which formed old dropper.

2. Tie loop in stiff mono to form new dropper.

3. Loop new dropper around standing leader above blood knot.

4. Snug tight.

Adding a new dropper to an existing leader.

can be cut from thin plastic. Plastic container lids or plastic coffee can tops work well. Cut spokes along the outer perimeter of the wheel. Weave the monofilament in and out of these spokes, around the wheel. The leader will stay nicely in place. Punch a series of holes circling around the circumference of the wheel just inside of the spokes to accept fly hooks. Such wheels were commercially sold abroad where multiple fly casts are common.

Once you've cast the multi-fly rig without fouling it, fishing is no problem—especially with a longer rod, which helps you to impart the proper action to the flies. There are several types of retrieves to use, but one of the best consists of V-waking three flies. To accomplish this, raise your rod tip to get the flies coming. If you're using a fly rod, make long continual pulls with your stripping hand. The hand-twist retrieve is worthless here.

Another method involves keeping the point, or tail fly, down in the water while the middle fly alternately skims, wakes, and drowns. The fly closest to you bobs and dances on the surface—which is how that fly became known as the bob fly. It's also known as the hand fly.

Another retrieve consists of keeping the two flies nearest to you on top. In this method, the bob fly is treated as a dry; it only occasionally touches the water surface. The middle fly dances up and down, and the point fly wakes. It's obvious that you can create a kind of excitement that's impossible when using just one fly.

Naturally, the more surface-oriented retrieves should be reserved for those periods closest to the actual hatch of insects in your lake, or just following the hatch or spinner fall. Another deadly surface retrieve requires a couple of well-greased, unweighted nymphs. After you cast them, allow them to rest a few moments. Then start them back with long pulls of your stripping hand, or a combination of rod lift and crank if you're using spinning tackle. The flies will duck beneath the surface, then pop back up. Repeat the action all the way back.

Earlier I mentioned the effectiveness of multi-fly casts for emerging caddis. A caddis pupa swims quickly toward the surface and, once it gets there, moves around in the surface film before emerging. A fast, 15-inch strip retrieve of a single nymph works well, but a skipping rise of two or three flies can be even better.

Besides the mayflies, midges, and caddis, damselflies can add significantly to lake fly fishing enjoyment. We're back to single flies here. Large, streamlined, active damselfly nymphs swim along the bottom toward the shore or any object that offers them a place to climb out, open their new wings, and dry them. Obvious stands of weed near deep water often are the starting points for these migrations. It's best to cast toward the deep water and retrieve toward shore. You can work from a float tube or boat. In some small and shallow lakes, anglers simply wade from shore. Sinking lines usually are preferred for fishing from a boat. Wading anglers can get by with sink-tip or floating lines. The strikes frequently come when your fly is beginning to rise near the end of the retrieve. Alternate between a fairly quick and longer pull-pause cadence as you retrieve.

Small, low boats such as open skiffs are ideal for stalking insect-feasting trout. The fish are even less sensitive to anglers riding float tubes. If you fish from a boat, electric motors are invaluable for positioning near weed-lines and other target areas. Trout are sensitive even to the low-noise electrics, so use them with discretion. Some electric motors are noticeably quieter than others.

Although too much breeze will clamp the lid on good surface fishing during a hatch and force you to go back to lightly weighted nymphs, you can use the wind instead of the electric for an even quieter controlled drift approach. If the wind is blowing from the correct direction to give me a good drift, I sometimes use a cone-shaped fabric sea anchor to keep my boat moving as slowly as possible. These devices are available from marine supply outfitters. You can attach them to the stern in a mild breeze, but don't chance this anchor location in a stronger blow. If you do, you're gambling with taking water over the transom. Instead, tie the sea anchor to a line off the bow.

Let's go back to our model lake again. Summer is approaching: Hatches slow, the surface grows warmer, and the lake begins to stratify more along vertical temperature bands. The trout begin going deeper to find cooler water. The exceptions are those far-wandering steelhead, which can still find acceptably cool water not too far beneath the surface, far offshore.

The fish in our lake are forced to travel some distance to locate deeper water, because the big basin they used earlier in spring does not afford depth. If, when using your depth sounder, you locate trout that are on the move, don't expect them to eat as well as they will when they cease migrating and begin holding in their summer territories. Once they do, you can expect a couple of different behavioral situations.

As insect hatches begin to taper off, the trout switch back to forage fish—first a variety of minnows, then smelt, ciscoes, or alewives. Trout frequently congregate on fairly deep underwater bars, reefs, or humps some distance from shore. But if you find deep water close to shore, and sections of its bottom are irregular and rocky, there's no need for them to look elsewhere. Trout can spend most of their time in the near-shore depths, then move closer in to shallower water early and late in the day to feast on whatever forage is plentiful there.

Many of the fish in our lake are now in 16 to 20 feet of water. Some big loners are as deep as 30 feet. Sometimes they'll take a cast, jigged, or trolled spoon at these depths in the morning or afternoon. Even better is to wait until gathering dusk cloaks the western shoreline in shadow. Just before dark, the trout are likely to move up into water that is clearly not their preferred temperature. Straggler insect hatches sometimes provide the evening meal, and methods earlier described will take fish. In other cases a variety of minnows become the bill of fare—but not smelt or ciscoes. After a bright, warm day, the water surface can warm as high as 70° to 74°, and those particular baitfish need 50° water. Of course, the feeding trout tend to cruise a few feet below the surface if the water is that warm, but they will take short forays into surprisingly warmer water if the food is there.

Conditions are close to ideal, though, if there has been a little breeze late in the afternoon to mix and cool the surface water. If there has, the water can go from the 70° range to 65° in a very short time. Obviously you must keep a sharp eye on the weather. If there are no hatches at dusk, try very small spoons, spinners, or streamer flies, both near the surface and several feet below, depending on the surface temperature profile. When darkness falls, don't go home. The early hours of the night can be grand for finding brown trout in the fast-dropping areas close to shore. Steep cliffs, islands, and points extending out underwater hold these fish. Even better for the brownies can be the period from false dawn to daybreak. Try trolling plugs that run a couple of feet deep, light flutter spoons, and big streamers. When experience has shown you the better spots, cast to them.

Once the hot weather has moved in for good, trout begin concentrating on the deeper schools of smelt and other coldwater forage fish. Looking again at our model lake, schools of smelt are now in 51° water at 50 feet. The thermocline (the area of most rapid temperature change) has formed at 45 feet. Now it's obviously a game for planing devices or, for complete versatility, downriggers. Your trolling will be in the preferred temperature zones of the most prevalent baitfish, or just above any trout you've located with a good depth sounder. The key areas will be bottom configurations that attract and frequently concentrate bait: reefs, valleys between underwater cliffs, humps, cuts between islands, areas off deep points, and steep bluffs not far from tributary mouths. Choose lures to match your trolling speed.

For deep-holding lakers and browns, I prefer to use light flutter-type spoons either by themselves or behind attractor tandem flashers (cowbells). Floater-diver plugs like Rapalas and Rebels are also very productive when used in the same manner as flutter spoons. Streamer flies or plastic squids are best used behind dodgers at this time to give them erratic action. When slow trolling doesn't produce, you should have a selection of spoons that give best action at slightly faster speeds. Finally, high-speed spoons like the Westport Wobbler, and seeker type plugs like the J-Plug and Pop-Top, should be tried. Obviously, you cannot team a fast-trolling lure with a slow lure and expect to have both working well. Match every lure swimming behind your boat to your trolling speed for maximum effectiveness.

Your next major period for trout fishing the lakes begins with the cool nights of early autumn. Surface temperatures begin to cool from a combination of colder nights and breezes that roil the surface. You'll alternately have warm hazy days and brisk clear ones. But when you get the feeling that "autumn is in the air," it's time to begin hunting trout in different places.

If the surface temperature has dropped into the 60° range, you'll find trout offshore working schools of young-of-the-year baitfish. Birds will tip you to the action, which usually occurs around reefs and off islands rather than the springtime areas closer to the mainland or in sheltered areas. Some of the most exciting sport at this time is casting small flashy flies or hard lures that resemble the baitfish prey. You can also cast live or rigged baitfish with a spinning outfit.

Late autumn finds most fall-spawning fish—browns and brook trout— first rolling in wide weedy river outlets or on shoals outside harbors or rivermouths. They then move up into dead-end bays and harbors, and finally rivers, if they can. Winter/spring spawning cutthroats behave similarly. By the time this movement begins, surface temperatures will be anywhere from the low 50's to 49°. During the late autumn period, big, bait-gorged rainbows will cruise near the surface and fairly close to shore. The better spots include beaches with some sand and weed, shorelines with small tributaries, and mouths of short bays. Possibly the most effective lures for them are spoons that can be trolled from medium to high speed, such as the Westport Wobbler, Eppinger Flutter Chuck, and Northport Nailer. The lures don't even need to be the same size as the bait, especially if you're trolling fast. Some of my most productive late-season rainbow trolling is with 3⅜-inch spoons, even though the young forage fish usually being eaten now are just a little over 2½ inches. Chrome/red/black, chartreuse with orange—any "hot" color or combination seems desirable to rainbows, while the browns seem to prefer silver. Blue and silver are favorites for lake trout. For big lake-dwelling brookies, excellent colors are silver, plain white, and sometimes silver and orange.

You might want to experiment with some of the billed diving plugs that can be trolled at high speed. The Rapala Shad Rap and Rebel Fast Trac are two.

With a willingness to experiment and search for areas and patterns that the fish are relating to, you'll find that trout fishing in lakes can be much more than merely a springtime fling.

Temperature Range for Key Forage Fish in Trout Lakes

Expect most species to concentrate within optimum temperature range

Species	Lower Avoidance	Optimum	Upper Avoidance
alewives	48	54	72
cisco	—	52–55	—
emerald shiner	—	61	—
rainbow smelt	43	50	57
yellow perch	—	68	—

(Temperatures in Farenheit)

chapter 7

Flyfishing Deep

*"Sure, I have effectively fished 100
feet deep—and a lot deeper than that."*

—HARRY KIME, *angler.*

The changes began tentatively enough with the increasing use of fiberglass rods in the 1940s. They gained momentum with the development of new line formulations during the tradition-shattering 1960s, and reached the current state of free-wheeling experimentation in the 1970s, with the use of carbon filament (graphite) rod fibers and dozens of newly engineered line designs and materials. The once-gentle art of flyfishing, the roots of which trace back to just after the birth of Christ, is today a whole new game.

Once innovative anglers discovered that rods of space-age materials could be pushed for extreme distance casting, and that incredible depths could be fished when these rods were coupled with new, quickly plummeting lines, almost no waters were considered unfishable. To date, fly anglers are catching fish of such size and variety from previously inaccessible places that it would no doubt have given Izaak Walton borderline apoplexy.

Ever since the second generation sinking line (Wet Cell II) was introduced in 1955, lines have generally gone down—deeper, that is, and faster, too. To date, the two largest fly line manufacturers—Scientific Anglers and Cortland Line Company—produce everything from very slow sinking intermediates (that float when dressed) to four densities of sinking lines. Beyond that, each firm produces ultra-fast sinking 30-foot shooting tapers. (Advantages and uses of shooting tapers, full sinking, and floating-sinking lines will be described in detail shortly.) Cortland's ultra-fast sinking shooting taper is a dense leadcore with tough, tapered outer coating. Called Kerboom, it comes in two sizes as of this writing. Scientific Anglers incorporates lead particles in the outer coating of the lines in its Deep Water Express series of ultra-fast-sink shooting tapers. These are also tapered, come in three weights, and are color-coded for weight identification (as are the Kerboom tapers). Cortland also markets level leadcore line (sold by the foot) with smooth tough vinyl coating. This line weighs 13 grains per foot. Several other firms still produce leadcore with an uncoated, braided nylon or Dacron outer sheath. Level leadcore is ideal for making custom mini-heads of various length for specialized fishing assignments, as we shall see further.

The four most popular densities of sinking lines from Cortland and Scientific Anglers come in full weight forward, double taper (sometimes even level) design, or as 30-foot shooting tapers. You should know that different weight lines within a given density type will sink at different rates. For example, a WF 6 Wet Cell Hi-D sinks slower than a WF 8 Wet Cell Hi-D.

Although there's not much of a problem deciding what rod to use with the lighter sinking lines or shooting tapers—they correspond well to the American Fishing Tackle Manufacturers Association line number designations—the heavier ultra-fast sink tapers have stimulated some debate. The AFTMA line designation is based on weight in grains of a line's first 30 feet. For years, the heaviest line was a No. 12 of 380 grains. What do you do now with tapers weighing 550, 700 and 850 grains? Cast them with a pool cue?

Today's best graphite rods are quite capable of handling a wide range of line weights. In fact, many anglers regularly use a line one size heavier than the rod's specifications, in order to quickly load the rod with little or no false casting. Still, you can overdo it. I know of some fishermen who persist in using a 550-grain high density lead-jacket shooting taper on No. 6 and No. 7 rods, which were designed for 160 and 185 grains respectively. The rods just aren't going to last long under that strain. Line manufacturers won't give rod recommendations for their heaviest tapers, except for statements to the effect of "for an 850-grain line, you need a very powerful rod." You bet. I've launched those 850-grain tapers with a rod I use for big saltwater fish. It does sail on out there, but as it whistles by I've often caught myself retracting my head into my jacket in fine tortoise style.

We need not worry about such problems here. Trout and bass fisher-

Big, deep holes with slow current are best fished with a floating line and nymphs or streamers, the leader weighted with lead.

men will be able to extend their subsurface flyfishing with these wonderful lines in weights typically no heavier than 250 grains (a No. 9 line). I have used a 450-grain and even a 550-grain shooting taper in windy conditions, with big flies for extreme depth, and in monstrous river currents for wilderness char and salmon.

Well, with all these superior new sinking formulations available, just how deep can you really fish with a fly rod? Pioneering West Coast flyrodders of my acquaintance have fished 150, 180, and 200 feet down in the ocean. It works, but these depths are extreme and, for my taste, very simply takes the fun from flyfishing. In lakes, I consider 35 feet as deep flyfishing. In rivers, 7 to 10 feet is deep—especially in strong current.

Despite these line advances, lead split shot, sleeves, or Twiston lead strips coupled with a floating line are sometimes still the most efficient means to sink a fly quickly under certain conditions. Lately, lead particles or wire inside braided leaders, and small sections of level leadcore line incorporated into leader construction as a mini-head have replaced clamp-on lead to an extent. The question, even among anglers experienced in other phases of fly fishing, is: Where and why do you use all this stuff?

Veteran fishermen develop strong attachments to particular line/leader systems. Further, there are waters and specific types of fishing where more than one system works. Given my particular prejudices, here is how I see the various sink systems at their best.

Full Sinking Lines

First of all, despite availability of double tapers and level line configurations in many full sinkers, I'll always go for a weight forward for fast and hard casting ability—with any size fly. I'm not looking for double taper delicacy, and I don't want to fight a level line when I need distance and good tip and leader turnover without false casting. I like full sinking lines in windy weather, when the finer diameter running/shooting lines that back up a shooting taper system are more likely to tangle. This is especially true if you fish in smaller boats not really designed for flycasting, and is worth considering even in good flyfishing skiffs. Standing on a casting platform, dropping coils of line at your feet in a healthy breeze, you're more likely to avoid tangles with the full sinker—especially if you're a newcomer to shooting tapers. I also prefer them in float tubes.

The full-sinking line that's easiest to obtain distance with is the fine diameter Hi-Speed Hi-D or Cortland's Type 4. You can cast these entire lines far easier than, say, a full floater with its larger diameter and greater air resistance.

Overall, a full line is easier for many anglers to handle. If you have not allowed it to sink too deeply, you need not complete a full retrieve in order to roll it to the surface for another cast. Besides, sinking lines—even the fast sinkers—are not used only for getting your fly to great depths. In many cases you need to get the fly just a few feet beneath the surface as quickly as possible in wind and rough water, or before current can sweep it far. The fast sinkers will do the job. They're also excellent for getting big bulky flies beneath the surface fast. Of course, you'll then need to begin the retrieve immediately and continue it at a relatively fast rate if you don't want the fly to descend deeply.

Classic situations where you need fast sinkers include trout or bass feeding on fish life from just below the surface to about 4 feet beneath it. Bass over shoals, shallow reefs, or around boulders where they're feeding on minnows or crayfish are other situations. A bulky hair fly like a Muddler Minnow must sink fast in a river to reach the holding trout. The full sinking line is effective in all these situations.

Shooting Tapers

Originally called shooting heads, these lines were first made of level sections cut from old-style leadcore line. Today they come right from the line makers in 30-foot weight-forward *tapered* lengths, and in all the popular sinking line classes. The ultra-fast sinking formulations are only available as shooting tapers. Special new level leadcore is available to create your own length shooting heads.

The taper of these newer shooters helps somewhat in both casting and turning over the leader and fly, but so does the very nature of the lines. Ultimate casting velocity means ultimate distances: Excellent fly casters achieve distances over 100 feet regularly. Call them what you will, shooting tapers or heads are so named because the 30-foot taper section is followed by 100 feet of coated, braid-core running/shooting line or 100 feet of monofilament running/shooting line. In casting, the main taper (head) is launched, and the finer line shoots after it. Credit is given to West Coast anglers for creating shooting systems like this at least as early as the 1950s. The lines quickly became standard equipment among steelhead and salmon anglers who needed both distance and depth in large, heavy rivers. And now, anglers fishing trout and bass around the nation are discovering the many benefits and diverse uses of shooting tapers.

Before exploring uses of shooting tapers, it is worth touching on the nature of running/shooting lines that follow the heads. Monofilament is preferred by many Westerners for ultimate distance and least water drag.

Many types of mono are used, and there are champions of both flat and standard round monofilament. Some want bright fluorescent finishes to better track their line; others prefer the more subdued shades. Most agree that overly limp mono is out of place as running/shooting line. Some anglers abhor monofilament for the shooting assignment, preferring the coated, cored running/shooting lines and their tendency to tangle less.

You may sacrifice some distance with a coated running/shooting line, but it is a little easier to manage in wind. It does produce slightly more water drag. Coated running/shooting lines come in floating formulations (.029-inch diameter), fast sinking formulations, (.032-inch diameter), and intermediate or very slow sink formulations, (.035-inch diameter). The latter is of 30-pound-test strength, while the others are 20-pound-test. The larger running/shooting line may be preferred by those fishing for giant chinook salmon. But for the fishing we're concerned with, the smaller diameter floating or sinking running/shooting lines are fine.

For all practical purposes, the .002 difference between the floating and sinking running/shooting lines is indiscernible. Deciding on whether your running/shooting line should float or sink may be likened to the long-running argument over whether your leader should float or sink. Actually, the sinking formulation may get your fly a bit deeper faster, if current isn't a factor. In most cases I prefer the floating running/shooting line. It can be mended, and the fast-sinking shooting taper brings down that portion of it that needs to get down for the majority of my fishing.

Many anglers avoid trying a shooting taper for fear it is overly difficult to master. A fisherman who has long used a full-length line will find it odd at first, but should quickly adapt. Beginners often catch on even faster, not having to re-educate their casting styles. In fact, Mel Krieger of San Francisco, one of the nation's best casting instructors, has advocated the use of shooting tapers (sometimes shorter than 30 feet) to help newcomers quickly learn the dynamics of flyrod casting.

The decreased water drag on fine diameter running/shooting line that permits your fly to swim slower and longer in heavy rivers will give you another advantage. Whether you're dealing with strong current or still lakes, the fact that fine running/shooting line cuts like a razor through the water will help put the odds for success in your favor when you've hooked a big, fast-running fish on a light leader.

Shooting tapers cost less than full lines, so you can afford to assemble a number of different density and sink rate heads to cover all typical fishing situations. If you use a loop at the end of your shooting taper and a loop at the start of your running/shooting line, you gain quick-change capabilities. Each shooting head is coiled (use twist-on plastic bag ties or bits of pipe cleaner to hold the coils) and ready for use without the need for extra

This is the kind of water where shooting heads of sinking line excel—big pools with swift current that would drive a floater to the surface.

reel spools. Because running/shooting line (especially mono) takes up less room on the reel spool, you have space for more Dacron backing.

If you primarily fish rivers for trout, steelhead, or salmon, you'll normally not need *quite* as many different shooting taper densities. Lake anglers who want to cover all bets need a complex system, including possibly a floating taper, a floating-sinking taper, an intermediate taper, and a variety of the faster sinkers. Anglers who really get involved often have a variety of tapers for several different rods.

You are the judge of the outfits for which you want tapers. As a guide, though, river trout fishermen should consider tapers for rods handling line weights from No. 5 to No. 7. Steelhead and salmon anglers need to think heavier. Lake anglers are usually covered by using No. 7 to No. 10 weight lines. You don't need a full range of tapers for each weight class; just carefully consider what you'll need in each weight category before you

Floating popper can be fished deep on a fast-sinking line. Popper rides just above cover when fished on a leader of proper length, long enough so the popper rides above the weeds.

begin building your collection. Many anglers are quite happy with a full range of shooting tapers for just one or two rods. The graphite or composite rods we use today are also capable of handling several line weights, so you can handle more situations with one outfit. Many fans of shooting tapers like to use a head one size heavier than the weight of line recommended for a given rod. The rod can then be loaded more quickly. We'll examine this more closely when casting the shooting tapers.

Although I stressed distance casting as one of the better features of shooting tapers, the lines also shine in many short-range situations. Such situations abound in the South for bass fishing and in the north for trout, salmon, or steelhead. The typical case is a tight-quarters river, a small stream, a canal, or a backwater oxbow. These places can be a nightmare of overhanging branches, leaning trees, or other vegetation where there's no room for a long backcast. If you were faced with conditions in which a floating line could handle the presentation, a roll cast might work to a degree. But we're dealing with deeper flyfishing here.

Let's say you have 25 to 30 feet of room behind you, but need to cast 55 feet or so. With a shooting taper, all you need do is hang from your tip guide an amount of head that will just clear the obstructions on the back cast, make one back flip, then shoot forward. In some situations you'll have even less room. If you regularly encounter true jungly areas, you may want to build shooting tapers even shorter than the standard 30 feet; perhaps 20 to 23 feet will do. If the shorter taper will load your rod, you'll get the needed distance again with one simple shoot. Just as vital, you'll get your fly to the proper depth.

Shooting tapers will handle virtually any fly—even big, wind-resistant streamers and poppers. Speaking of poppers, one of the more effective techniques for big, deep-holding bass is to fish a super-fast-sinking head with a standard high-floating cork, plastic, or balsa popper attached to your leader. The fast-sink shooting taper gets quickly to the bottom, dredges through weed, brush, rocks, or timber, while the bug floats and dances behind. If you incorporate foam in the body of a streamer, those flies can also be used for bass or any of the salmonids. Adjust your leader's length according to how high over cover you want the bug or streamer to ride.

Floating-Sinking Lines

Dual-density lines incorporate a front sinking section (fast-sink or super-fast-sink formulation) of 10, 20, or 30 feet, with the full remaining length of line being of floating formulation. The 10-foot sink section line is a Wet Tip, the 20-foot sinker a Wet Belly, and the 30-foot sink-float combo a Wet Head. The lines were developed to circumvent inherent problems with full sinkers, even shooting tapers. With those designs, the deeper the line sinks, the more of it you need to bring back in order to pick up and cast again. If you have not permitted a full sinker to sound too deeply, you can bring it up to the top for the next cast by rolling it. In river situations, however, the resultant commotion can alert fish. The floating-sinking lines are easier to pick up for the next cast, which translates into being able to cover more water faster. The longer the sinking portion of these lines, however, the more difficult it is to get them up to the surface. The type of water and the depth you need to achieve will determine which dual-density line to choose.

Floating-sinking formulations are at their best in rivers with complex currents, where critical line control via concentrated mending is required. They help you follow the travel of the fly, and detect the movement that indicates a strike. Some anglers prefer to attach weights to their leaders, and persevere with a floating line. This does work but, as you increase the weight, casting becomes progressively more difficult until you are restricted to roll casts. Floating-sinking lines permit far easier casting, but they are not best for the longest distances. With lighter floating line behind the wet tip, belly or head, you'll experience a hinging effect if line speed is not up to maximum. In short, you have to work harder to aerialize a lot of floating-sinking line and cast it far. A full floating line is easier to cast far and, of course, a shooting taper will go farther even easier.

Floating-sinking lines are somewhat limited as to the depth you can obtain, because of the effect of faster-moving surface water. Remember, as soon as current catches a line or as soon as you begin a retrieve, that line ceases to sink at its normal rate. That's why mending is so critical. Remember too, that full sinking lines and shooting tapers are also similarly affected.

I like to fish floating-sinking lines up and downstream or slightly quartering across. They lose a lot of their effectiveness when casting directly across a good current, unless you mend fast and continually. The dual-density lines are excellent for nymph or streamer fishing in pocket water or other concentrated areas 6 to 8 feet deep, where your retrieve will be short but you need to sink the fly quickly. They are good lines for slower currents and when river levels drop to a point where a full sinking line or shooting taper would be out of place.

These lines are wonderful for lake and pond fishing from boat or shore when you want to simulate a rising nymph. You can do the same thing with a long weighted leader or fly, but the floating-sinking lines with a shorter leader in fast-sinking density usually will get the fly down quicker. You'll not need to weight the nymph either, thus allowing it to swim more freely, and you won't have to worry about fussing with lead weights and having weeds catch on them.

When bass or trout are feeding on crustaceans or minnow life in relatively shallow water over reefs, rock rubble, or gravel, the floating-sinking lines work splendidly. With an unweighted fly, you'll be able to work a snag-covered bottom. The line will pass through the snags while the fly rides just above and behind. Don't be afraid to use extremely short leaders with the dual-density and other sinking line formulations. Many anglers use leaders as short as 2 feet, even for trout. If you use too long a leader, the fly tends to ride up even though the line is deep or on bottom. Obviously, you'll have to use a longer, finer leader where a most quiet presentation is needed but, if fish are nearer the surface, you won't be concerned with sinking the fly so deeply.

Some anglers even make shooting tapers from sinking tip lines. Using the first 30 feet or slightly less produces a line that will give greater cast distance or the advantages of shooting tapers in tight quarters, while still maintaining the benefits of the short sink section.

Cannonballs, Rolling Heads, Mini Shooters, and Lead Leaders

Let's say you've got the fish—big trout, steelhead, maybe Pacific salmon—cornered. They're in a tight little hole behind boulders on the bottom of a deep run, with surface water so fast that it could whisk away a mule as easily as a drinking straw. Or maybe they're back behind the leading edge of a logjam that breaks the current just a little. Or maybe they're somewhere even worse. The key problem with each of these holding areas is that it is so small and surrounded by so much faster water or snags that it is impossible to get a drift long enough, even with a super-fast-sinking shooting head, for the fly to reach bottom where the fish are holding. What to do?

Until now, the accepted way to present a fly to fish in short runs or other holding holes surrounded by powerful currents was to cannonball them. You fixed three to five big split shot to your leader or dropper. Then you kind of lobbed everything out with a power roll cast just scant feet upcurrent from them. The heavy weight would immediately sink the fly and the whole rig would bump along the bottom. An alternative was to use straight mono with lead clamped on it—no fly line at all. This method is generally used in more moderately sized streams. The mono can be hard to handle, though, and if you must go that far, it's silly not to use a proper spinning outfit to begin with.

The technique does work; it can be deadly. But the main problem with cannonballing is the weights, even if you don't use the kind with those little re-opening tabs that cause excessive snags. Even clean, round shot will hang up eventually. Some improvement has been achieved with those little cylindrical sleeves of copper or lead. They're a little more compact and more streamlined than standard shot when crimped to a leader. They too can snag, however, and obviously there was room for improvement over the clamp-on weight system. Ardent steelhead angler Ray Schmidt first came up with the idea.

The Manistee, Michigan, angler and his fishing partner Bruce Richards, a supervisor at Scientific Anglers, felt that the answer somehow lay in the floating-sinking line concept. A coated floating section could help mend line in the difficult currents. It was obvious to them, though, that the full 10 feet of sinking section found on a normal wet tip line would not be necessary—that much sink section was actually a hindrance. At first it was thought that the solution might be simply to shorten the sink section of a wet tip. The two began experimenting in the Pere Marquette, the Little and the Big Manistee, and the Betsie rivers—tributaries of Lake Michigan into which big steelhead and salmon run and seemingly enjoy seeking out some of the more difficult places I've described.

The shortened wet tips didn't work. Even the very fast Hi-Speed Hi-D tip would not take the fly 6 to 8 feet to the bottom in the places they needed to fish. The shooting taper concept seemed to hold promise, but the anglers knew that no 30-foot head or long casts would be necessary. They reasoned that if only a very short sinking section were used as a kind of a long flexible sinker ahead of a floating line, the No. 8 rods they preferred should be able to handle the combination for short casts.

Bruce immediately homed in on his company's Deep Water Express shooting tapers, which have bits of pulverized metal in the coating material. He elected to use the heaviest, 850-grain taper because it would sink fastest. Now the trick was to determine how much of the heavy material to use. Initial experiments proved that upsetting the balance of a normal floating line by adding a section cut from the Deep Water Express was going to make casting difficult. The anglers remember standing streamside festooned with ribbons of line so they resembled bizzare human maypoles.

They did not need to cast more than 20 to 30 feet. A simple roll cast should have done the trick, but the point and front taper section of the weight-forward floating fly line were not enough to turn over even a short section of the 850-grain lead-jacket line. The anglers then began cutting back the floating line, finally severing 8 feet from its front. This left them with the heavier belly of the floater. They now began attaching the various lengths of 850-grain sinker to the thick floater.

The new design worked. Roll casting is no problem; in fact, the lines can be cast much farther than you can roll them. When I first tested these lines, I found that if you can handle a normal 30-foot shooting taper, you can get good distance with the rolling head. Roll casting is still safer—that heavy, free-swinging fast-sink tip could slap you severely.

Ray and Bruce finally settled on using tip sections that were 1, 2, 3, and 4 feet long, depending on water depth and current. They used loops in the end of the floating fly line and the 850-grain tips. The loops are formed by bending over the coated fly-line ends, then nail-knotting two short pieces of monofilament line around the tag end and standing part to hold the loop in place. You can strip the coating from the tag end if you want. Two coats of Flexament or Plyobond make a smooth flexible finish and keep the monofilament knots from fraying. Spliced loops will work also.

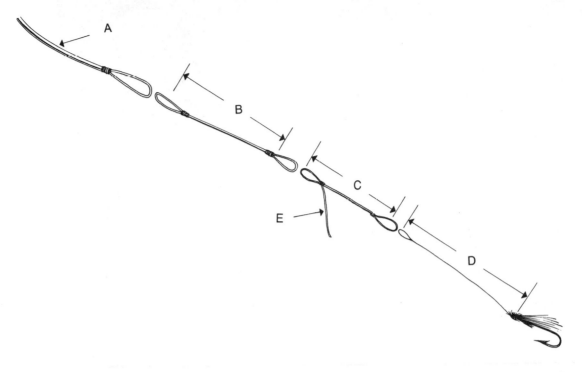

This diagram shows how a rolling head flyline is constructed.

A: Floating flyline with approximately 8 feet of point and front taper severed.

B: 1 to 4 feet (depending on water conditions) of 850-grain Deep Water Express or leadcore line.

C: 18 inches of 35-pound-test mono.

D: 3 to 4 feet of 4–10-pound-test tippet.

E: Leader butt loop tied with 3-inch tag to which split shot may be crimped for severe conditions.

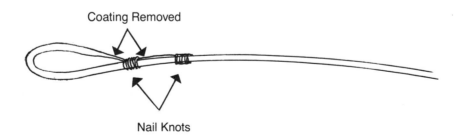

Construction of loop in coated flyline or leadcore line with vinyl jacket. Two nail or uni knots are tied with 15-pound-test mono, trimmed flush, then coated with Flexament or Plyobond glue.

Jerry Gibbs rollcasts an ultra-fast-sinking rolling head flyline.

One 30-foot taper of Deep Water Express will yield many rolling heads, but don't forget that it is tapered. For a more consistent sink rate, avoid using the small diameter parts. If you do, attach the thinner sections to the floating fly line. The smaller diameter sections sink slightly slower and are also easier to loop.

Use loops to connect the other elements of the system, too. The reel end of the floating line is looped and a large loop is also formed in the Dacron backing. Now you can quickly disconnect the whole ststem. Short leaders form the remainder of the system.

The leader butt that Ray and Bruce settled on is an 18-inch section of 25-pound-test mono. It is looped at both ends. The loop at the front of the leader butt is tied to leave a 3-inch tag sticking out. In conditions so extreme that even the 850-grain tip isn't enough, a big split shot can be clamped on this tag. If the shot hangs on the bottom, it will pull free or the tag will break. The bottom line is that you'll save rerigging.

The leader tippet section is 2 or 3 feet of 4 to 10-pound-test mono. You can attach the tippet to the butt with another loop or a twice-through clinch knot. The entire leader is only 3½ to 4½ feet long. Although you

The rolling head line is capable of casting light spinners, spoons, plastic egg imitations, as well as flies.

should go to lighter leader material in clearer water, the shortness of the leaders again does not seem to bother fish.

Rods lighter than a No. 7 are just not powerful enough to handle these rolling heads; even with a roll cast. Further, it's easier using a longer rod when most of the presentations will be via a roll cast anyway. Bruce and Ray typically use 9½-foot graphites. You may find a 10 or 10½-foot rod even better.

"The system is fished like any wet tip line," maintains Bruce Richards. "It just gets deeper faster." It also catches fish.

Skilled flyfisher George Harvey, once dean of Pennsylvania's Spruce Creek, developed a system that employs small sections of fast-sink line. I've come to refer to his as the mini-shooter system. Though I've used the mini-shooters in water that's not as vicious as that typically fished with the rolling system, George's mini-shooters can be used in the severe water just as well.

The system consists of incorporating various lengths of super-fast-sink-

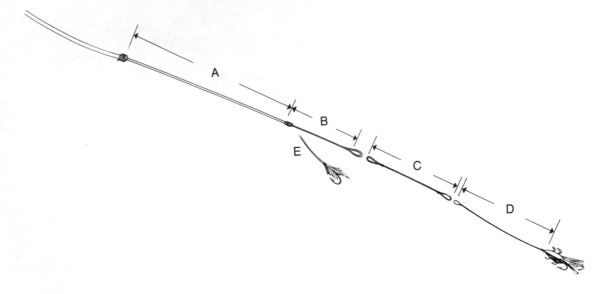

Construction of mini-shooter head sinking line.
A: 28–30 inches of mono or braided leader butt.
B: 12 inches of 2X mono.
C: L.C. leadcore to match water conditions.
D: 12-inch tippet
E: Optional dropper 10 inches above leadcore, if leadcore is under 2 feet.

ing line right into your leader. George settled on using Cortland's L.C. 13 vinyl-coated leadcore. He attached the mini-shoot heads after the first 3 or 3½ feet of leader. The sections of fast-sink line are matched to water conditions. Harvey used them in 6, 12, 18, 24, and 36-inch lengths, and also in 4, 6, and 8-foot lengths. To the end of the sink section goes a 12-inch section of leader to which the fly is tied. Sometimes a dropper fly is tied in 10 inches above the point fly when using sink sections that are 2 feet or shorter. George used his mini-shooters for fishing streamers primarily down and across current, and for casting nymphs upstream in pocket water. All the flies are unweighted, except for nymphs used in very fast pocket water. These have lead incorporated in the dressing, and seem to track better behind the sink line.

In shallow water, mini-shooters of just 6 inches are often perfect. If you use this system, you'll most likely find yourself adding and subtracting various length sections of fast-sink during a typical day. To facilitate a quick-change of mini-shooter heads, both ends of the fast-sink should be looped. If you use something like the Deep Water Express line, make loops as described for the rolling heads. If you use Cortland's L.C. 13, you can nail-knot mono loops onto the line or, for a more finished head, strip a bit of the vinyl coating from the braided core of the L.C. 13 with acetone or some other solvent. Remove 1½ inches of lead, and bend the braided core tag end back over the standing part to form the loop. Either tie in two monofilament nail or uni knots, or whip finish using tying thread. Then coat the connection with Flexament or Plyobond.

Like the rolling head, the mini-shooter can be cast quite well. It also gets your flies down quickly and doesn't snag with the frustrating frequency of split shot or lead sleeves.

Sink Leaders

Just when you think you've got all bases covered in this business of subsurface flyfishing, something new comes along. Actually, it is a new treatment based on a foundation going back to the origins of flyfishing. The ends of ancient lines—the leaders—were once made of braided horsehair. Now, along comes braided monofilament leader butts. They were originally intended for dry-fly fishing because, with their multiple filaments, they are tremendously efficient in transferring fly turnover energy from the fly line. They also stretch more, acting as a shock absorber when light tippets are used. And the butts are hollow. They can be dressed with a variety of floatants when a high-riding leader is desired. For our purposes, though, they can be built by incorporating lead pieces.

To date, the Orvis Company of Manchester, Vermont, and Dan Bailey's of Livingston, Montana, have braided leaders with built-in lead. More are sure to be available at a later date. These leaders can handle slow to moderate stream conditions and many lake situations, although you'll still need to use one of the other systems for extreme depths and currents.

Casting and Fishing

We've already discussed roll casting with the short rolling heads, but the subject is far from dead. For all full sinking lines, some situations with floating-sinking lines, and any shooting taper, the roll cast becomes part of virtually every presentation. There is just no way you can pick up 30 or 45 feet of line that has sunk a good way underwater and flip it up into the air for a backcast.

What you must do is strip in enough line to enable you to roll the rest up to the surface. Depending on your rod (and skill), usually about 20 feet of line may still be underwater. The next step, unless you are fishing a floating-sinking line at close range and could spook the fish, is to continue the roll, laying the line back out on the surface. Do not let it sink. Immediately lift it up for the back cast. The resistance caused by pulling the line from the water loads your rod without the necessity of false casts. In most cases you need only one backcast before shooting the line out once more. The technique is called a water haul.

If you are using a shooting taper, do not attempt to roll up the head until the shooting line-shooting taper connection is inside your rod guides. Some anglers prefer to have this connection in their line hand before picking up. Then, on the roll, the connection is extended 4 to 6 feet out past the tip guide.

When you are first learning to use a shooting taper, extend this junction—often called the overhang—only a foot or two. The more overhang out, the more critical cast timing becomes, but you must have a little of the running/shooting line out. If not, the junction may snag in the tip guide on the power shoot, causing all kinds of nasty things to happen.

To make the water haul in the first place, of course, you must get your line or shooting taper out. All sinking lines, especially the faster sinking variety, feel heavier than a floating line when you cast them. Sinking lines are denser, have less air resistance, and tend to begin dropping in the air faster than a full floater. This is more noticeable with a shooting taper, on which virtually all weight is in just the 30-foot head.

To cast these lines properly, you must know how to double-haul and

CASTING A SINKING LINE OR SHOOTING TAPER

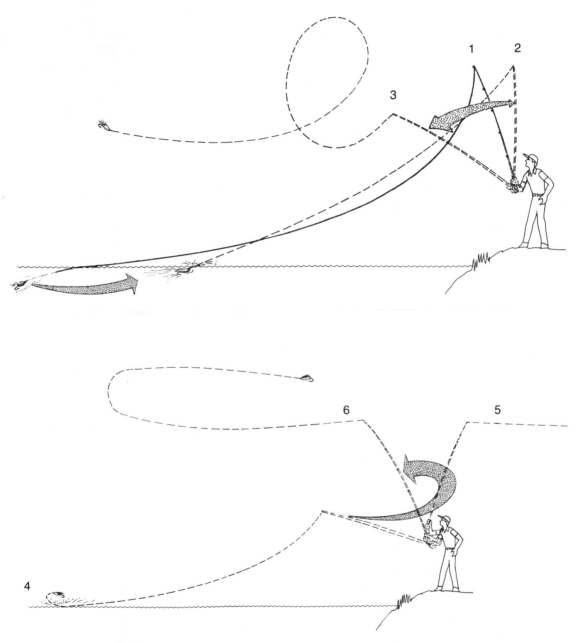

After stripping the line close to the surface (**1**), raise the rod and go into a roll cast (**2**). Allow line to straighten out (**3**) above the water's surface. The moment line splashes to the surface (**4**), pick up line in normal backcast (**5**), and go into a forward cast (**6**), shooting line and fly to the target.

constantly remind yourself not to force the cast. Think slow, smooth, and easy, and you'll soon master extremely long casts. Strip out running/ shooting line. On the back cast, do not power stroke sharp and hard. Make it a short and easy energy application. As the line goes back, drift your rod well back with it. Now push your rod forward smoothly, picking up speed gradually. Make the forward power application with the rod tip out in front but high, aimed for the horizon. Stop the rod tip quickly at this point. A little trick that aids distance here is to raise your rod handle so the butt is nearly parallel to the water. This lessens friction of the guides on the shooting line.

All your movements should be a little slower when casting the dense lines and shooting heads. Let the rod dictate speed as it loads and unloads. Don't drop your rod butt during your forward cast or your line loop will open, thus decreasing distance.

When you're getting used to the heavier lines, try to cast with the wind coming head-on, from the back, or over your left shoulder if you cast right-handed. This way you'll avoid being clonked if your timing goes off and an errant puff of wind pushes a fast-traveling lead-weighted line too close to your noggin.

Although much stream trout and salmon fishing revolves around dead drifting, lake fishing for salmonids and bass requires a variety of retrieves. All speeds are used. Often the ultra-slow hand-twist or short strip is employed when using a floating-sinking line to simulate rising nymphs. Streamers, of course, are stripped at a variety of speeds and worked in and around cover or places where fish have the bait corralled. Here's one tip to keep in mind when using one of the denser lines.

If your stripping or line hand has moved too far back when a fish hits, you'll obviously come back with your rod to help set the hook. When you do, be sure to keep the line under control with at least one finger of your rod hand. If you ease off too much to let the fish run, the heavy taper will quickly zip from the tip guide, sag in a slack curve to the water, and your fish may come off. This same feature can be beneficial if you think you have a hit, discover that it is instead a snag, and you are able to pull your fly free immediately. If you've struck upwards with your rod, simply lower it quickly while easing up with your line-control finger. The heavy sink-taper will immediately drop down, getting your fly back to the target zone for the remainder of your retrieve.

The dense, fast-sink lines also enable you to fish flyrod-size hard lures: the ultralight metal spoons, spinners, and a variety of plastics. All told, the new line and leader formulations we have today put flyfishing right in there as a method that competes favorably with spinning and conventional gear. It's just a whole lot of fun as well.

Fly Line, Leader, Butt, and Backing Connections

Line Type	*Connection*	*Connection Type*
Coated, high-density braid core lines	Line to leader butt	Needle nail knot or small loop
Coated, high-density braid core lines	Line to backing	Small loop
Plastic-coated leadcore	Line to leader butt	Regular nail knot over plastic
Plastic-coated leadcore	Line to running line	Loop. Remove plastic coating. Remove section of lead wire, double braid section back on coated section. Wrap with thread, then coat with rubber-based cement or fly head cement
Straight leadcore with braid casing	Line to leader butt	Modified nail knot. Make three turns with leader butt, lift up leadcore tag end, make one turn of leader butt, replace leadcore, complete turns. Alternate: remove section of lead wire, make loop
Straight leadcore with braid casing	Line to running line	Loop. Remove section of wire, fray casing, double back, wrap with bobbin and thread, coat with rubber-based cement or fly head cement

Typical Sink Rate of Faster Sinking Lines

Line Type	Line Weight	Approximate Sink Rate Range (in inches per second)
High-density coat	AFTMA 9	3.70–3.98
High-density coat	AFTMA 11	4.22–5.0
High-density coat Scientific Anglers Deepwater Express	550 grains	7–8
High-density coat Scientific Anglers Deepwater Express	700 grains	8–9
High-density coat Scientific Anglers Deepwater Express	850 grains	9–10
Leadcore with tapered coating— Cortland Kerboom	450 grains	7.0–8.75
Leadcore with tapered coating— Cortland Kerboom	550 grains	9.5–10 plus
Level leadcore, nylon sheathed	366 grains (falls between AFTMA 11–12 line)	7.73
Level leadcore, nylon sheathed	513 grains	8.66
Level leadcore, nylon sheathed	606 grains	9.30

(Rate is dependent on line design, brand and weight)

chapter 8

Big Bad Browns

I long ago lost my heart to the trouts as my favorite species to fish for, and of all the trouts I put the brown at the top of the list.

—JOE BROOKS, *Trout Fishing.*

We had left the pretty portion of the stream a long time ago and, with it, what seemed to be all the fishing we would have. From a bubbling free-stone stretch, the river had turned slow and shallow. There was no cover and not a sign of life in the water.

"Just a little farther," my friend Ed Taylor persisted.

Bowing to his long-time knowledge of the little river, I continued to slog through the shin-deep water in the blazing sun, my rod over my shoulder, with no faith.

Ahead lay a sharp bend. Perhaps 60 feet before it was a little V-cut into the bank.

"You try it," Ed offered.

"Try what?" I demanded.

"Look a little closer," he persisted.

Upon more careful inspection, the tip of a submerged tree branch barely poked above the surface, discernible mainly in the gentle current break it made in the slow-moving water.

"Could be something," I agreed. "But you're the one who knows the tricks here. Show me."

He tried to insist that I take the cast, but we split the difference when I agreed to work the next spot that he was sure lay just around the bend.

Early in the day we'd been dry-fly fishing upstream, but had switched to spinning equipment for this lower water on Ed's suggestion.

Conditions were not what he had hoped, however, and we had not cast for quite a spell. Now he eased into position, brought his arm back horizontally across the water surface, and fired the little gold spoon on a low trajectory. It landed softly on the upcurrent side of the cut but deep enough in so that, in a moment, Ed twitched his rod tip and started the lure out. It came to the place where the branch poked through, and almost made it past. A brown-gold shape snaked from the sunken tree, plainly visible in the amber water. The fish pounced on the ultralight spoon, turned back toward the cover, felt the hooks, and cartwheeled through the surface.

"Nice brown!" I shouted. "This place isn't completely dead."

We were to prove that around the bend in a nearly identical spot, and this time it was my turn. The two fish were almost twins, measuring 15 and 15½ inches respectively before we slid them back in the river. They both were nearly copper in hue, with fine markings, and both were far leaner than they should have been for their length. The stream was not overly rich in forage here, but these fish had nowhere else to go. The upstream sector we'd fished earlier just did not have the holes or cover to support larger fish. As it was, these two had taken over the only real cover for a very long way. Fishing on downstream later, it looked like an aquatic desert.

The incident points out several important characteristics about brown trout, especially those having reached over a foot in length. First, they are survivors. Long after brook trout, cutthroats, and even rainbows have given up a barely borderline environment, browns will continue to hang on. They'll not simply live out a genetic lifetime, they will strive to reproduce if they can. Second, many of the larger browns in a river are loners, simply because they need the giant's share of the cover, water depth, and available forage from the better holding spots. Third, despite the insistent complaints of some that wise stream browns are uncatchable, they can be taken by any reasonably competent angler who pauses to think before fishing. They are likely to fall to a hard lure or natural bait. Fourth, you really can't count on the creatures to *consistently* hold true to normal behavioral patterns. For instance, we caught those two fish in bright daylight and hot weather, when everyone knows that any self-respecting brown trout almost always eats at night or during false dawn. "Almost" is the catch word. Depending on the environment and the time of year, I've taken about as many good-size browns outside of the witching-hour period as during it.

Still, if I were forced to generalize on the best time periods and/or conditions to catch big browns, I'd settle on pre-dawn to dawn, dusk, some portion of the night, overcast weather, or almost any time following a good summer rain. Low light conditions can also be simulated by roily surface water over a river's deeper, slower-moving water.

There are other grand times to catch big browns with fewer of their defenses up. One is just after ice-out on a lake. Another is prior to and during the fall spawning run. The most popular of all, of course, is during and immediately following a major hatch of large insects. In summer, when the fish have moved to deeper water slightly offshore, one of the best times is during the approach of a storm when wind has picked up following days of heat and haze. (Remember, though, that graphite rods are highly conductive of electricity.)

Brown trout mature at 2 or 3 years of age. Stream browns typically live from 7 to 12 years, while the incredibly fast-growing fish of our Great Lakes and other large waters may die following their first inshore migration to spawn—typically at age 3. The fish are frequently afflicted with fungus during this period. Despite a short life span, these big-lake browns have enjoyed a bountiful feeding existence, and usually weigh 7 to 10 pounds by the end of their third summer. Some lake fish wait until their fifth or sixth year to spawn, and they are huge. The growth of river browns is slower than that of their larger lake peers. Depending on the fertility of the river, though, it can vary considerably.

In the U.S., brown trout spawning usually occurs between late September and February, influenced by water temperature and shortening daylight periods. Whether they are lake residents or stream dwellers, browns seek out and run up smaller and smaller tributaries to build their gravel beds. Lacking smaller water, though, the fish will utilize large open rivers, lakes, or estuaries if some form of gravel exists. Once brownies are established in an even somewhat favorable environment, they tend to become self-supportive. The supplemental stocking of other trout is not necessary.

The brown trout is intrinsic to the evolution of the most exacting fly-fishing developments both abroad and in the U.S. The fish's often incredibly selective feeding, for example, turned anglers to the study of entomology and the refinement of tackle. Although finicky feeding—especially in fertile rivers and rich smaller lakes—is typical of browns, the larger specimens with which we'll be dealing can be far less delicate. They will eat an incredible variety of larger insects, most forage fish small enough to be consumed, mollusks, crustaceans, and even mice, birds, frogs, and other small animals on occasion.

The bigger fellows are quite opportunistic. If a choice-looking morsel becomes available when big browns are in a positive attitude, they tend to eat it. This gives the hunter of large browns more latitude in how and what he can fish, thus improving his odds for catching a big fish when compared to anglers matching the hatch with an emerging nymph, dun, or spinner on the surface. This does not mean that larger browns lack the wariness for which the species is famous. Far from it.

Even when small, browns in rivers tend to seek the deeper riffles, holes, and of course, pools. As they grow older and more solitary, they favor increasing amounts of cover. Brown trout that normally live in lakes may be even more aware of their exposure than river residents when they run upstream prior to spawning and are confined to shallow water.

Until recent years, most of the very largest browns have fallen to natural baits (alone or in concert with various artificials), spoons, plugs, and spinners. Some, of course, were caught on larger nymph patterns and streamers fished by fly anglers but, compared to those fishing hardware or bait, they were far fewer. The confines of traditional flyfishing were largely responsible. Today's modern flyfishers are increasingly innovative, however. They are equipped with tackle that permits the sport to be practiced in places undreamed of in the past. They are possessed of an unbridled desire to experiment with both technique and an amazing array of new fly materials. They are thus probing the inner sanctums of the most reclusive old river browns, as well as the giants of our inland seas.

Whether you choose to hunt trophy brown trout with hard lures, bait, or flies, you need to adopt strategies built around specific fish patterns that vary for lakes and three distinct types of river environments. Let's look at these situations as they exist across the U.S. and abroad.

Lakes

With the exception of peak hatch periods, and some unique, highly fertile inland waters (primarily in the Western U.S.), lake-resident brown trout that reach gigantic proportions tend to do it by feasting on a variety of high-protein, non-insect forage. In some waters that may include various types of amphipods (shrimp) or crustacea such as crayfish but, by and large, it means other fish life. Primary forage typically includes ciscoes, alewives, smelt, and shiners, but the trout will feast on other readily available prey as well. Sculpin, chubs, young perch, and other small trout—especially the less-than-savvy stocked rainbows—are all fair game.

Feeding and locational patterns for browns vary from lake to lake because of forage, bottom structure of the lake itself, climate, and vegetation. Still, general patterns exist. Big browns are inshore and shallow for longer periods in early spring and autumn. The fish continually follow their key forage, however, and in warmer weather this means depth—

though not necessarily extreme distances offshore. Browns tend to locate within 10 feet of the thermocline during warmer weather, and are especially prevalent where the thermocline approaches the bottom. Unlike salmon and rainbows stocked in our larger lakes, browns don't range as far. In fact, they tend to be almost what you could call resident fish,

Trophy-size brown trout often feed on alewives. These can be imitated with trolled Rapalas, Countdowns, Flatfish or flutter spoons. Tandem blade flashers often produce in deep water.

moving off prime inshore grounds until proper forage-holding temperatures and bottom configurations are located. In many lakes, this may not be far at all from spots that hold the fish in spring and fall.

Big browns can be taken from deep water—50 feet or more—but are among the most difficult fish to entice at those depths. One theory has it that with huge schools of cold-water forage fish virtually locked into a narrow survival zone, the browns find it easy to consume as much as desired with precious little effort. Therefore, why bother chasing an angler's lure? Browns are also able to handle warmer water. In late spring and early summer they periodically work the surface to about 15 feet deep, even though bigger forage concentrations are elsewhere. It is in this shallower water where they are most susceptible to an angler's offerings. I have caught good browns close to shore just before dark when schools of smelt were 50 feet deep and farther offshore. Small trout, shiners, and young perch were feeding on insects in the shallows. The browns were ambushing the smaller fish from below.

Other keys to locating browns in lakes include bottom and shore structure, plus tributary flowages. The physical features that form the hot spots include shoals and reefs, rock-gravel-sand flats with deeper channels through them, ledges, underwater cliffs, points with nearby deep water, and rocks and boulders close to shore or a few yards off. Don't overlook shoreline brush or low-sweeping tree branches that concentrate insects and tiny bait upon which larger forage species feed and, in turn, become prey to brown trout. In spring and fall, man-made harbors, coves, and bays—especially those with current—pull in big browns. So can sand bars, weedlines, and some sand beaches if spawning forage fish are using them. Normally, though, these gently sloping areas are not productive.

Each lake will vary slightly as to the best depth to fish shores and bottom structure. The age of a lake can influence those depths. For example, Ray Johnson, the dean of brown trout fishing in Utah's Flaming Gorge Reservoir, specialized for years in fishing just several feet of water, tight to shore. In lakes with fast drops, this is possible. In Lake Michigan, fish come from a variety of water, both near-shore shallows and drop-offs some distance out. Nothing in fishing is ever finite but, if I had to pick prime depths for active shallow browns, I'd work the 10 to 20-foot water columns with deeper water close at hand.

Although it's not the most exciting fishing method, trolling is overall the most efficient one for lake browns. The saving grace for what could otherwise be a deadly dull pursuit is that a *good* troller is constantly thinking. A casual angler too often simply drops his lures back and succumbs to the drone of his outboard engine. The effective troller is much like a computer. Mentally, he is constantly running through a list of alternatives if no trout are forthcoming. Under analysis are lure type, size, color, depth, amount of line out, speed, troll pattern, and area type (bottom and shore). He will already have learned that light line is necessary for browns. Nothing heavier than 8-pound-test should be used, and preferably 6-pound-test must be connected to lure or bait.

In spring or fall when the fish are shallowest, working into harbors or over shoals, bars, and rock rubble in water 6 feet or less, I much prefer to troll single plugs, spoons, and sometimes streamer flies with small dodgers ahead of them. Favorite lures include floating Rapalas with a little weight 2½ feet ahead of them, Countdown No. 9 or 11 Rapalas, U20 or X5 Flatfish, and ultralight flutter spoons. If you troll the 10 to 20 foot-water, your best bet in spring is often tandem blade flashers (sometimes called cowbells or lake trolls) with bait or lure 16 to 18 inches behind. Natural minnows or other forage fish sewn with a baiting needle onto a leader can be deadly in early spring. As an option, try removing the treble hook from a spoon and tying on two tandem hooks (single or treble). Drape a nightcrawler on these two hooks. The action of ultralight spoons will be curtailed by the bait addition, but the natural offering makes up for it. Using the old faithful red-and-white Dardevle with copper underside will enable you to maintain spoon action. These spoons need slightly faster speed, however, and I like them a little later in spring, then on through summer.

The business of speed is a critical one. Like lake trout, big browns normally want a lure or bait presented slowly. They want to simply ease up from below or the side to attack, and will not chase down the offering. Boats with big engines need a smaller one to troll with. Smaller boats often use electric motors, especially in the extreme shallows. Small skiffs powered by electric motors are one of the best inshore trolling rigs. The recommended lures necessitate a slow troll speed, because they just will not run correctly at a faster clip.

Also critical is the distance the lure is trolled behind your boat. The minimum should be 125 to 150 feet. You can work back from there. Some brown trout trolling specialists go to the extreme and send their offerings back 300 feet or more. Precise lure presentation is impossible with so much line out. Your turns and zig-zags will present the lure or bait over the holding and feeding places only part of the time, but the risk of spooking a trophy-size brown in the shallows will diminish. Two rods are all you should use for distance trolling, or much of your time will be devoted to untangling lines after turning.

Although I use rod holders for much of my trolling work, hand-held rods are an advantage when fishing for big browns. Unlike rainbows or salmon, these trout often hit with just a slight bump and you must be always ready to strike. When using side-planing boards, you'll have to rely on your release to do its job. The release should be set to pop easily. Boards are a great help to work a lure through areas that you cannot motor into, and should be part of your overall technique.

Trolling is generally more productive, but big browns can be taken by casting. The better fish-concentration spots can be worked from shore, boats, or float tubes. In fact, when the fish move into the extreme shallows, roll slowly on top, or rip the surface while chasing bait, casting often produces best. Many lakes around the nation offer casting potential. Channeled weed beds in the fertile Western lakes are an example. So are rivermouths like Lake Ontario's Oswego Harbor, plus jetties and breakwaters on many big lakes around the nation. One of the more fascinating and productive areas for casting is Wisconsin's Door County peninsula, which thrusts up into northwestern Lake Michigan. The area is one of the premier spots for browns virtually all season (if you move offshore in summer).

The perfect fishing rig for inshore casting here is a low-slung skiff with an auxiliary electric fishing motor. You could fish the cuts between rocky flats, the shoals, and the harbors with it in spring and fall. By careful stalking with the sun out, you can visually locate fish in the ultra-clear water. But you do need sun and calm water to do it. Without it, and when the browns move slightly deeper, you still do not cast haphazardly. Because the water is so clear you can still see the shoal edges, craggy rock pinnacles, or places where two different bottom types meet. These places are visible as a change in water color when the sun is gone.

Some friends and I did some pioneer belly-boat fishing in this area. We employed a large "mother" boat and float tubes for each angler. I'll never forget the look of the lady at the motel desk when our caravan rolled into the parking lot with a cluster of six belly boats lashed to the high observation/casting platform on the big boat. After questioning us closely, it was clear that she believed the whole operation to border on the transcendental. Several days later, when we reported our growing success, she rolled her eyes to the heavens, obviously wanting no truck with such black-hearted story tellers. But we had been catching fish, and doing it by casting big streamers with fly rods.

It was April, and the successful method that developed was to use Hi-Speed Hi-D lines. Not only did these ultra-fast-sink lines permit working depths over 20 feet, they also permitted long casts and, when the retrieve was commenced immediately, were no trouble working the flies over shoals and boulders as shallow as 5 feet. We caught the fish at various times, including high noon with the sun shining gloriously. Cool water and heavy inshore schools of alewives and smelt had much to do with that.

Larry Dahlberg scored on a big brown from a belly boat in Lake Michigan. Belly boaters can have field day by launching from any open shoreline.

When we began our little operation, the water was 38° to 40°. During a week of fishing it warmed to 45°, then into the low 50°s inside harbors. When that happened, the harbors grew less productive and shoreline structure produced best. The browns shifted position daily on these in-shore grounds: they'd be up the cuts and on the flats one day, cruising scattered boulders off a point in slightly deeper water the next. As the forage moved, they moved.

When the sun disappeared and wind increased wave action, it was impossible to visually locate fish-holding structure from the low-riding belly boats. Even though the low profile and inherent quiet mobility of the floats meant few spooked fish, we found ourselves kicking into shallow rocks or knolls with our swim fins—spots that we should have fished. The answer was to somehow mark the feeding places. Ever the innovative angler, friend Larry Dahlberg came up with the idea of inexpensive and expendable party balloons.

What we did was scout the areas from the high vantage point of the big boat, dropping inflated balloons attached to tire-balancing weights via a length of string. After the turns and cuts of an area were marked, we retreated and marked another area, returning some time later to fish in the tubes once the area was rested. It was an effective system.

Very early in the spring, the float tubes have another advantage. As ice-out commences, some shorelines—especially some flatter ones that attract spawning smelt—open up before the harbors and ramp areas where boats can be launched. Belly boaters can then have a field day by walking to any open shore's edge and going in. The fish are there and, with no competition from the trollers, an angler bobbing in his tube can cast flies, plugs, spoons, or spinners to his heart's content anywhere he chooses.

Vital to all this cold-water float tubing are neoprene foam waders over polypropylene underwear. Polypro—as it's called by its fans—is preferred over long underwear of other materials because of its near zero moisture absorption characteristics.

Trolling, of course, gets the nod for deeper water fishing in summer, except for those periods mentioned earlier when the big browns work the surface both inshore and off. Few anglers want to be in belly boats during rough weather, but I have friends who take exception and have their finest innings in conditions that would terrify the faint of heart. Rough or calm, inshore or farther out, float tubers have learned the consistent effectiveness of light floating-diving balsa plugs and darting stick-type plugs during the periods when the trout come back up near the surface to feed in warm weather. Flyfishermen are discovering that they can score with, of all things, surface poppers—especially the longer, more streamlined variety designed for saltwater bugging.

I'll never forget my first experience popping for big browns with red-and-white bass bugs on a huge hydroelectric impoundment. Of all unlikely places, it happened in southwestern Tasmania. The fish here grow large. Ten-pounders are caught with regularity and 20-pound-plus fish turn up each year. Whatever the browns take the noisy bugs for, they eat them quite well. In the blackness of night, the browns came close along a near vertical dropoff into vast depth. They wallowed and thrashed as they

Bragging-size browns hit bass poppers at night. This one is especially appealing. As it's made of soft foam, trout will hold on longer after hitting it.

fed. Treading carefully to avoid falling in and trying not to snag backcasts on the invisible scrub willow back up on shore, I worked my little bugs while feeling rather foolish about it.

It soon became evident that the trick was to attract the browns with sharp popping and burbling sounds, then retrieve the bug with a steady swim. I found this out after having several monsters crash and miss on an erratic stop-go popping retrieve as I set the hook into blackness while my heart pounded. The steady swim retrieve that follows the noisemaking at the start allows the trout to track the bug and catch it. Whether it's a Northeastern water or one of the vast Great Lakes, you'll find that feeding browns will take the popper at night as you work from a float tube or cast from a point or jetty thrusting into darkness.

In autumn, lake anglers find great numbers of browns moving back inshore on attempted spawning runs. Moving from the 40-foot depths, they use the long points, bars, and tributary currents to direct their migrations. Anglers in small skiffs or belly boats can easily work the transitional routes. At the approach to large and small rivermouths and harbors, shore anglers take fish. Bait anglers now find salmon eggs and spinners sweetened with nightcrawler tails to be effective. Spinning enthusiasts continue to score on balsa minnows, light spoons, or spinners. Fly anglers often score with small nymphs having a bit of bright color in the dressing, and on egg-imitating flies as well as large sculpin imitations or big bushy streamers. In many cases you'll be casting to visible fish cruising hard by the shoreline.

One other situation has become an increasingly important factor in today's big-water brown trout picture. The phenomenon is no quirk of nature, but man-made warm or hot water discharges—typically from industrial cooling operations and sometimes nuclear energy plants. The effect of such discharges is to attract bait and big browns, which follow the plumes of warmer water like the Gulf Stream out into the lake. The fish tend to approach the warmer streams closer in cold weather, up to the point where the temperature is uncomfortable. They approach in two ways.

Some of the fish nose directly into the heart of the current. They tend to do so within a few feet of the surface, and can sometimes be detected rolling or grabbing bait there. As a rule of thumb, these fish are a bit smaller than those that move along the edges of the thermal plume. The larger fish often approach close to the bottom. The plume edges are, of course, easily located with thermometers, but often are identifiable as surface disturbances—swirl and eddy patterns.

Browns move into the flows, feeding, until they reach a point of discomfort or forage runs out. They'll then drift back and work the area again, much like fishermen. Thermal outfalls are productive in winter and very early spring. They are one of the first places hit by urban ice-out anglers. In some areas, anglers drag aluminum boats out over the ice to reach open water slots created by hot water plumes. The open sectors provide good fishing in January, February, and March, or until general open water occurs.

Thermal plumes are easily fished. Boats are anchored strategically and anglers work the near-surface or deeper fish. Various long-profile crank plugs or floater-divers are cast or drifted downcurrent, then worked back. For the deep fish, jigs sweetened with natural bait and slip-sinker rigs with minnows and blade attractors can be bumped along the bottom. Heavy spoons and weighted spinners can be cast, then jigged off the bottom. If the thermal discharge is substantial, the proper weight spoon or spinner

Though usually used for rainbows or steelhead, egg-imitative flies like this one produce big browns in fall and early spring.

Del Canty finishes a high bunny fly designed to imitate a mouse. Big brown trout regularly fall for such outsize flies.

In tailwater fisheries, one of the most productive techniques for big browns is to dead drift fly-jigs or tiny shrimp-imitative nymphs beneath a strike indicator—the tiny floats shown here—using a long flyrod and a 6-foot leader.

can be dropped to the bottom, then allowed to tumble with the current under angler control. If the flow is slow to moderate, flycasters with fast-sinking lines can score on the bottom fish. In swifter flows, the browns holding closer to the surface can be regularly taken. Thermal outflows can be fished by day, or at night when the fish will hit quite close to your boat.

Rivers

Several quite different river situations exist in which to hunt large brown trout. Let's first take what can be the most difficult: the slow-current limestones, spring creeks, or meadow streams. Though the names vary geographically, we are dealing with a basic river type. Subtle differences exist, but basically these are rich, alkaline, slow-moving waters that gather here and there at bends for a brief rush of current before reverting to slow, steady, and dignified movement. Frequently, this type of river has abundant vegetation in the water, and few or no shade-making bankside trees.

This is the kind of water that was instrumental in the development of exacting flyfishing techniques in England and the U.S., and for good reason. The brown trout in such rivers have precious little cover to give them security, and thus become extremely wary. When actively feeding they can be completely exposed, and therefore seek virtually anything that gives them the slightest suggestion of cover. That is the key to locating them.

Most obvious are the deep pools graced with the occasional willow, alder, or cottonwood tree—living or dead—that has a root network thrusting into the water. Perhaps the tree trunk itself will have fallen and now lies slanting into flow, its branches forming an intricate maze behind which fish can lie. This is the classic big brown hide, usually the domain of the one old hook-jawed monarch. Fishing it can be the epitome of frustration, because trout that typically use such cover move only scant inches from their lairs, waiting for current to bring food to them.

An angler stands the best chance to hook a large brown from such cover early in the night or again before dawn when the fish has moved a little from its sanctuary. This not only makes presentation easier, it also gives you a couple more moments to get a hooked fish away from the cover. The strongest line or leader that can be used for an acceptable presentation should be employed in such places. Flies, floating plugs, and natural baits are your best bet here. They must be drifted naturally. A careful study of the complex currents around the roots or branches must first be made before a bait or lure is cast.

Subtle current is the key to locating large browns in other lies in the meadow stream. In many small limestones or spring creeks, the fish hold beneath sheltering umbrellas of various weed types, or in channels snaking through matts of vegetation. The fish are not randomly distributed here, however. Careful study of the situation will reveal that certain spots in the weeds are touched by tongues of current. These are the places to fish, because the currents bring an endless array of both terrestrial and aquatic forage tight to the weed edges. Browns, especially the larger and more cautious individuals, hardly move to feed in such places. Other seemingly likely weed edges hold smaller fish or none at all, only because the currents do not bring food close enough.

Fishing this cover has developed into an art among flyfishers. The trout are selective, feasting primarily on a small variety of aquatic and some terrestrial insects. Fishing at night is close to impossible, and other forms of tackle and baits are usually out of place.

Possibly the easiest meadow stream lies to fish with both fly and spinning gear are the banks. That is, they're easy *if* your casting is supremely accurate. In most every situation you must present your offering not 3, not 4, but 1 or 2 *inches* from a bank. Sometimes the only presentation that takes a streamwise trophy is one in which your lure hits the bank, falls from it, and bumps the edge as it drifts along.

The banks hold the fish because they are deeply undercut—sometimes several feet. Muskrat holes provide shelter in some places. In others, streamside grasses bend into the water and the fish hold not quite so far beneath the banks. In either case, grasshoppers, other terrestrials, aquatic insects, and forage fish of various types sweep close by and are greedily consumed. Rarely are both banks of the stream simultaneously productive.

Study the water and you will see that the outside bends, where the current sweeps and carves the bank, provide the deep, favored sanctuaries. Sometimes bars and islands guide the current to form the lies. In a few straight runs, both banks can hold trout, but usually smaller ones.

The trophy hunter can work with natural bait, in-line spinners, or small and light balsa floater-diver minnow plugs. The latter will have periods of effectiveness both on the surface and deeper, with a little weight added to get them there. Fly anglers will catch numbers of fish with a variety of dries, especially hopper imitations and small, sparse Muddlers (No. 12 to 14 hook), which suggest a number of edibles. Occasionally a large trout will be taken this way. If your goal is a truly large fish, however, your best weapon is a deeply sunken Muddler or sculpin imitation, a fat Wooly Bugger, or a large streamer.

Your best approach on foot, regardless of tackle, is usually upstream because of the dirth of cover and the gentle, clear water. In much of my fishing in other types of water these days, I fish downstream, but rarely will I do so in the small limestoners. Rarely, too, will wading be required; in fact, it is often a disadvantage because of the disturbance created. I usually spot-hop, crossing the stream as needed below the suspected lie to get in position for a perfect presentation. Two anglers working either side of a stream can leapfrog, alternating spots.

The absolute best bank area for a huge brown trout is the outside bend, with a very strong thrust of water carving against it. The best spot on this bank will be just below the place where the full force of the current hits. However, you should begin fishing such a bank below this area in slower

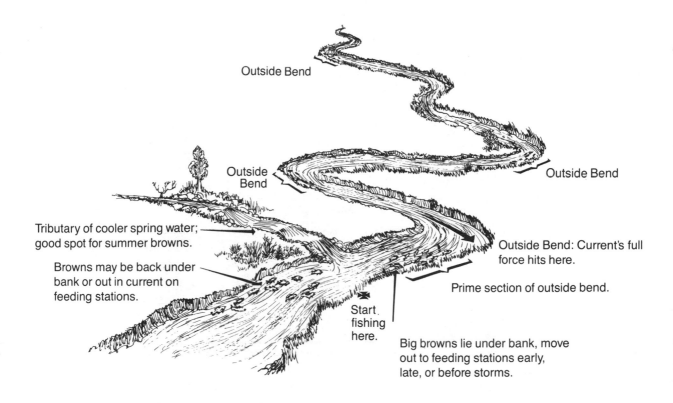

Outside Bend

Outside
Bend

Outside Bend

Tributary of cooler spring water; good spot for summer browns.

Outside Bend: Current's full force hits here.

Browns may be back under bank or out in current on feeding stations.

Prime section of outside bend.

Start fishing here.

Big browns lie under bank, move out to feeding stations early, late, or before storms.

Prime brown trout lies in a meadow stream without trees or other bank cover.

water, then work up. The big fish may have moved down, or another slightly smaller brown could be in residence below the prime lie.

If there is a deep run broken by several rocks or a gravel bar directly off a prime outside bend, active fish sometimes move into it. Their cover is the broken surface and, when they do leave the security of the bank to move into such a run, it is rare when they will not take. These runs can be productive at night, too, and anglers who fish banks by darkness will find their presentations need not be quite so close—a good thing, too, for much of their time would be spent tying on new lures.

Freestone or mountain rivers offer a wider variety of lies for big brown trout. While the occasional slow-moving stretch along a bank will call to mind the meadow stream, freestoners are generally a mixed bag of other kinds of holding areas. Many freestone stream banks lack good fish-holding cover. There are exceptions, such as wherever deadfalls lie in the water, but generally the fish will relate more to structural changes farther out in the river.

The real key to finding large freestone browns is to search for areas of deeper water. Obvious will be the larger pools at the ends of fast runs, or at the base of falls or ledge drops. Just tossing out a bait or other lure is not enough in these places. The target areas are edges of the main current in a pool. Another prime location is the tail end of a long glide where the current runs swiftly over large rocks or boulders before it tightens into the next whitewater riffle section. The trout here will usually be behind the boulders and a presentation must be upcurrent enough so your offering has reached the trout's level as it skirts the rocks.

Less obvious, but often harboring very large browns, are smaller deep-water sections frequently bypassed by anglers intent on plumbing the larger holes. These mini-holding areas are usually home to just one good fish. The spots can consist of glides, holes, or short channels in the stream bed that is otherwise shallow. Deep riffles that seem to offer no true lie frequently do, in the form of occasional rocks behind which a trout can rest. Fast, riffly pocket water is something Western anglers are at ease with, but too often overlooked by fishermen from other areas. The water is fast, often dancing with waves that can curl into little whitecaps. There may be a rare boulder here and there, but these are not the chief holding places. The pockets are truly depressions in the stream bed, sometimes in concert with a few rocks, sometimes just one. The rocks will normally be completely underwater.

What's working for us in pocket water is a fast surface current with slower water deeper beneath it. Wading is tricky and best done down-stream (frequently the only way possible) with a wading staff. The pockets, as well as other isolated mini-lies (holes, glides, and channels) are evident if you seriously scan the water through polarized glasses. They appear as slightly darker, sometimes much darker places in the river. Pocket-water browns will rise to take large dry flies during a substantial hatch, but more often they will fall for a deeply drifted nymph or streamer. Spinning enthusiasts take big pocket-water fish with a variety of natural baits, jigs, and jigs-plus-bait. Fewer spinning enthusiasts experiment with spoons and plugs, but those who do often produce very surprising results.

Some of the most productive public fishing for big brown trout today is found downstream of dams. These tailwater fisheries often provide excellent year-round angling because of the continual supply of cold water spilling from the dams. The tactics for fishing these areas center around the water flow coming from the dams or through turbines. Tailwater fishing can be likened to fishing the tides in saltwater.

Tailwater trout reposition themselves with the changing flows to both obtain more energy-efficient holding areas and take better advantage of drifting food. In low flow periods, for example, a tailwater river can resemble any moderate freestone stream in its upper to middle reaches. Fish will hold in pools, pockets, and deeper riffles, all related to the main river channel. They can also be along steeper-breaking banks. With the start of a water release, they usually become active for a little while as an increase in food occurs. As the flow becomes stronger and the water level rises, they move to more sheltered areas.

The spots may have been shoals or bars at low flow. Sometimes they are backwaters—setbacks and oxbows. They can be banks with a lot of cover present to offer current buffers. The fish could simply move farther downriver during a heavy discharge. Once high water occurs, it usually takes several hours for the trout to stabilize and resume a positive feeding attitude. In some normally prime areas, the high-water/full-flow period is just too much for effective fishing.

Once the current is turned off, fishing can be hot for a time while the trout are still in the high-water security areas. Fishing around logs, trees, points, big rocks near shore, and the mouths of backwaters can be great. If you wait too long, though, the browns will have begun relocation and you'll miss the action until they once again take their low-water stations. The time frame varies in each tailwater and each location within a prime tailwater. It's something you'll have to learn on-site.

Although it was previously touched on in this river brown trout discussion, nighttime fishing needs a little more attention. Whether your after-dark or before-light fishing is done in a freestone, tailwater, or meadow type environment, in most cases it is best to fish down or down and across current. Your downcurrent presentation will quickly telegraph the feel of a hit on a tight line.

Because darkness can be the prime period for big browns, you'll be fishing with larger flies or lures. Huge sculpins, Muddlers, and popping bugs that seem better suited to saltwater fishing are tops. They create maximum water disturbance and give the trout an easier target in low-visibility conditions. Large brown trout have and do eat things like mice and bats, so there's little you can throw with a fly rod that they won't be able to take.

Light floater-diver plugs are great for spin fishermen. The plugs can be cast across and down, alternately twitched and cranked. The method seems odd at first, but it can result in fast action—especially on fish that see a lot of angling pressure. Denver angler Charlie Meyers developed it to perfection with plugs, high-floating hair flies, and bugs, too. The method can be used by day as well, in heavily fished clear waters.

The basic retrieve is none at all. With plugs, Charlie calls it the dead cigar technique. The fly or plug is cast to drift over potential feeding areas and simply allowed to float. When it reaches the target zone it can be held in the current or permitted to float on by. Flies are often best fished by holding them in the flow where the current can gently work on them. The plugs are normally hit when they are simply drifting with no wiggle at all, like a cigar stub tossed into the water. One reason this technique may be so effective on heavily worked fish is that the browns have learned, through experience, to avoid the fraud of actively worked lures. In any event, it's effective. Bait enthusiasts will find that live or dead minnows worked this way are also very productive.

At night, even the biggest browns tend to move into extremely shallow water to feed. Try the pool heads and tails, the shoals, and the riffles that are just too shallow for big fish during the day. Evening into dark is the prime time for some big fly hatches or spinner falls like the brown drake, the famed Michigan caddis (really the *Hexaginia limbata* Mayfly), and, of course, the unintentional fall of big moths. Big browns feast greedily on the big bugs and, if you're not a long-distance caster, you can still get in on the action. Being able to cast a big fly imitation just a little way out into close feeding lanes will produce fish. In fact, all your night fishing should be close range, both to maintain control and to enhance strike effect. Long-distance presentations at night result in too long a delay between sensing the hit, striking, and hooking. Working your offering 25 to 30 feet away is just fine.

Browns tend to feed hard and fast at night once they begin. When they quit, it's usually over until the pre-dawn or dawn period. Veteran night fishermen have also learned that a fog rolling in over the river will cause the browns to stop feeding early. Take a break, catch some sleep, and go to it again in the early morning.

The autumn spawning run of lake-dwelling browns continues up both freestone rivers and meadow streams. Big browns, used to the space and depth available to them in lakes, are terribly skittish in rivers. They will seek any hint of cover available, even if it won't hide them well. A small sapling in the water may be a temporary holding place for a very large fish. Part of what makes this such fascinating fishing is that you can visually stalk them. The chief concern must be a super-quiet approach with attention to sun angle and your height above the water. If a big fish is holding near a logjam or blowdown, you'll be lucky to see a part of its body shape to give him away. In some situations, you'll see nothing and will have to fish the cover blind. In other cases, the running browns will hang in riffles and channels that are a couple of feet deeper than surrounding water. If gravelly bottom is close at hand but no fish are present, search the slightly deeper adjacent riffles. Watch them carefully. From time to time the surface will curl and smooth, giving you a brief, almost magical look below. That view can frequently be just enough to show you if a large trout is home.

If salmon use the same rivers to spawn, there may be some confusion with identification at first. Although the browns will be right out in the open later in the run when the salmon are spawning, the trout will usually hold in small glides, pockets, and any obvious cover downstream from them.

In the early stages of the upriver run, the spawning browns will be more responsive to your lures. Their feeding reactions are gradually eclipsed by the spawning urge. They will feed less, and it will become increasingly obvious that they will only take an offering that drifts just

Typical Seasonal Brown Trout Locations

Early Spring	*Spring*	*Summer*	*Fall*
Bays, harbors	Reefs	Deeper reefs, deeper in-shore water: Points, other structure.	Bays, harbors
Gradually sloping sandy beaches if smelt, other forage spawning.	Underwater boulders	Trout generally hold 0–10 feet off bottom.	Tributaries and mouths.
Underwater boulders.	End of points.		Underwater boulders.
Shallow flats.	Channels in flats.		End of points.
Underwater points.			Underwater points.
Channels in flats.			

inches from the streambed. They will be more inclined to take brightly colored egg imitations or real spawn, although sometimes nymph imitations will be accepted.

In the end (or the beginning, depending on your viewpoint), loner browns begin to pair up on the spawning gravel. There will normally be a female plus a dominant male, and several other smaller males in attendance. Before the actual redd-making and spawning takes place, all these fish will hold out in the open, sometimes being visible only when the surface currents smooth. A careful stalk and presentation of natural spawn, bright egg-imitating fly, or sometimes a marabou or fur streamer, will usually attract the attention of the downcurrent males. The stimulus is more one of competition or annoyance rather than feeding. During and immediately after the actual spawn, the leading players are best left to their reproductive activities.

Quite a few browns die following the spawning period, but many more survive. They drift back either to their deeper river lies or, if they are lake fish, try to reach the home water or pools deep enough to shelter them until they can again attain the lake and grow for yet another season—larger, and possibly even more cautious. Big brown trout are one of the more fascinating and very much one of the more challenging gamefish that exist.

chapter **9**

Float Tubing
Comes of Age

Observing trout anglers in belly boats "walking" across the water of Idaho's Silver Creek, Ernest Hemingway was moved to observe that to accomplish this feat the fishermen were undoubtedly equipped in nothing less than Christ pants.

Let me tell you about the time that the world's largest snapping turtle fell in love with me. Well, perhaps it wasn't the world's largest, but it seemed so then.

A friend of mine had elected to fish from a steep shore on the far side of a weedy cove in a backwoods lake we had discovered. As for me, I thought the little lake would be a perfect test site for my newly acquired belly boat. Back in those days, we didn't use skin-diving flippers to move about in the inflatable fishing tubes. Instead, I had strapped to my wader heels a set of plastic side-fin kickers. Their rigid wings locked into position when you kicked your legs backwards, then folded against your heel on the forward stroke.

I entered the water and began kicking back into a weedy cove that seemed to hold promise for a good largemouth bass or two. From the corner of my eye I caught a movement that corresponded with a rather seriously sounding splash. Jerking my head in that direction, I saw an extremely ugly head emerging from the water.

It stretched up, higher and higher, one glittering eye fixed upon me. It was a snapping turtle, and if it could support a head of the size I was seeing, I did not care to know about the rest of the creature. Floating there, the inflatable doughnut around my mid-section, I somehow did not feel as secure as I would have in a boat with a rigid hull. I began to kick out of there fast without looking back. Upon reaching the steep bank where my friend was merrily casting, I told him about the huge brute, but was not sure he was convinced of the dimensions I described with wild gestures. Nursing my questioned integrity, I kicked on up the lake and did catch some bass.

An hour or so later I returned to the put-in spot near the cove. My friend had also returned after working his shoreline.

"Did you really see a big turtle back in there?" he shouted down. "I thought I saw something huge moving back near those lily pads a little while ago. Maybe it was a fish."

With the courage born from my friend's proximity, I eased a little way into the cove. "He was right back there," I said, pointing with my rod. As if on cue, the beast breached once again.

"Good grief," my friend said.

The turtle rose up so I could see most of its shell. I couldn't believe it. Then it turned and headed for me. I began kicking madly. I cleared the cove mouth and headed for the nearest firm bank. I glanced once over my shoulder and saw the front of the brute's face, two tunnel-like nostrils focused directly at me like torpedo tubes. The turtle was gaining. I am sure a hunter who has been charged by a rhinoceros could not have felt any worse than I did at that moment.

In fact, it only broke off the chase when I gained footing and heaved myself ashore to scamper back into the trees, the belly boat around my middle like some bizarre skirt. All this time, instead of coming to my aid, my friend was laughing hysterically. In retrospect I can empathize with his feelings. I couldn't then.

Turtles aside, a lot of people think that the whole concept of churning through the water with a giant doughnut around their middle is pretty silly to begin with. Float tubes may not have the dignified aura of a properly attired angler-and-ghillie team on an Atlantic salmon river in Scotland, but they do very much more than provide comic relief. They can be the most effective means for getting you into otherwise unfishable areas. They can enable you to make the proper presentation to trophy fish, in terms of both precise placement and stealthy stalk, that is impossible unless you are being guided by an expert who lets you do all the casting. Today's float tubes have evolved into angling systems with an array of ancillary support gadgets that make it possible to fish anywhere from urban ponds to wilderness waterways. Actually, the inflatable personal vessel has been serving man for a long time. A few of the early devices were quite remarkable.

Copper carvings from about 2300 B.C. show hardy Assyrian fishermen plying their trade while astride inflated devices made from goatskins. Both Assyrian and Babylonian armies used similar inflated skins to navigate across the Tigris and Euphrates rivers. A soldier would lay upon the skin, kicking with his legs and paddling with his hands. Periodically, he would blow into one of the skin's legs to maintain proper inflation.

Take a mega-leap forward to 1892. It was then that the Goodyear Company introduced what may be the first float tube designed expressly for fishing and hunting. It had a built-in rain cape so gentleman sports might keep from getting too wet in inclement weather. In the early 1900s, a two-tiered tube affair for fishing was marketed in France. By the 1950s, anglers were experimenting with all sorts of homemade, sling-seat-equipped fabric covers designed to go over car or truck tire inner tubes.

Truly sophisticated versions of the covered inner tube represent one of the two schools of contemporary belly boat design. The other is the tube-less style. It first was offered commercially in the late 1960s into the early 1970s by The American Safety Company, but was soon taken over by an innovative engineer from Leadville, Colorado. The man is Del Canty, widely acknowledged as the dean of contemporary belly boating. Through continued experimentation by Del and his fishing cronies, belly boat fishing has been pushed beyond the realm of what would have been thought foolhardy at best only a few years ago.

Today's tough belly boats put you in reach of those deeper oxbows and sloughs of a river that are beyond the capabilities of a wading angler. Belly boats permit you to become intimate with narrow channels in heavy weed or moss, both in river and lake. You can position yourself so that you can cast up into such spots that couldn't be waded to, and are too shallow and narrow to be worked using a boat. They are absolutely the best devices to fish small wooded streams that have banks too overgrown to permit walking, let alone casting. I have floated the deep stretches of such rivers, casting ahead as I drifted, stopping on gravel bars or tying on tree branches to work particularly promising areas, and getting wonderful fishing in close-to-city areas I knew weren't fished. Backwoods beaver ponds and high country lakes are obvious and popular places for float tubes.

In some ways, fishing floats have advantages over even small skiffs and canoes when fishing alone or with a friend. For example, because you maintain position with your legs, your eyes never have to leave target— such as the exact spot where a fish rose or swirled. Both hands are always free to fish, so your presentations are more accurate. As in wading by yourself, you get the first crack at an area. There's no need to alternate with your partner for the front-of-the-boat position or, in a canoe, the paddling chores. There are no arguments with friends over where to fish. Everyone goes where he wants and comes in when he likes.

Although float tubes find their biggest number of enthusiasts among lake and pond fishermen, the tubes are ideal for working small to medium-size rivers, especially those streams with brushy banks where it's impossible to walk the banks and wade. Trick is to float deep areas, then wade and fish the shallows.

Belly boats are quiet. Not only is there no engine noise to deal with, but there's also no splashing or banging of oars or paddles, plus no grinding of a pushpole on a hard, irregular bottom. You present the lowest profile possible, thus chances of spooking a fish are greatly reduced.

When traveling, the tubes take up little room when deflated. For instance, the tubeless floats pack up into a bundle approximately 4 inches by 20 inches, weighing 3 pounds. The units are easily maintained, are far less expensive than any decent boat, and can be as safe.

Even some saltwater fishing grounds have been sampled by adventuresome enthusiasts of the doughnut fleet. Pioneering West Coast flyfisherman Harry Kime has plied the Pacific off Baja, battling outlandishly-sized fish in his float. Of course, extreme discretion is advisable when belly boating in saltwater. Kicking along in a float anywhere in California's infamous Red Triangle between Monterey Bay, the Farallon Islands, and Point Reyes—currently the nation's shark attack capital—is definitely not worth considering. Nor would I want to float some of the inlets and reefs in the Southeastern part of the country. It's interesting, though, that belly boat use in big open water is definitely on the increase. The Great Lakes, huge reservoirs, and big brawling rivers are seeing more frequent use by fishing float enthusiasts. That's a distinct change from the early days of the sport.

Tubers of not long ago avoided going too far out, fearing that their little floats might deflate or overturn in rough water, or that they might be blown far away, stranded, with a strong wind going and rain or snow on the way. Modern tube designs plus accessory safety equipment have taken the teeth from these former potential disasters. The better fishing floats that are built around inner tubes have a backrest compartment in which a second, partially inflated motorcycle tube is sequestered for comfort and wave-splash protection. That little tube is also a second flotational device.

Some anglers use non-inflatable auxiliary flotation in the backrest compartment. Bob Rifchin, who regularly floats the New England coast in search of bluefish and striped bass, stuffs his backrest pocket with closed-cell foam—the stuff used as backpacker sleeping pads. There's no need to worry about leaks at all.

Some long-range belly boaters are now carrying flare guns, portable radios, or devices that give out homing signals to rescue teams in case of an unlikely mishap. Bob Rifchin carries a 2-pound mushroom anchor and 50 to 60 feet of small-diameter nylon line to keep from becoming legweary when he fishes moving tidal water.

Anchors are called for anywhere you want to hold in a given spot for some time in wind. Some systems are built around nylon bags that are filled with rock or sand. These are closed with a drawstring and carried in secondary anchor storage bags attached to the float, usually via Velcro tabs. Some anglers use quick-release systems—either snaps or slip knots— so they can instantly unhitch from the anchor line when fighting or beaching big fish, or working a fish from heavy cover. The surplus anchor line is coiled around a floating line winder that bobs in the water over the anchor after you unhitch, just like a marker buoy. It is then a simple matter to return to the anchor to continue fishing, or pick up and move to another spot.

Not every float tube has everything you may desire, but certain other safety features should be incorporated. The center seat safety strap that prevents you from sliding down through the tube should have a quick-disconnect buckle of reliable design. If the float is equipped with suspenders—very handy when walking a shoreline or toting the float—they, too, should have quick-release buckles. Floats built around covered inner tubes should have a valve arrangement that would not interfere with fly lines, or snag in case of an emergency ditch operation. The covers should have grommeted drain holes that allow water accumulated between cover and tube to spill out.

I've seen some package tube units that, at first glance, seemed to be a good buy. At least the cover looked nice. On closer inspection, though, most of these lacked safety features and had tubes of inferior quality. One came with one of those vinyl tubes usually used in a child's backyard wading pool. I'd hate to be caught miles offshore in something like that.

In the tubeless type pack-in floats, no one has done more in safety and also practical fishing design features than Del Canty. Del and his fishing cronies, whose ideas are regularly considered and often incorporated in the ever-changing Lunker Hunter Fishing Systems, have chalked up an enviable record on huge fish taken while belly boating. In the basic circular belly boat that these men use, there are two separate air chambers. Either one of them can float you. Optional inflatable sea cushions can act as another flotational device. The deluxe float called the Super Lunker Hunter looks more like a one-man backpacker boat with no bottom. It features three flotation chambers and has a 500-pound load capacity when all three chambers are filled. This unit is ideal for long-range trips and running big rivers. It can even be fitted with miniature hand paddles or oars for increased speed.

Aside from fishing, travel efficiency, and convenience, speed can also be a safety factor, if you need to run for shore. Both of Canty's floats are generous in diameter for increased stability. The deeply slung seats put your center of gravity low, further reducing tip-over hazard. Canty claims that in swimming pool tests, two men could not overturn him in the standard belly boat. The tubeless floats can be inflated orally on the water in case of slow leaks. The feature is also good when you're out in rough water and want to deflate the units slightly. A slightly soft tube lets the float give and wallow in high waves, rather than being knocked about as would a unit inflated to the point where it is hard. Until you try it yourself, you won't believe the rough weather that these floats can handle. Why would you want to be bobbing around in swells and whitecaps anyway? Fish are the reason.

Fish regularly turn on and can be taken on the surface or in very shallow water at the start of a blow, which oxygenates the water and pushes bait where it can't do very much to help itself. Big trout typically exhibit such behavior, and Canty has made it a regular practice to hunt these fish in wind as strong as 30 miles per hour.

"I haven't found weather bad enough to flip me," Canty says. "When the fish are cruising the big swells so you see them as the water curls up and you sink in a trough a little ways away, that's when I want to be there."

Del Canty drifts a nymph from one of his tubeless pack-in floats on Eleven Mile Lake, Colorado. Tip-overs are reduced by the float's large diameter and the deeply slung seat that lowers the angler's center of gravity.

A slightly soft float tube can also take more abuse without puncturing. Sometimes even a puncture need not mean deflation. One angler who was using one of the tubeless floats fell as he was descending some rocks to the water. He landed in the shallows unharmed, fished the entire morning, then returned for a lunch break. He noticed that one of his air chambers seemed a bit low. Upon leaving the water, the chamber began deflating. The man's fall had opened a neat gash, but water pressure had kept much of the air in.

Tubes can be affected by volatile chemicals, such as solvents and paints. Keep them away from such products while traveling or in storage. Always bring a patch kit with you, and always carry a flashlight both for seeing what you're doing at night, and, just as important, signaling fast-running boats that otherwise would not see you. The light will also help keep you in contact with your other belly-boating friends. In sunny weather, do not inflate your float—especially the tubeless variety—to maximum, then leave it on the beach. The rising temperature can over-inflate it to the point of seam failure. Always let a little air out before taking a break.

Swim fins are the most efficient means of propulsion for float tubing. The rigid side-fin kickers are rarely used nowadays, except in small ponds. If you should lose just one of your swim fins, though, you've effectively lost your means of propulsion. At the least, it means a serious inconvenience. But it could also mean real danger for you, depending on the circumstances. Most foot fins sink. You should have some sort of safety strap running from fin heel strap up around the calf of your leg. I've been using Force Fins marketed by the James-Scott Company. They are the most comfortable I've found for belly boating, and their design even allows you to walk forward (rather than backward) once you're ashore—something close to impossible with all other swim fins I know about. These fins have a grommet built into each heel strap. I like to fix a piece of elastic to the grommet, then sew another short piece of elastic to the end of the first section to form a T configuration. To the end of each arm of the T, I sew and glue a piece of Velcro or other similar fastener material. The T-piece goes around your calf and is fastened by the Velcro.

Even in summer, you must be concerned with keeping dry and warm. It's doubly important in cold weather. Rain, snow, splashing waves, leaking waders, or insufficient insulation can all lead to hypothermia. I've even experienced the initial stages of this rapid cooling of body temperature and impaired function after being caught without protection in heavy summer rainstorms, or after being long in the water with waders that did not have any insulative qualities. Shaking is an early warning signal. That's soon followed by an obvious clumsiness that you should

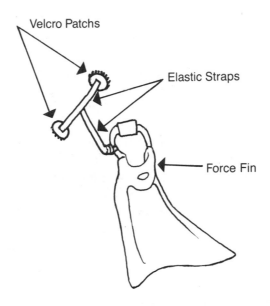

Velcro Patchs

Elastic Straps

Force Fin

To prevent losing foot fins, attach elastic safety strap as shown, with Velcro patches to secure strap around calf.

instantly recognize as a symptom. There need not be any problem, though, if you consider the following points.

With a tube type of float, the high backrest does much to guard against splashing from waves. Anglers using floats without the backrests have taken to gluing splash guards to their chest-high waders. These are simply bibs of coated nylon wader fabric or thin neoprene foam. Attached to the front and back, they effectively raise the protective height of the waders. Your wader suspenders then will have to be fastened to new buckles or Velcro patches on the bibs.

If you're fishing when the air temperature isn't extremely warm, you should wear a short rain jacket. It will act as a wind and rain stop, plus keep your elbows dry when you lower them to the sides of the tubes to fish. You don't need the splash guards if you're wearing a jacket.

Probably the most vital equipment, especially in cold weather, is garb made of neoprene rubber. This is the material from which scuba-diver wet suits are constructed. You can even press an old wet suit into service. Several firms have begun producing the rubber wear that can serve float tubers so well. The James-Scott Company of El Segundo, California, makes a jacket that has zipper sleeves, a high collar, and optional hood. Canty offers a three-piece hypothermia suit with short-sleeved jacket. The pants extend just below the knees so they don't hinder your kicking or cause chaffing. Long or short neoprene booties are worn outside over thin stocking foot waders.

If you opt for neoprene stocking-foot waders, you naturally do not need the pants section of a hypothermia or wet suit. You should still wear an additional pair of neoprene boots over the wader stocking feet for abrasion protection and foot comfort. Several firms now market so-called tuber booties. The best ones have a harder, non-skid sole. You can also glue some sort of improvised sole to your wader-protective booties. Such soles are vital because you'll regularly be walking to and from the water, and along shores or banks.

In more moderate temperatures, a diver's sleeveless wet suit vest can be a handy undergarment. You'll find yourself varying the neoprene garb you wear to match water and air temperature. A short rain jacket should always be with you, however. There are some rain jackets designed especially for fishermen, with pockets to hold your small fly or lure boxes.

Floating rivers in a tube can get you into some fantastic fishing. If you run heavy water, it can also get you into some dangerous situations caused by rocks and sweepers. All canoeists and other river runners are familiar with sweepers, which consist of logjams or tree branches thrusting from shore down into the water where heavy current sweeps against them. If you were thrust against one you could become pinned. The current could force you under and, if it's strong enough, there is no way to push free. Running in white water through rocks can be as bad. Wedge a foot between two boulders, and heavy water can rip you from your float and pull you under. As in any river running, advance scouting of whitewater stretches is a must. So is one more piece of life-saving equipment.

The item is a simple pad of closed-cell foam, slightly narrower than your chest, and about as long. A piece of backpacker sleeping pad would work. Just slip it down inside the front of your waders against your chest. This little piece of foam rubber could do more than some life vests to save you in a lake, and especially a river situation. Why? If you were unconscious, it would turn you face-up in the water.

Combination camping/fishing trips by belly boat are becoming increasingly popular. They require you to rough it with a minimum of creature comforts. If you use one of the inner-tube type floats, you'll have to stow gear in the built-in pockets of these units, plus in a small backpack. Some anglers even lash another pack or a couple of nylon storage bags to their tubes. If you plan a trip where some take-out and hiking is involved, the tubeless floats are better. Because of their small size and the fact that you can orally inflate them, they make it possible to hire a bush plane or horse pack outfitter to bring you to remote spots from which you'll launch your trip. The Lunker Hunter units, for example, have three 10 × 10 × 13-inch auxiliary camp-storage bags of the same tough neoprene-coated nylon from which the floats are made. They attach to the rear of the floats via Velcro tabs on short elastic pieces. To keep gear dry in these or any packs or bags lashed to the innertube type floats, place it in one or two heavy-duty plastic trash bags first, just as you would for a canoe or raft float trip. For further water resistance, coat the storage bag or pack zippers with stick-type lip balm.

For his personal long-range trips, Del Canty uses three camp-storage bags. Into one goes a 2-pound down sleeping bag. Into another goes freeze-dried food, basic cooking gear, and a backpacker's cook stove. The third bag holds emergency clothing but, with the neoprene rubber clothing already being worn, not much is needed.

There is another part of Del's system that is extremely valuable for long-range trips, overnight excursions, or as emergency shelter should an unforeseen mishap occur. It consists of a so-called bivouac inflator bag, plus a hood unit.

The inflator bag is made of urethane-coated nylon. Using a small valve at one end, you can attach it to your float tube, open the bag, catch air in it, then fold open the bag mouth. By squeezing the bag you inflate your belly boat quite quickly. But for use as the aforementioned shelter, you slide your sleeping bag into the bivouac inflator. It reaches chest level in the sleeping position. A second hood section attaches to the bivouac inflator via Velcro fastener material. The hood is also of coated nylon, but has a strip of Gortex in the middle along its entire length. The Gortex is to avoid breath condensation—to use the hood, you pull the entire unit up over your head and face like a sheet. The four corners of the hood section have pockets in which you place stones or sand for weight to hold the covering in place in a wind. For further comfort, a thin ground cloth and foam sleeping pad can be placed beneath everything.

Properly equipped, the float tube is a surprisingly comfortable, secure, and relaxing vessel from which to fish. Canty often tubes and fishes 8 to 12 hours in a stint. He frequently goes night fishing, especially the wee hours before dawn when some of the largest salmonids are on the prowl. He may start fishing in the evening. Around midnight, when the action slows, he'll just doze off there in the tube, drifting if there is a gentle breeze.

"There have been many times," he says, "when I just fell asleep and woke up on the other side of the lake when my tube nudged the shore."

To keep from losing a rod while catching a nap, changing flies, or working on tackle, a safety strap is advisable. To make one, attach a 30-inch length of elastic to your vest, rain jacket, or possibly the float itself. Sew and glue two patches of Velcro a couple of inches apart near the end of the elastic. These will then go snugly around the lower part of your rod handle. The 30-inch elastic length is long enough so it won't hamper your casting.

Float tubing lends itself to virtually any tackle you prefer: fly, spinning, or baitcasting. If you're a flyfishing enthusiast, you'll find a longer rod—9½ to 10 feet—a definite advantage because of your low placement to the water. One effective fishing method, when you are just tired from casting long hours, is to grip your rod with two hands, thrust the rod out, and rest your knuckles on the tube. Then slowly paddle with your fins. You can use this "trolling" method with a nymph or other fly, a little action-tail jig, or natural bait.

Casting is a lot more fun, though. Spinning and baitcasting present few problems, but the flycaster is presented with the problem of where to stow excess line. Modern belly boats are equipped with so-called aprons that attach to the tubes in front of the caster. They are a tremendous help. As tables on which to place line stripped from the reel, they both facilitate casting and keep loose line from tangling around your legs where it can cause a lost fish.

Besides using a longer rod, a flyfisherman can increase his cast distance from the low belly boat by other means. Expert fly angler Chico Fernandez has used a system for many years that he calls the long-ranger line. You might call it a very long shooting head that lacks the problems inherent to those heads. To work it, the *rear* section of a weight-forward fly line is cut back. The length to cut is determined by how much line you can hold in the air with your rod. An average caster might cut the line back so it is 50 to 55 feet long, while a very good caster could work with a fly line cut to 70 feet. Now, tie in enough 30-pound monofilament to the rear of the cut-down line so the two combined measure 100 feet. Thirty-pound mono is right for fly lines as light as No. 6; for anything lighter you might want to use slightly lighter mono. Use a nail knot to tie the mono shooting line to the fly line, and coat the connection with flexible cement. Tie a loop knot in the end of the mono to interlock with a loop in the Dacron backing.

When casting, you do not allow the mono to extend past the tip guide, as you would with a shorter 30-foot shooting head. You can hold any desired amount of the fly line in the air, changing false-cast direction immediately. You are also not as committed to making the cast once you have the line in the air, as you are with a shorter shooting head. If you're

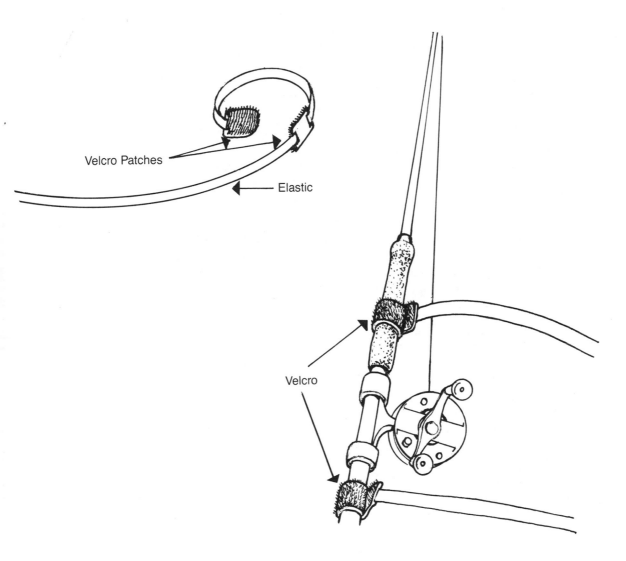

Safety strap of elastic/Velcro can be attached to rod above or below reel, the other end affixed to your jacket or vest.

using a floating line, you need not strip the entire line back before picking up for the next cast. Besides all these advantages you have the original one of increased distance. The long-ranger system is just simpler to use all around.

The average caster can add 20 to 25 feet to his cast when he shoots the monofilament through the guides instead of the normal fly-line tail of coated running line. A very good caster can add even more distance.

The system is excellent for fighting large fish. The monofilament running line slips smoothly and easily through the guides and its stretchability and low drag in the water insure far fewer breakoffs. Most record seekers are using this system for that very reason. And, because you are not using as much monofilament as in a normal shooting-head arrangement, there is less pressure on the reel spool that occurs when stretchy mono is cranked in under pressure and then contracts.

Another system that is used by some belly boat enthusiasts is the special shooting reel designed by Del Canty. Although it is a single-action reel, the similarity with normal fly reels ends there. The reel is designed for use with shooting heads backed with monofilament. The cast is made in the normal way, but then the mono running line shoots directly from the reel. The line comes through an opening in the side like an old spincast reel. If you are interested in records, it should be noted that the International Game Fish Association will not qualify for fly-rod records any fish caught using a reel from which the line is cast directly. A fish taken with such a reel would be considered for the normal line-class categories.

When retrieving with this shooting reel, you do not strip in the mono running-shooting line. Instead you crank it directly back on the reel using the handle. It is also necessary to alternate cranking direction on every other cast to avoid twisting the mono. You'd crank away from you one time, then toward you on the next retrieve. The rig has special pickup arrangements to make this possible. The reel also has two handles. One is located near the center of the spool for slower retrieves, the other near the spool rim for faster retrieves.

Teflon-impregnated gasket material forms the drag, which is adjusted for your tippet with a set screw and will not deform if pressure is not relaxed. It has been successfully tested to 1500 revolutions per minute. Secondary drag is applied by palming the reel, almost as you would a baitcasting reel. Palmed, your fingers reach around and touch the edge of the stainless steel spool. The reel frame is dura-aluminum. When used in saltwater, it is recommended that you touch the frame screws with a zinc solution or other protective lube coating to avoid corrosion. These reels are available from Lunker Hunter Systems, 4039 Highway 91, Leadville, CO 80461, on a thirty-day free-trial basis.

Adventuresome anglers have thus far taken their belly boating systems from the Arctic to Australia, and show no signs of stopping. There's no reason to. We've come a long way from the age of the inflatable goatskin.

chapter 10

The Coming of the Flylures

"The way I look at it, if I put a hook in my vise and build something on that hook from bits and pieces of natural or manmade materials, then paint it or finish it into a fine and pleasing work, then it's a fly; especially if I fish it on a fly rod."

—HAL JANSSEN, *fly tyer/fisherman.*

It was summer, hot and still even on the U.S.–Canadian border, and the smallmouth bass were not having anything to do with whatever my fishing partner and I offered them. In freshwater, my friend Albert is almost exclusively a fisher of salmonids, and he prefers to use a dry fly for trout or salmon whenever possible. It had been a major accomplishment to get him bass fishing in the first place. Flyfishing had been my only hope to lure him. But now we sat nearly defeated, sizzling in the late-afternoon sun.

The weather was obviously too hot to use poppers or hair bugs, although something might start on the surface at dusk. The streamers we'd been dredging down deeper didn't work. Even my favorite crayfish drew a blank. At this point most fisherman begin to rummage through their tackle instead of think. That's what I did, and this time it paid off.

What I came up with was a little delta-winged creation with a V-shaped nose and banana-shaped bend to its body. It was all plastic and had a little clip to which you tied the leader. I had several of them in a variety of colors. The one I chose was white with a splash of red. I turned my back to Albert while I tied it on.

The bass hit at the mouth of an inlet—a place where it should have been holding for food and cooler, moving water. It was a nice bass and, when my pal netted it, he plucked the successful lure from its jaw and turned to me with an accusing eye.

"What *is* this thing?" he demanded.

"Frisky Fly," I said. "Been around a long time. Fifteen years. Maybe more."

"Give me one," he said.

I didn't show him the other soft, molded-plastic creation. It was like a little squirmy porcupine with propeller-like wings in the back and skinny arms that stuck out in all directions. When you cast it, the pitch of the wings made it spin in the air. Then, when it hit the water, the twisted leader would unwind and cause the creation to struggle like a living thing. The Southern gentleman who invented it used the lure mainly for big panfish, but it catches a lot of bass—both largemouths and smallies. It's called the Cajun Fly. When the Cajun and the Frisky Fly were first introduced, they ran full bore into the tradition-bound barrier of the period's unliberated flyfishermen. Things have changed since then.

Ron Bargin is a hard-core largemouth bass angler who, at this writing, holds the total weight record for a limit of largemouth bass from California's Lake Isabelle. The five fish weighed 51 pounds, 6 ounces. One of the tricks Bargin uses is to clamp a split shot on his spinning line, and tie to the line's end one of Dan Byford's Zonker flies. The fly is one that's made with foam beneath the shiny Mylar tube body for flotation. He also may use a bit of cork ahead of the Zonker to perform the same function. Ron uses the rig to fish for suspended bass. He might set the split shot as much as 8 or 9 feet up the line. He obviously does not cast. With a long spinning rod, he allows the rig to descend to the bottom, then begins shaking it. The technique is called doodling.

The point here is that he uses a fly. Well, perhaps not a fly by some standards, but the Zonker certainly meets more of the traditional standards than the Frisky or Cajun flies of molded plastic. The coming of the flylures was a spinoff of the natural progression in the use of synthetic materials for traditional fly patterns. As popular natural materials became unavailable, creative tyers found a limitless supply of man-made materials that not only took their place, but also could be used in new and different ways that were even more effective than many of the older fur or feather supplies.

As just one example, look at the success of Gary LaFontaine's use of DuPont nylon Antron or American Cyanamid's Creslan orlon to build sparkling caddis patterns. Or, consider Monty Montplasir's Craft Fur Muddler, and his Stillwater Hex—a dry with synthetic wings, body, and tails. Economical, usually non-allergenic, rot and insect-proof synthetics—mostly from the petrochemical industry—are extremely adaptable. Today we have flies tied with tails or legs of nylon paint-brush fibers, crustaceans with shells formed of heat-melted synthetic dubbing, worms and leeches of processed leather, bugs made of plastic meat trays, nymphs with rubber balloon stomachs, dry-fly bodies of plastic leaf-bag material, and more.

Certainly the first use of synthetics was in more familiar fly styles. Then spinning and casting enthusiasts discovered that some of the materials could be incorporated in existing plugs to give them more flash or, in the case of large eyes, to target strikes by game fish. They also found that several of the materials formed excellent jig or spoon skirts—both in subdued hues and brilliant, flashy finishes.

Truly free-thinking tyers like Hal Janssen, Dave Whitlock, Dave Chermanski, Chico Fernandez, Al Troth, Ralph Kanz, Lefty Kreh, Dick Nelson, Dan Byford, Larry Dahlberg, and Monty Montplasir are among many that saw the versatility of the new products they were using, and began the process of creating totally new designs. Some of the patterns they developed incorporate features of lures used in non-flyfishing techniques. Traditional they are not, but they catch more fish. To give credit where it's due, past years always produced a scattering of individualists who were ahead of their time in the design of non-traditional flies. Lee Wulff's salmon stoneflies, which were formed initially of plastic drinking straw, typifies the breed. But now, with so many more creative souls at work, plus an unfettering of angler attitude, we are truly in a new era and can expect more innovative patterns and techniques each year for some time to come.

The new flylures make the taking of virtually all game species on one type of lure a more consistent reality. As with more conventional patterns, many designs work on a multitude of species. Because the focus here is on trout and bass, we'll concentrate the discussion to that end, although you'll no doubt see a variety of applications. All of the flylures discussed are available through the major retail outlets and mail-order companies listed later.

The hair bass bug has been around a long time, but it was given a sudden face-lifting and boost in fish-catching qualities when, some years back, Dave Whitlock launched his multi-colored, wiggly-legged series of clipped hair attractors. Whitlock may have been the first bass-bug tyer to employ hollow plastic doll's eyes with little pupils that move around inside their clear plastic spheres. A lot of anglers shook their heads, and said "Well, now. . .". But this seemingly simple innovation was to have long-lasting effect. At first, the eyes were assumed to be cake frosting. But anglers with a scientific bent soon began to relate them to protective deflector patterns on fish, insects, and other living things. A lot of creatures, including many species of fish, have eye-like markings at the edges of their rear portions. These markings are larger and more attractive than the true eyes, and serve to direct predator attack away from the head. When used on streamer patterns, the plastic doll eyes also offer slight built-in flotation, which can cause a slight bobbing action as the fly is strip-retrieved.

Whitlock also applied his doll eyes on a new minnow pattern called the Prismatic series. The sides of this fly are formed from pieces of stiff Mylar film with a glittery prismatic finish—the same kind of adhesive-backed tape now so commonly used on spoons, spinner blades, and some plugs to add flash. The only natural materials used in the pattern are marabou wing and a few peacock herls as topping. In appropriate sizes, the streamer is very effective for both bass and trout, as well as other species. The big eyes are now found on a variety of Muddler ties, as well as patterns of other tyers.

Four original flylures for freshwater game fish: (top) Whitlock's Water Pup, Flashabou Muddler with doll's eyes; (bottom) Dahlberg's chamois tail salamander imitation; Whitlock's Prismatic Minnow.

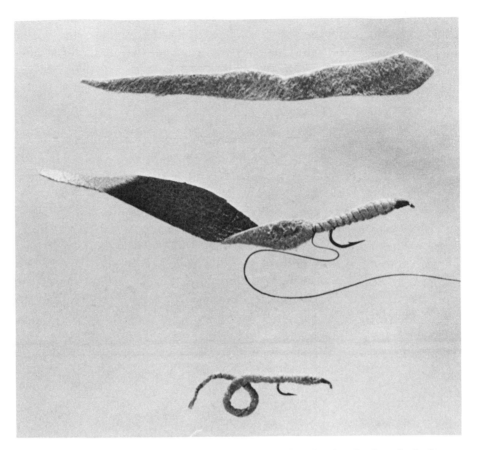

Pete Ross's worm fly is tied with a piece of leather (top), which is locked to a hook with tying thread (center), the thread then wound along the leather so it forms a wormlike tube (bottom).

Leather—usually chamois or the thin tongues of old shoes—has lately been finding its way into a variety of patterns. Whitlock's chamois leeches, with an extended tail-like body of the stuff behind a collar of squirrel tail and metal bead-chain eyes, is one example. Then there's the worm fly. No, this is not some imitation of a grub or inchworm that trout so love, but a bonafide earthworm simulator.

Peter Ross, the guiding light of Wood River Fishing Bags in Santa Ana, California, made the bogus crawler by simply laying a strip of chamois along a hook, locking it in place with tying thread, then winding spaced thread wrappings down its entire length. The thread wrapping curls the leather into a tubular, wormlike configuration. The wrapping includes the tail section, which extends on past the hook bend. The pattern doesn't have much action, but is successful when drifted or allowed to sink slowly with occasional, very gentle twitches. Some anglers like to anoint it with one of the commercial scent attractors so popular today. It takes stream trout and smallmouths readily.

Mylar Fly Lures

Perhaps the most innovative new flylures to come along are built with new, ultra-thin strip Mylar wing materials in an array of shades, and new patterned Mylar body tubing in a variety of highly innovative body constructions. Frequently, construction centers around the use of several materials beneath one another to give not only a fantastic variety of subtle shade changes, but also a three-dimensional effect, with body markings showing through surface coverings.

The thin, flexible, wing-material strips are available as Flashabou from most major fly tackle outfitters or direct from its marketer, Flashabou/ International Hairgoods, Inc., 6811 Flying Cloud Drive, Eden Prairie, MN 55344. Tel. 612-941-0500. The Orvis Company of Manchester, Vermont has a similar material they call Fly Flash. Rogue River Anglers of Gold Hill, Oregon, and Traun River Products of West Germany, are also marketing a similar product available through many dealers. The wing material comes in bundles about 9 inches long, in a variety of interesting shades including pearl, gold, silver, copper, red, light blue, light olive, black, purple, green, pink, white, orange, and possibly more by the time you read this.

The most obvious use of the thin strips is to mix them with other

Hard on the heels of the wing materials came an exciting new version of the braided Mylar tubing that has been used for bodies on such relatively recent fish-taking patterns as Dan Byford's Zonker, as well as some old standard streamer patterns. The older Mylar tubing we had handily available came basically in silver, possibly gold, or other solid hues if you were lucky and could find it in millinery shops. This new tubing, introduced by Larry Dahlberg, has been dubbed Flashabou Minnow Body. It is truly eye-catching for both humans and fish. Unlike the older solid colors, Minnow Body possesses an iridescence and is also translucent. Turn it this way and that in the light and you'll see it change its primary hue, dispersing and refracting light prismatically.

Because of its translucence, you can alter the overall tone of Minnow Body by using solid-color tubing, prismatic tapes, or other variously colored materials as an underbody beneath it. Some makers of flylures, like Californian Hal Janssen, take advantage of the material's translucence in a different way. They build underbody forms that are marked and painted to produce fish-like markings that show through the Minnow Body.

The tubing comes in a variety of size as well as colors. Pearl may be the most versatile, for it is light enough to allow most other colors and patterns to pass through. The pearl color is an iridescent weave of pink, silver, blue, and green. It is the basis for all the other colors that are produced by an overlay braid or cross-weave, which quite nicely simulates the patterns of fish scale. The other colors include goldtone, silvertone,

HOW TO TIE THE MINNOW BODY FLYLURE

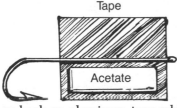

1. Lay hook on aluminum tape which is stiffened with acetate or other material.

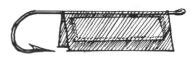

2. Fold tape over hook shank and pinch tight along shank

3. Cut tape and stiffener to minnow shape, being sure not to block hook gap.

4. Tie off ends and cement. Coat body with epoxy and let dry. Trim front only.

5. Tie in optional strip of 1/8″ fur at same points body was tied. Add eyes, doll's or painted.

6. For snag-free version, invert hook, sandwich lead strip like a keel between tape and stiffener.

coppertone, greentone, bluetone and blacktone. Smaller sized tubing produces flies up to ¼-inch deep, medium results in flies up to ½-inch deep, and large can make flies an inch or more deep. The largest size is suitable for slipping over plugs and other hard lures to change their finish.

Early use of braided Mylar tubing was quite simple, and is still used in the original Zonker pattern. The proper length of tubing for a 3x or 4x-long hook is cut, slipped over the hook eye, and slid down the thread-covered shank. It is then tied off at the head and tail end just forward of the hook bend. More anglers these days are beginning to use body forms beneath the tubing in order to produce a more realistic configuration that is broader toward the head-shoulder area, and tapers down toward the tail end as does a natural minnow. The deeper body also has the advantage of presenting a larger side profile and, naturally, more flash.

The body forms are most commonly formed of aluminum tape, available at hardware stores or departments. The tape has an adhesive on one side, covered by a peel-off backing. A piece of tape is cut long enough so it may be folded tentlike over the back of the thread-wrapped hook shank from a point ³⁄₁₆-inch to ¼-inch behind the eye to just ahead of the hook bend. Using fingernails or small pliers, pinch the tape snug along the shank. Now that the rectangular piece of tape is hanging below the shank, you draw the outline of the distended belly and rear taper on it. Then, using strong scissors, cut along the outline. Make sure the rear taper gives plenty of room between the shank and hook point—if not, you'll have a closed hook gap that will result in missed fish. Without a 3x or 4x-long hook, you would not derive the full benefit of the body form because the taper would have to be too severe in order to not block the hook gap.

The standard aluminum tape is, of course, a silver color. For hotter color, you may prefer to use prismatic tape—the kind frequently used on spoons and spinners. None of the tape is overly stiff and, for more rigidity, Larry Dahlberg prefers to use a little piece of acetate beneath the folded tape strip. Both tape and acetate—a celluloid or clear plastic-like sheeting—are then cut together to make the body form.

The cut piece of Minnow Body tubing is slipped over the hook eye and over the form. Then it's tied down, first at the head end, then at the tail end. The little leftover tubing behind the rear thread wraps can be frayed out to give a little tail-like effect. You now have the body base for many flylure patterns. One of the most popular consists of a simple wrap of soft hackle at the head end. Then a wing of rabbit, skunk, mink, or muskrat hide with the fur attached is tied in at the head. The thread is cut and the fur strip is tied down at the rear of the hook just ahead of the hook bend. Make the fur tie-down wraps over the wraps that hold the body material at the hook rear. The fur strips should be cut from the underside of the skin, holding the hides in a clamp and cutting with a razorblade so you won't cut the hair as you would with scissors. Strips 3/16-inch wide will suffice for hooks in sizes 2 to 6, but many prefer 1/8-inch wide strips.

The Mylar tubing unravels easily, so some tyers like to put a coat of head cement like the new Flexament at the spot where the body section is to be cut from the length of tubing. Let the cement dry a few seconds, then make a sawing type cut. Also, if you expect the body material to hold up through a few fish, the body should be coated with epoxy before adding a wing or hackle. You can use any popular epoxy for the coating, a brand that won't yellow with age is Hi-Build, Hi-Gloss from the Epoxy Coating Company, Union City, CA 94857. It's available in good craft shops.

Other tricks can be used to make a Minnow Body flylure even more versatile. For example, after you have fastened and cut the tape or tape-acetate body form to shape, and before you slip on the Mylar tubing, lay a thin strip of foam along the top of the hook shank. Then proceed as

MINNOW BODY FLYLURE WITH MYLAR TUBE UNDERBODY

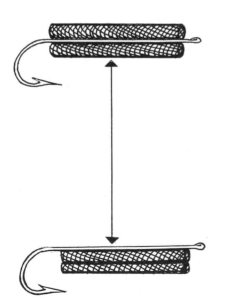

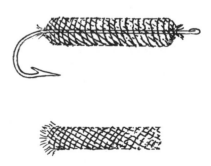

2. Tie off tubing the usual way, then slip larger diameter Mylar tubing over underbody, tie off.

1. Cement two pieces of small-diameter Mylar tubing either above and below, or below, hook shank.

DIVING BILL ON MINNOW BODY FLYLURE

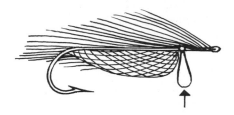

1. Wrap the ends of a loop of fine wire around the hook shank. Then fill the loop with Bond 525 cement to form a clear bill.

2. Finish off in usual way, including foam back strip, and bend bill down.

previously described. This will result in a floating minnow imitation that will dart on the surface with gentle retrieves, but dip beneath it with more vigorous strips of the fly line. Forming the underbody with a cork cylinder covered with Minnow Body will result in a lure that rides even higher.

Dahlberg has been experimenting to obtain even more action. Before the body form is affixed to the hook, he forms a little wire loop by tying two legs of wire to the top of the hook shank. The loop, sticking out past the eye of the hook, is then bent just below the eye and filled with Bond 525 Cement. The body and foam strip are then built in the above way. After all is completed, the cement-filled loop is bent down in front of the body to form a bill like that found on floating-diving plugs. Precise location must be subject to experimentation but, once you get it right, you'll have a flylure that will dive like one of the popular balsa plugs.

To make a flylure that is fairly snag-free, invert the hook so it rides point-up in your vise. Build the body form of tape or tape-acetate in the usual way, but sandwich a little lead wire or Twist-On lead strips at the bottom of the body form, much like the lead keel on a sailboat.

A fuller, more rounded body shape can also be created. Rather than the tape form underbody, use two solid color Mylar tube pieces. Usually a darker color Mylar tube goes on the top of the hook shank while a lighter color tube piece rides on the underside of the shank. The solid color tubing pieces can be glued and tied on the shank. Use the small-size tubing for the underbody. Then the larger size Minnow Body tubing is slipped over the two underbody tube pieces. The solid colors of the underbody tubing pieces will show through, affecting a subtle change in the outer body hue.

The Fry Fly

Another outstanding flylure is Hal Janssen's Fry Fly. This little lure must be seen to be appreciated. They are being marketed now in several patterns to imitate various fry eaten by trout and bass. There is a threadfin shad; little rainbow, brook, and brown trout; plus a little largemouth and little smallmouth bass. A series of very bright finish Fire Frys is also available. The underbody form for these little fry curves both above and below the hook shank. It is made from Grumbacker No. 7123 Bristol board in flat finish. Bristol is a fine, smooth pasteboard available in art supply stores. Silver Mylar tubing is stretched over the cemented-on forms. A tail of marabou is also featured. Once the Mylar is in place, an exacting paint job takes place. All these Fry Flies are carefully hand-painted to produce the markings and color of the species they are to represent. The only exception is when the translucent pearl Mylar tubing is used. In this case, markings are made first on the Bristol board form, which show through the pearl tubing. Beautiful little parr are thus fashioned.

After the painting—including eyes—is done, the Fry Flies are coated with the non-yellowing Hi-Build, Hi-Gloss epoxy previously mentioned.

Janssen prefers not to produce the Fry Flies on hook sizes larger than a No. 1. Beyond that, he says, the lure begins to lose the darting life-like action that so helps it attract gamefish. Also, these flies are rarely weighted. The epoxy, hook, and Bristol board produce the perfect weight proportionate to the lure size. Various sinking formulation fly lines are necessary when you need to get these flylures deeper.

All of the previously discussed flylures can be used by spinning or casting enthusiasts for ultralight teasers on tandem lure rigs behind spoon, spinners, and especially plugs. Usually a short length of monofilament line is tied either to a hook hanger eye or one of the hooks of the main lure. The heavier lure, which gets the teaser down deep, is either trolled or cast. Trout and bass anglers who fish tandem rigs frequently use ultralight jigs or very small spoons as the teaser. Very often it's the big lure that causes the commotion that game fish come to investigate, but it's the little lure that the fish end up eating.

The flylures have the advantage of being lighter even than the small jigs often used on tandem rigs. They tend to suspend better or run higher

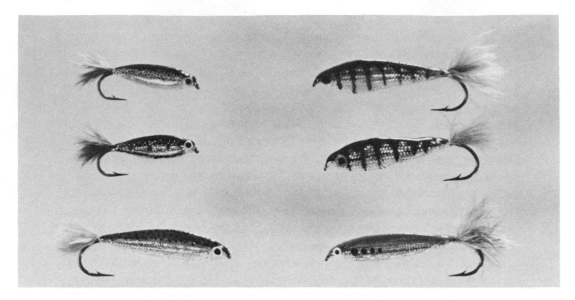

Hal Janssen's Fry Flies are made by stretching transluscent Mylar tubing over Bristol board forms which have been painted with dots or stripes. The tubing is then given a coat of epoxy.

than the jigs or small spoons sometimes used. They also rarely affect the action of the main lure, and are more easily cast. Of course you can use them alone with split shot on spinning tackle, just as bass expert Ron Bargin does in his deep vertical jigging technique described at the beginning of this chapter.

The Balsa Dragonfly Nymph

When trout are feeding on emerging insects or nymphs rising up from the bottom of some quiet lake or pond, they tend to develop a distinct feeding rhythm. They are slow and deliberate, taking what they want exactly when they want because of the enormous availability of food. But with other forage, it's usually a different story. Free and fast-swimming minnows must be attacked right away before they can escape. A slow-swimming leech is another example of something trout tend to attack right away, but not because they move fast. High-protein leeches are just not so readily available—especially in daylight hours—and the fish cannot afford to be so cavalier about when to take the creatures. The same is true for big, plump dragonfly nymphs. When they get the chance, trout will usually gobble them. Keying on this knowledge, Hal Janssen created a super dragonfly nymph out of balsa. The finished product looks almost like a bass bug, but it is not popped and gurgled on the surface.

Hal generally fishes the floating dragonfly nymph in the shallow areas of lakes or ponds, where the naturals are found. He uses an intermediate or slow-sinking fly line and a leader up to 15 feet long. Floating line with long weighted leader, or sink-tip line with a shorter leader, may better fit your particular local conditions.

The trick is how the nymph is retrieved. Hal eases it along slowly with

HOW TO TIE THE DRAGONFLY NYMPH

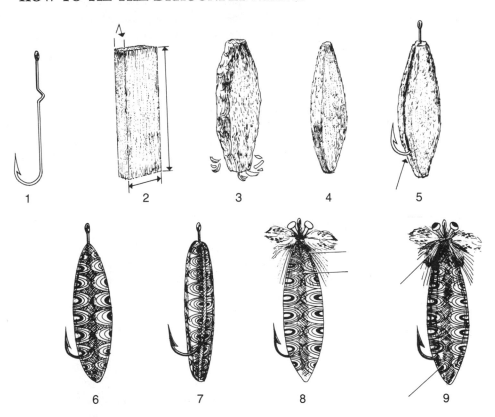

Use a No. 4 or 8 bass-bug type kink hook (**1**). Start with a piece of balsa wood about the dimensions shown (**2**) and rough-cut it to shape (**3**). Sand the balsa smooth (**4**), then split the wood to accept the hook and epoxy it in place (**5**). Paint body olive and rings green, brown, and black (**6, 7**). Tie in eyes of artificial flower pistils, then guinea-hen hackle, and finally fibers from peacock herl—eyed section (**8, 9**). Coat back only with Aero high-gloss clear dope.

The trick is how the nymph is retrieved. Hal eases it along slowly with hand turns as the sinking fly line or leader weights bring it down. Occasionally, he'll twitch it forward in a short burst. This action causes the nymph to dive briefly, but also gives a quick moment of slack during which the fly may slowly rise a little with a wiggly action that's very attractive to trout. Many fish hit on the rise.

The accompanying illustrations show the steps in building Janssen's balsa dragonfly nymph. For painting, use a model dope such Aero Gloss by Pactral Industries of Los Angeles, CA 90028. The flower pistils used for eyes are available at good craft shops, as is the paint. The other materials are obtainable from good fly tying material specialists. The dragonfly nymph catches more than trout, by the way. I'd also try it when largemouth or smallmouth bass are working the shallows or are near the surface in deeper water. Even if they are feeding on minnows in the latter situation, they do not become so locked in on one type of forage as trout can during a major hatch period, and are just as likely to eat the dragon if it seems easy to catch.

The Dahlberg Diver

One other pattern needs to be considered. It's another of Larry Dahlberg's fascinating creations, called the Dahlberg Diver. The pattern is part streamer, part popper. In use it behaves very much like a jerk plug designed or muskie fishing, which is exactly what Dahlberg had in mind when he designed it. It has accounted for a share of muskellunge, by the way. But Larry also discovered that, in slightly smaller sizes, it would take smallmouths in the rivers he fished, and good largemouth bass in the large sizes. I saw it take very big brown trout. After that demonstration I began using it regularly for several species.

The fly features hackle wing-tail, with strips of Mylar or Flashabou winging strips for attraction. The front part of the head is of clipped deer hair like that of a muddler minnow. But then comes the feature that sets it apart. Behind the head is a splayed collar of deer hair. The collar sticks at least ¾-inch out and back from the clipped head. It is not just for looks. The fly is made to swim gently on the surface, its wedgelike front end causing a good wake. Then, when it is quickly stripped in, the head and collar make the little lure dive with a bubble wake. Because of the buoyancy of the deer hair, the Diver will again pop to the surface. The up-down commotion, plus the look of the creature when a gamefish arrives on the scene, is usually sufficient to result in a strike. The fly will eventu-

The Dahlberg Diver, shown here in four variations, is part streamer, part popper. Originally designed for muskie, it's effective for largemouths as well, and in smaller sizes, for smallmouths.

ally become waterlogged, but a few false casts are usually enough to get it doing its thing again. Even if it does pick up enough water to submerge it during a retrieve, the thing still catches fish swimming beneath the surface.

With the continual introduction of new materials in other industries, fly makers have just begun to explore the frontier of fascinating new concepts that may be applied to our long rod fishing. And now that we are no longer bonded by rigid thinking, who knows what intriguing new fish-taking patterns will emerge just a little way down the river?

Flylures Sources

L. L. Bean Inc.
Freeport, ME 04033

Bass Pro Shops
Box 4046
Springfield, MO 65808

Cabela's
812 13th Avenue
Sidney, NE 69160

Kaufmann's Streamborn
12963 S.W. Pacific Hwy
Tigard, OR 97223

The Fly Shop
4140 Churn Creek Road
Reading, CA 96002

R. Monty Montplaisir
Box 212
Colebrook, NH 03576
(Flies only)

The Orvis Company
Manchester, VT 05254

Umpqua Feather Merchants, Inc.
Box 72
Idleyld Park, OR 97447

chapter 11

Visual Fishing

"Fish comin', said the guide. "Eleven
  o'clock."
"Where?" asked the sport in near panic.
"Get ready to cast."
"Where?"
"OK, now's your shot; they're crossing.
  One o'clock!"
"Where, 0!°$%!"
"Well. . .they're gone."
"—."

Nowhere has the art of stalking visible fish been more highly developed than on the shallow flats in clear saltwater. In fact, regulars of this environment commonly refer to all other angling as blind fishing. Even casting to cover or other underwater bottom convolutions you can easily eyeball falls into this category—if you don't see the fish.

There's no argument that the tropic marine flats offer the finest opportunity to stalk sighted fish but, in reality, much inland fishing for trout and bass both in lakes and rivers can be done visually. Sometimes it may consist of casting to fish you can actually see; other times it may be presenting to risers, cruisers, sounders, or to visually located underwater objects. I do not call that blind fishing. In any case, though, few freshwater anglers have bothered to develop visual fishing techniques anywhere near to potential. Too bad; sight fishing in its many forms is one of the more fascinating aspects of the sport, and it can appreciably increase your hookups.

Two basic equipment items are vital to success in the visual fishing game: polarized glasses and good binoculars. There's a wealth of specifics to consider with both pieces of equipment. These will be discussed later. First let me whet your appetite with some of the interesting ways to use your aided eyes to catch fish.

Increased height is an obvious advantage, yet it is routinely ignored by too many bass and trout enthusiasts. It was not overlooked by early native Americans who regularly climbed river or lakeside cliffs to peer into clear-water depths. They learned all kinds of things about their home waters that way, and often spied fish, too. Modern steelhead and some salmon anglers do a bit of the same thing; it's an intense part of overall angling tactics for those at the top of their game. Aboard fishing craft, however, methods for increasing line of sight have seen greatest development in saltwater. Let's look at some of those developments, then consider the application in freshwater.

Nineteenth Century whaling skippers understood, if not the mathematical theory, the end result of placing a lookout in a masthead perch. He could see things farther off and before anyone else aboard ship, which is how the term crow's nest came to be. Big game pioneer Zane Grey rigged a crude crow's nest on a short mast back in the 1920's. The flying bridge came into vogue about 10 years later, and makeshift structures were hastily constructed by charter boatmen on their fishing craft. Renowned charter skipper Tommy Gifford built a tower of 2x4's on his boat back in the 1930's. The numbers of towers for tuna and swordfishing increased during the late 1940's, along with the development of somewhat better remote steering, shift, and throttle controls bolted to the high perches. Lightweight, small-diameter aluminum combined with good design made scaled-down towers a possibility for smaller and smaller boats. The so-called teeny towers proliferated in the early 1970's and are considered normal equipment today. They are widely found on center-console, outboard-powered boats down to 21 or 22 feet. Boats the size of popular bass rigs—17 to 18 feet—are equipped with mini-towers or poling platforms attached to the transom over the engine. The platforms are standard equipment among skiff anglers who regularly fish shallow saltwater flats. As we'll see, they have direct application for bass and trout fishing.

Increasing line of sight through height was and is the main purpose of towers on both the larger boats and the 20-foot, center-console, pocket sportfishermen as well. Seeing farther helps locate things like birds, breaking or rolling fish, and other boats that are on fish. On a clear day, an angler seated in a boat with eyes 3 feet above the water can gaze about 2 miles. With line of sight raised to 7 feet, the horizon is 3 miles distant. Get to 19 feet on a larger tower and you can see 5 miles.

Increased sight distance is not the only benefit of height. A higher perch also increases your circle of vision down into the water around your boat. This especially appeals to shallow water marine anglers whose whole sport centers around visually locating species such as tarpon, permit, bonefish, sharks, redfish, and other species. Before the innovation of the poling platform, some early skiff guides in this environment were known to bring a stepladder in their boats. They'd then set it up to pole from and hunt fish.

Freshwater bass and trout anglers aren't so fortunate to find fish in shallow clear water so often, although it is a distinct possibility some of

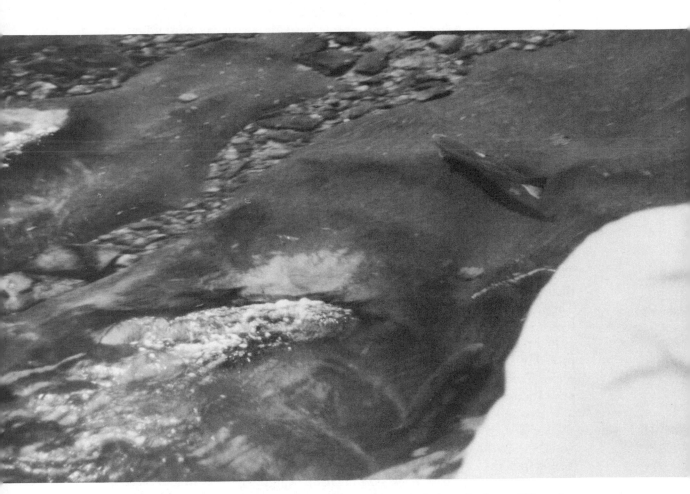

In a stream, fish on a plain bottom are easy to see with the naked eye. When the bottom is mottled with rocks, bars, and weedbeds, binoculars or polarized glasses are helpful in locating them.

the time. What we can do is combine a bit of increased elevation with high-quality binoculars and polarized glasses to locate a variety of natural and man-made cover, plus bottom changes that act as fish magnets. If you've ever flown over a lake or reservoir, you know what I mean. Stretching before you are underwater points, reefs, shoals, and bars. Channels are revealed maplike by changing color and, in clear water, by the actual rocks, mud, and clay bottom makeup. You'll see areas of submerged weedbeds; perhaps the ancient pilings of a bridge or wing dams will become evident. Things aren't quite so clear down on the water in a boat, but you'll still be able to locate a surprising number of fish-holding areas with your optic-aided eyes. You only need sun and a little bit of clarity to the water. A great amount of wind, of course, will spoil things.

I've been trout fishing when no rising, breaking, or slowly porpoising fish were in evidence, yet I could still locate long points extending from mainland or island shores, channel cuts through shoals, and all manner of dropoffs, gravel banks, sandbars, and deltas formed by tributary streams. These are all places where trout pass, hold to feed, or congregate when getting ready to make a spawning run. In smaller lakes and ponds I've felt the surge of excitement that followed my spotting of dark, ever-moving schools of trout.

The smaller waters are sometimes the best places to start. Contrary to popular belief, trout don't simply make routine circuits of a small lake's shoreline. Instead, they move in from deeper water onto flats and near coves or weed edges where baitfish congregate or insects hatch. Fall-spawning trout move up to the mouths of tributaries or to areas of lakes with gravel, current, or spring holes where spawning will take place. They'll cruise an elliptical pattern, perhaps along 150 feet of shoreline, then disappear as they turn into the deeper water to circle back around. They'll probably not move more than 25 or 30 feet away from the attractive area on their sweep, and may confuse you by reversing direction.

In breezy weather when you cannot actually see moving fish, you'll probably still be able to make out the shoals, flats, and bars that attract them. Trout can still be there and may take underwater lures and flies, even though they are not rising.

If bass in lakes have been relating to vegetation that rises close beneath the surface, you have a distinct advantage for this visual fishing. Move your boat so the angle of the sun penetrates the water, lighting the plants. You'll spot not only the inside and outside edges of the weedbeds, but subtle turns, points, cuts, pockets, and channels in the beds as well. Other hotspots in the weeds will often be evident. I've found stumps, old trees, cribbing, drowned fences, rocks, and the like amid vegetation beds this way, before moving in too close and spooking the fish. Once you have a good idea of the lay of things underwater, reposition your boat for the best presentations.

In the past, I sometimes worked promising-looking weedbeds with little or no success, reasoning each time that the fish weren't biting or there simply weren't any there. One day, smack in the middle of a large weed-clogged area that failed to produce, I decided to take a break. It was a lovely day for loafing; the sun was high and the wind was calm. I grabbed my binoculars, dug out a sandwich, and climbed as high as possible in my boat. In between bites, I used the glasses to check more distant areas that I normally fished to see if any other boats were working them. For no reason in particular, I happened to train the binoculars down into the weeds nearer the boat. I was amazed. First I began to see a large number of forage fish suspended not far beneath the surface. Some were just hanging there; others moved about slowly, unconcerned. Then I spotted a bass—just his head sticking from behind a stalk of coontail weed. The fish lay deeper than the minnows. I took the binoculars away and could not relocate the largemouth. Continuing my inspection I found still another bass. This one was was simply lying on what looked like a mattress of moss, appearing totally at ease.

I cannot recall what happened to my sandwich, but it doesn't matter. I had been fishing the area with spinnerbaits and weedless spoons, swimming them over the matted weeds. I switched to a jig trimmed with pork rind and went to work—sometimes flipping, sometimes just casting and working an up-down swimming retrieve that was far deeper than I had fished earlier. It was clear that the fish were not in an aggressive feeding state, but I managed to pull three of them out of that bed before I was through. Spotting the bass with polarized glasses and binoculars had given me the confidence to continue fishing an area that I was about to give up. Today, when conditions are right, I never leave an area that ought to yield fish without visually checking it first.

Besides all this relatively close-in hunting, trout and bass anglers can use the advantages of height, binoculars, and polarized sunglasses just as offshore, saltwater, big-game anglers do to find far-off fish. For example, flying birds often tell the tale of working fish on the surface. You can usually spot them without binoculars, of course. When a school of fish sound, however, they frequently come up not too far from the spot where they disappeared. Birds know this, so they regularly hang around for awhile, setting down on the water. Riding the surface, they're a lot harder to see. Enter the binoculars and a high perch.

Another example: Let's say you're on a new lake or reservoir, spot flying or sitting birds, and head for them. The place could be laced with a maze of drops, cuts, shoals. Wind can set up complex currents to which bait and gamefish relate. With your knowledge of fishing, it's obvious that each situation must be cast or trolled in a different way. Just as saltwater anglers read currents and rips before fishing a spot, so can inland anglers. Checking the place visually before you reach it will greatly increase your chances for success. Use your glasses and higher perch to scout things out, then move in to fish.

Having made my case for a high scouting perch aboard your fishing boat, I should add that height is relative. Even a little helps. There is no intention here for you to lash a stepladder to your favorite canoe. The device would soon assume the keel position, with you forced to straddle the now skyward-facing canoe bottom.

The ladder trick does work in broad-beamed johnboats, however. If you want an ideal setup, one of those mini-towers or poling platforms used in skiffs that ply the saltwater shallows is great. They're suitable for boats in the 16 to 18-foot class. For more information on the platforms, which can be adapted to many open, skiff-style boats, write to the following manufacturers: Salt Shaker, Inc., 2635 Northeast 4th Avenue, Pompano Beach, FL 33064; JMC Outfitters, Inc., 1301 Yorktown Street, DeLand, FL 32724; Pipe Welders, Inc., 413 Southwest 3rd Avenue, Ft. Lauderdale, FL 33315; Marine Island Products, Inc., Box 2806, Vero Beach, FL 32961.

An even simpler method is to securely fasten a strong, flat-topped cooler to deck, seat, or other area in your boat. Reinforce the lid with a piece of marine or exterior plywood. It should cover the entire lid and be easily glued on. The unit makes a handy perch from which to scout and cast. Strong, flat-topped tackle boxes work the same way, but do not offer as wide a standing surface.

Some anglers have taken to making their own tackle storage container that serves as a good standing platform as well. Such a unit is basically a wood box with stock aluminum angle pieces inside. Drawers from commercially built tackle boxes slide over the angle stock. The drawers that fit the Plano 777RN or 777N tackle boxes are ideal. Build your wood box with a wide enough platform on top to stand on. The ABS box in which the drawers initialy come is not big enough for standing purposes. Drawers are available from Plano Molding Company, Plano, IL 60545-0189.

More small V-bottom skiffs are being built these days with forward and aft decks. Standing on these decks alone gives more height than the bottom of the boat and is obviously more secure than standing on a cross seat. Your cooler or stand-on tackle box can be fastened to the decks. If you have a boat with no such decks or platforms, it is not a difficult task to construct them from marine plywood, cut to fit the configuration of the hull. The decks simply cover the cross seats, giving you storage below and a place to sit as well as stand.

Visual fishing should be as much a part of a wading angler's gameplan as it is for the boating angler. This is no news to ardent steelheaders who regularly climb cliffs and trees to locate their quarry. Jim Teeny, the human heron from Oregon, spends long, intense periods scouting for his fish before ever wetting a line. Like salmon, the migratory rainbows can be here today and gone tomorrow, so why fish hard over a nice holding spot that harbors no fish? Teeny designed special polarized glasses to spot fish better. If you're a trout or bass specialist who normally fishes streams and rivers, scouting underwater structure and cover likely to hold fish

Jim Teeny of Oregon has developed visual fishing for steelhead into a fine art. He never fishes unless he has first located the fish. He developed special sunglasses designed to reduce peripheral glare for maximum vision into the water.

should be done with binoculars and polarized sunglasses in the same manner as for lake fishing.

Locating individual fish or groups of them is sometimes even easier in shallower river environments than it is in lakes, if the water is fairly clear and you search areas where the current smooths from time to time. The trick is not to expect fish to appear as they do above water. Once you learn to mentally ignore the surface, search for shapes that appear as gray ghost-like forms or brownish-olive torpedos, depending on the fish, the water, and surroundings.

From the stream bank or the side of a small hill, you can gain invaluable information on rising trout with your binoculars. Not only can you locate those fish which are rising very delicately, but by careful examination you can also often determine at some distance whether they are working emerging nymphs or duns. Sometimes you can even identify the insects either by actually spotting them on the water or in the air, or by the rise-forms of the trout. You do all this before ever disturbing the water by wading or casting. Of course, if you do much hiking down steep banks or cliffs, binoculars can help find the best way down in a strange area. And, by searching the water below first, you usually can tell whether it's worth hiking down there in the first place.

Sunglasses

The sunglasses and binoculars that you choose influence your angling success—and over short periods they can cause or protect against eye strain. Over a long period of time, sunglasses may help reduce chances of acquiring serious vision impairment, such as cataracts. Because you're on the water a lot, you need to be concerned about protecting your eyes against the harmful effects of invisible ultraviolet radiation, as well as extreme light intensity and reflection. Even when glare is not a problem, UV radiation still can be. Haven't you ever found yourself on the water during overcast conditions, squinting if your glasses were off? That's the result of UV rays being scattered by millions of water particles in the atmosphere.

Glass acts as a filter of UV and infrared radiation as well. However, in order for plastic sunglasses to filter UV rays, an ultraviolet-inhibiting chemical must be added as the plastic lenses are made. Manufacturers of better plastic glasses do this.

There are other considerations when choosing between glass and plastic. Good quality synthetics work well, but eventually scratch and need to be replaced. Distortion has been more of a problem with the synthetics—

mainly the very cheap glasses that have been dumped on the market. Chances for distortions in high-quality synthetics are far less. Fine glass, especially optical glass, has traditionally been even more free from distortion.

Try this trick when you're choosing sun-glasses in a store. Hold the glasses in front of you so an overhead light reflects from the front of the lenses. Move that reflection around the lenses. If at some spot the reflection appears to jump or wave, the glasses probably have a distortion problem. Your eyes try to compensate and, over a full day of wearing them, you can develop a mean headache.

Also try this test. Put the glasses on and observe yourself in a mirror. If you can easily see your eyes, the glasses will not do much by way of protecting against light intensity. That doesn't matter under some light conditions, as we'll see. But when the sun is bright it does.

Good glass lenses are more expensive, but last longer. Custom-made glass polarized lenses are the most expensive of all. The Cable Car Sunglass Company of Hollister, California, was the first to produce good quality, glass, polarized lenses at moderate prices. They are widely sold at fishing specialty shops around the country, and they now offer a variety of specialty designs specifically for anglers. Other firms noted for their optics are also designing high-quality sunglasses for fishermen.

The reflection-cutting characteristics of polarized glasses both reduce eye fatigue and help you to see below the water, as most fishermen know. The polarizing filter in sunglasses is formed by introducing iodine crystals in a thin matrix, which is then sandwiched in glass or plastic so the crystals are aligned along a single axis. Few anglers will argue over having polarized glasses; the right color for those lenses, however, is a subject for much discussion.

The best colors for fishing sunglasses are yellow (sometimes called amber), brown, and gray. Yellow and brown lenses increase contrast and help you locate fish better. They do not reduce light intensity as well as gray. Many anglers have worried about not getting enough eye protection, especially with the lighter yellow lenses. There's no need to. Good yellow or brown lenses absorb ultraviolet radiation along with the short blue and violet wavelengths. Orange and red—shorter wavelengths—are not blocked, which means that infrared radiation gets through. Much was once made of the need to block infrared (heat) radiation, but it is not considered as important today. The fact that light yellow glasses do not do much for reducing light intensity is not so important on overcast days or along toward evening. And, because the lenses are polarized, reflected glare will be cut. The table will help you choose the correct sunglass tint for your specific needs.

Lens Tint	Effect	Use
Yellow	Absorbs shorter wavelengths like blue, violet. Transmits orange, red, yellow.	Good contrast. Helps in picking out subsurface objects. Most effective in lower light conditions, early and late in the day.
Brown	Absorbs shorter wavelengths as above yellow lenses, but reduces light intensity better.	Excellent contrast. Aids greatly in picking out weeds, fish. Good all-around tint under most conditions.
Gray	A neutral density filter. Best reducer of light intensity. Permits all color values to come through equally. Besides ultraviolet elimination, tends to block infrared radiation as well.	As a polarized lens, permits viewing underwater, but does not cause objects to stand out as do yellow and tan. Best in extremely high light intensity for sensitive eyes. Often preferred for offshore use.

I prefer the more natural appearance that objects have through gray lenses, but realize the benefits of increased definition using brown lenses. I generally use brown for river and all my shallow water work, or in slightly deeper water. Offshore, I use gray.

There's another option as well: photosensitive lenses that lighten and darken according to sun intensity. Photochromic glasses are now available with polarized lenses from several sources. Some anglers swear by these; others feel the photochromics don't become quite dark enough. They are available in a variety of tints.

Until recently, anglers wearing prescription glasses had a tough time getting specialty fishing sunglasses. There are now several sources for both photochromic and non-photochromic polarized glasses built to your prescription. Some firms offers polarized bifocals in various shapes and sizes from very small to a long, rectangular-shape. You can have the "second lens" area located anywhere on the main lens that you'd like. Why would you want to move it from the standard bottom position? Some anglers who do a lot of wading have found it helpful to have the close-up lens located at the top, so they can see normally when they're trying to step through a river in tricky current. Everything's in focus. When the time comes to tie on a fly or lure, it's a simple matter to hold materials in front and look up. The upside-down bifocals could also be an advantage in boats for netting and gaffing, or just working around all the gear that generally clutters up a fishing rig.

Quality sunglasses are also available for those who don't wear prescription lenses, but have reached the age where they find threading small hooks and tying knots isn't quite the snap it used to be. If you need to wear reading glasses, Cable Car offers a pair of polarized fishing glasses in either tan or gray, with small magnifiers located in the low, standard bifocal position. These are available in three magnification strengths.

Sunglass frames are important, too. More than anything, you need comfort. Glasses that you must fuss with all day take away from pleasurable fishing. Look for frames that incorporate lightness and strength. I like a rigid main frame with rear-temple pieces that can be bent to fit the odd contours of my skull.

Other accessories are available that can give your glasses a better fit. Nose pads are one example. Tiny O-rings that slide over the earpieces and slip over the hinges can provide a tighter grip. Cheap frames will soon loosen, break, or even change shape if you leave them on the dashboard of a closed vehicle in the sun. Some of the light nylon frames found on skiing glasses are good.

Some specialty fishing glasses are designed to keep out peripheral light by side shields attached to the temple pieces or by wraparound lens design. Side shields should be large and of polarized material. Opaque side shields cut out your peripheral vision and should not be worn while you're driving. Very tight-fitting wraparound designs can cause a problem by not allowing air to circulate. Your glasses can easily steam up when you exert yourself.

Have you ever cupped your hands around your eyes to cut down glare? There are some specialty fishing glasses available that are built around that principle. The Teeny Nymph Locator Glasses are of wrap-around design, but also have opaque frame sections above and below the front lenses to further reduce all unnecessary ambient light. They are plastic, come in gray or amber, in both regular or clip-on style, and are polarized. Teeny developed them especially for spotting salmon and steelhead in rivers, even under poor light conditions. Take them off when you walk any distance on land, though, or you might trip.

Sunglasses to be used on the water should have a restraining device so you can hang them around your neck or to keep them from falling into the drink if they're accidentally knocked off. You can also make your own with a piece of heavy monofilament.

Binoculars

Once you make a proper comparison between high-quality and mediocre binoculars, you will notice quite a difference. Try comparing instruments of different quality but of the same magnification (power) and exit pupil, and the first thing you'll notice is a difference in light-gathering ability. Objects will appear brighter through the better glasses.

A quick test for sharpness (called resolution) can be done at a store with the help of a friend or salesperson. Take a page from a book or magazine that you haven't read and back up until you can just read the print using the binoculars. The instruments that enable you to read the print from the farthest distance have the best resolution. Eye fatigue after continued use of the binoculars will be far less with those having the better resolution.

Corrosion resistance of exposed hardware and fittings is vital. Most good modern glasses are at least tight enough to prevent minimal spray or drizzle from harming them. Best for water-oriented use, though, are glasses that are totally fog-proof and waterproof, and are monitored during manufacture to make sure of the fact. For example, the waterproof models of Bausch & Lomb receive rigorous shake tests while immersed in tanks of water. You won't be storing the binoculars in a bait well, of course, but hermetical sealing and nitrogen purging eliminate condensation and fogging. Condensation not only hinders use under changing weather conditions, it can lead to the growth of fungus, which will eventually destroy your binoculars. Totally waterproof glasses can be stowed just about anywhere for instant use.

The neoprene armor coating of some binoculars is not just a sales gimmick. The armor helps protect against shock, corrosion, and chipping of the finish. It also helps protect from oil, gas, and other chemicals that might affect the standard vinyl that covers most binoculars. On slick fiberglass or a varnished boat shelf, it can keep the binoculars from sliding and taking a spill. Other important features include good design to help avoid fatigue and hand shake. Quick focusing is nice, and close-focus capability is very important—especially for river and stream use.

Center (single) focusing is an advantage because, once initial adjustment for your eyes is made, you don't have to continually fool with both lenses. Rubber fold-down eyecups are great for the fishing tactics already described. With the cups in the down position, you can use the binoculars with your polarized glasses. Your field of view will be less restricted the closer you can get your sunglasses to the binocular lenses.

The best power is probably 7X, which magnifies objects seven times. I sometimes use 8X, but 10X is just too difficult to hold steady in a boat. The larger the objective lenses—the ones that face the target—the wider your field of view and light-gathering capabilities. For years, 7X50 binoculars were the standard for boating use. They are tops for dawn, dusk, and night work. But they are big, cumbersome, difficult to stow in small boats, and will be left behind when you fish afoot.

My feeling, therefore, is that the better compact binoculars are the best choices for fishermen. Most only weigh around a pound. If the optics are superior, even the 7X26 or 7X24 format are fine in surprisingly low-light situations. Among the compacts, there has been a demand of late for the roof prism design, mainly because they are slightly smaller. Not all compacts are roof prisms, though. According to engineer Al Aiken of Bausch & Lomb, manufacturer of both porro and roof prism glasses, the latter are difficult to make properly. The angle of error of internal prisms can be 300 times greater than that of the porro design. Therefore, roof prism glasses require painstaking hand finishing, which greatly increases cost. Roof prisms, because of their critical tolerances, are more subject to getting out of alignment when shocked. Also, internal refracting surface coating requirements on roof prisms can result in light transmission loss of 12 percent. With the high-quality compact porro prism glasses now available, there seems little need to go into a roof-style binocular.

Here's a final tip. If you've become involved in photography, you should not be without a polarizing filter for your camera lens. That way, your pictures will look as great as you remember seeing things with your polarized sunglasses, and you may be able to capture an outstanding portrait of a fish in shallow, clear water. Who said lake or river fishing needs to be blind?

Manufacturers of Specialty Optical Products

Amway Corporation
Ada, MI 49355

See Spray, A handy lens cleaner that cuts through and cleans off saltwater spray in a jiffy. Comes in convenient small containers.

Dan Bailey
Box 1019
Livingston, MT 59047

Sells a wide selection of polarized glasses including Cable Car, clip-ons, and photochromic type.

Manufacturers of Specialty Optical Products

Cable Car Sunglasses
Hollister, CA
(Products available from sportshops, ski shops, major department stores, flyfishing specialty shops.)

Fisherman's model sunglass comes in brown or gray. Has polarized side shields, polarized glass lenses, eyebrow light shield, bendable temple pieces. Hole formed for attaching monofilament or other keeper device.

Croakies Division
Life-Link International, Inc.
Box 2913
Jackson Hole, WY 83001

Nylon-covered foam rubber device that fits over temple pieces and keeps glasses snug.

Fish-Eye Optics, Inc.
360 Harbor Court
Key Biscayne, FL 33149

Non-prescription or prescription polarized photochromic glass lenses. Brown, gray, green, and yellow available. Bausch & Lomb wraparound frame or Ray-Ban pilot frame available. Polarized bifocals in different sizes and locations on lenses.

Bud Lilly's Trout Shop
Box 698
West Yellowstone, MT 59758

Eyeglass keeper of nylon cord with snug-up loops that attach to ear pieces.

Orvis Company
Manchester, VT 05254

Sells Cable Car Sunglasses, plus variety of other models including polarized photochromic, prescription or non-prescription. Amber or gray. Bifocals available.

Polar Eyes
Box 17AA
Key Largo, FL 33037

Glass or plastic polarized lenses, prescription or non-prescription. Polarized side shields available. Frames are nylon composition, light yet tough. Will retain shape in extreme temperatures. Special gripper temple pieces for fishing.

Simms Product Division
Life-Link International
Box 2913
Jackson Hole, WY 83001

Optically correct, polarized photochromic glass lenses in tortoise-shell imitation frames.

Teeny Nymph Company
2281 S.E. Kelly
Gresham, OR 97030

Makes special Locator glasses with narrow field of view to reduce most ambient light. Polarized. Plastic lenses.

chapter 12

Side Pocket Fishing

"There doesn't seem to be a limit on what we can do with these things in fresh water or in the ocean. Why, sailfish—even marlin—could be next."

—Brady Bounds, *charter boat captain*

"Salmon King, this is the *Last Chance,"* the voice crackled over the radio.

"You got him," answered the King.

"I've been following this boat a little while now. He's got some strange, sophisticated-looking equipment aboard. Looks like a little mast sticking up on his forward deck. Two lines come off it and go out to either side. I can't get a good eyeball on him, though. He keeps turning away from me."

"Maybe it's a spyship," suggested the King.

"I dunno. Maybe he'll fire a salvo across my bow, but I'm going to reel in and go chase him."

Not far into the exchange I realized that the two fishermen were talking about me! I don't know why it never occurred to them that I might have a radio aboard, but I didn't want to spoil the fun. I waited until the *Last Chance* had pulled in his lines and roared over to me. He was bug-eyed with curiosity. Pacing me on a parallel course, he held up two hands spaced conservatively apart, in the universal fisherman's gesture of inquiry. I turned, reached into the livewell, and withdrew a very nice rainbow. Now he was really interested. I picked up the microphone and began to explain. . .

The reaction to side-planing trolling boards on many inland lakes can still be like that today, although it's becoming rarer. Even remote lakes have begun to see initial use of boards. Once word gets out on the success that fishermen are having with them, they'll be close to commonplace. Still, a lot of fishermen continue to deal with half-truths and incomplete information concerning planing devices. It's about time to clear up the confusion.

When the late, great, and irascible charterboat skipper Tommy Gifford pulled his boat *Stormy Petrel* away from dock one morning back in 1933, he began to attract instant attention. The sudden interest by other boats in those Bahama waters focused on two 50-foot poles jutting skyward from each side of Gifford's vessel. The poles gave the 26-foot *Stormy Petrel* the look of some giant water bug. In fact, they were the prototypes of the world's first outriggers, soon destined to take the first blue marlin in the Atlantic on sport tackle.

Of course, outriggers are standard equipment on today's bluewater boats and large sportfishing craft in big inland lakes. They have been appearing on smaller center-console vessels as well, but there's a practical limit. You obviously can't fit a small skiff or cartopper with such devices, although anglers who use such craft have yearned for their advantages.

Outriggers help a fisherman keep trolled lines away from his boat, and keep them from tangling on turns. They enable saltwater anglers to troll big live or rigged bait to tempt huge gamefish. Freshwater anglers aren't concerned with the size of baits used in the ocean, but they do want to be able to troll hard-digging lures on light lines with reel drags set very lightly to avoid breakoffs on solid strikes. The solution came from a very unlikely source: commercial trawlers.

For years, conical trawl-net mouths have been kept open via two so-called otterboards or trawl doors, which planed out from the commercial fishing vessel. Sport anglers in the Great Lakes began to experiment with such boards to take out their lines. With the explosive salmonid comeback in those waters beginning in the late 1960's, interest in the boards began to grow quickly and shows no signs of quitting today. There is good reason. Not only do the boards spread lines to fish lures over a wider area, they also allow for several fishing lines to be trolled from each board tow line. They keep fishing lines from tangling on turns, and they tow lures away from boat and engine commotion that can spook fish in certain situations.

Initially, the primary use of planer boards was for trout and salmon. It still is. As anglers experiment, though, it is becoming clear that the devices can be used for virtually all freshwater species—even bass. The boards are also less expensive than outriggers; some are compact enough to be taken on remote trips, and all can be used on the smallest open fishing boats.

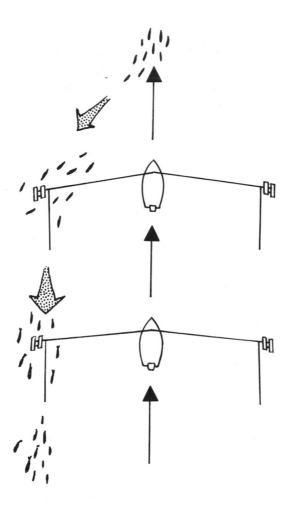

How planing boards help catch fish that ordinarily would be spooked by boat and engine noise. Boat spooks fish (top), which veer to the side and encounter planing boards and trolled lure/bait. Since boards are silent, fish are not panicked and may strike lure/bait.

Today's refined versions of the old otterboards fall into several categories. There are large single or double boards, which are usually 24 to 28 inches long. There are smaller, 8½ to 12½-inch boards, designed to be towed with your fishing line, and there is the Hot Shot Side Planer built especially for river bank fishermen. Each fits a particular need.

The larger planing boards work on a principle similar to flying a kite. The boards are rectangular in shape. A line-tie device of various design extends at a right angle from one side of the board. The front edge of the board is cut on an angle to help the board run out from your boat. A heavy tow line is fastened to the line-tie device. As this tow line is let out, forward boat motion and force of water against the board causes it to swim farther away form your boat—just like sending a kite out with the wind. Your fishing line, with a lure already trolling back behind the boat, is clipped into a line release once the board is the desired distance from the boat. The line release is hooked over the board tow line. The angle of the tow line (going down toward the board) and the force of water against the lure pulls the release along the tow line out towards the board as you

A selection of popular boards: the Super Ski Twin; the Sea Skee, which can be used as shown as a double board, or as a single; and the smaller Rover board.

free-spool line. You can stop the lure at any point along the tow line. When a fish hits, the line pops from the release and the release slides on out to the board.

Calm, smaller waters; light, delicate baits; and slow trolling usually call for smaller boards. The better models, however, can handle surprisingly bouncy water. Rougher water, big lakes, and heavier lures usually are best matched with the bigger boards, particularly the double boards. Under these conditions, proper balance in the form of ballast is extremely important to keep boards upright, pulling well, and running true. Internal or molded-in ballast is located along the bottom edges of the boards. The Sea-Ski boards made by the Wille Company use a system of cells for ballast. These are filled with water. If heavy weights or big baits are to be trolled, the boards can be adjusted with nose-heavy water ballast to compensate. Ballast that's off as little as 30 grams can adversely affect board

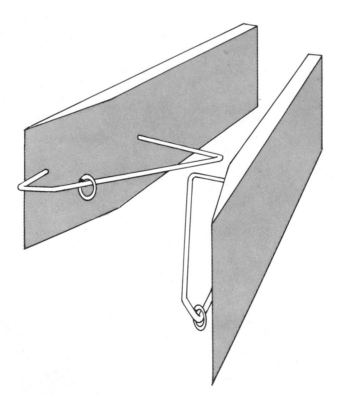

Yellow Bird boards have triangular metal bars on which a ring slides. One board is for the port, the other for the starboard side of the boat.

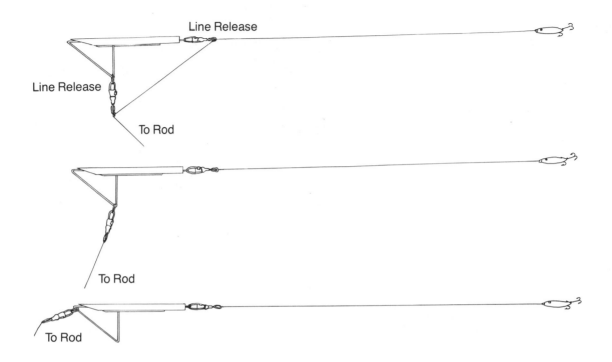

Top view of Yellow Bird boards showing two methods of rigging them. In top drawing, a line release device is attached to the bar and another to a ring at rear of board. Line from rod is clipped first to one release, then the other, so lure is trolled behind the board. When fish strikes, the line slips from the release and the angler plays his fish from the rod. Boards are retrieved later. In the middle drawing, the line is attached to the ring in front and a line and lure are attached to the ring in back. When a fish hits, the ring slides up the bar to reduce drag (bottom drawing). There is no release.

performance. So can the location of the line-tie attachment on the board.

The smaller boards are commonly attached directly to your fishing line rather than a separate tow line. They can be rigged so they stay attached even after you hook a fish. A variety of mechanisms then allows the on-line board to swing off-plane once a fish is hooked. This results in greatly reduced resistance, but you will still be reeling in both fish and board on the retrieve. Obviously, the fish's fight will be curbed and, in cases of a really large fish, the hook may pull out because of drag produced during

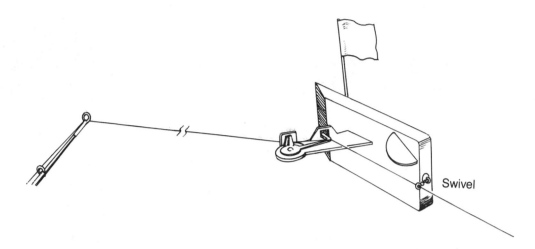

Rover boards have a built-in release mechanism. Board is set so it will remain on fishing line, sliding down to sinker or swivel after fish strikes. By not putting line through swivel, board can be released entirely.

sudden, violent surges of the fish. Of course, if you had not used the board, you might not have hooked up in the first place.

The original, commercially-produced, on-line type boards were the Yellow Birds. They are fitted with a triangular bracket or elbow to which your fishing line is attached via a sliding ring. The boards used to be fished with just this ring. You sent out the board with the ring located so the board would plane away from your boat. When a fish hit, the ring would slide forward on the elbow, killing the planing action and permitting easier retrieve. Today, most anglers use any of several popular downrigger release mechanisms that allow the fishing lines to pop entirely free of the board when a fish hits.

Another board with a built-in mechanism that allows for quick line attachment or pop-free release is the Rover. It can also be adjusted to remain fixed to your line. You need to use line of no lighter than 12-pound-test with this unit. Like the Yellow Bird, the Rover floats when it pops free of the line, thus acting as a temporary marker of a school of fish below. With the free-floating board as your guide, you can try casting the area as well. The board does eventually have to be picked up, of course, which can be a little tricky if it is floating over shoals in rough water.

It's very likely that the board will be in the shallows, because the smaller models create little surface disturbance and are ideal for trolling plugs in skinny water where surprisingly big fish can be foraging. Even if you were able to drive a boat through the shallow spots, doing so would spook the fish out of there. The boards won't. Some anglers prefer to rig the small boards so they will not pop free when working such areas; then there's no hassle over trying to get them back. Because of their compactness, the small boards are the ones to carry with you on trips to remote areas where trolling may be done.

As mentioned earlier, the larger boards are run from tow lines fixed to your boat. I have seen such tow lines attached to sailboat masts or shrouds, and even from downriggers. Best of all, though, is to use a tow line attached to a retrieval system specifically designed for use in board fishing. Once the trolling boards are sent out, they remain there during your fishing.

Retrieval Systems

The retrieval systems to which your board tow lines are fastened can be homemade or commercially manufactured. There are a number of retrieval systems in use, but they all have the basics in common. They consist of a pole or boom normally 4 to 8 feet high. The purpose of the boom is to keep as much tow line as possible off the water, thus reducing drag that can affect board performance.

The tow line is normally 125 to 200-pound-test, coated, braided Dacron. It runs from the board to the top of the pole, then down to the bottom of the pole where it is stored on a cleat or, preferably, a large-diameter, single-action reel. A reel makes it easier to bring in boards or send them out. The retrieval reels can be fitted with a drag mechanism, which is as practical as it is on downriggers.

On smaller fishing boats, it's advantageous to locate the retrieval system forward. Boards tend to angle back from your boat as they're trolled. With the retrieval system forward you'll lessen this effect. On larger boats, the problems of getting around cabins or other structures to tend the board lines make it practical to locate the retrieval system along gunwales closer to amidships.

There are a number of ways to attach the retrieval system to your boat. The best methods all allow for quick removal. Most of the commercial rigs come with plates or brackets to which you fasten the retrieval boom base with knobbed bolts, just as are used with downriggers. Four bolts hold

Retrieval system for planing boards consists of a boom, tow line and reel. The boom is mounted on the gunwales or bow of the boat.

each retrieval unit. Some manufacturers of retrieval systems have designed their units to fit into the sockets that hold outriggers on larger boats. Even big boats equipped with outriggers have found boards to be an advantage at times.

Another mounting technique is similar to one used for a series of downriggers. The method utilizes an 8-inch-wide plank cut to fit the width of the boat from gunwale to gunwale. The plank can be clamped to the gunwales with the existing oarlock sockets, or fastened to interior boat decks. One or more retrieval systems are bolted to the plank along with rod holders. The plank with all the attached equipment is easily removed once you're finished trolling. Some anglers simply fix a pole to the forward deck using a socket and braces. The pole can then be pulled out when you're finished board trolling, although the socket remains and may be annoying unless it is mounted flush with the deck. Using these systems, port and starboard planer boards can be sent 60, 80, even 100 feet or more off your boat, depending on conditions and boat traffic.

Once your boards are out the desired distance from the boat, it's time to get your lures or baits in the water. First, make sure your boat is running at the proper speed for the lures you intend to use. Then, feed the lure out to the distance you want it to troll *behind* the boat. Next, clip

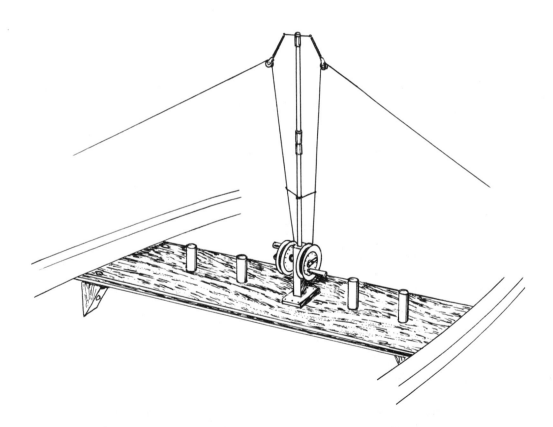

For trolling larger boards, one set on either side of the boat, a boom with a double reel can be mounted on a plank which is then bolted to the gunwales of the boat. Plastic tubes glued in holes in the plank serve as rod holders.

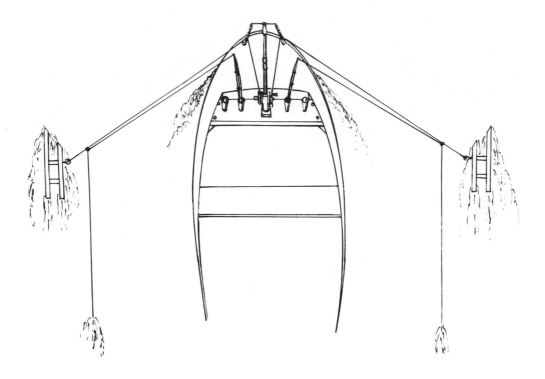

Top view of a double-reel boom trolling two planing boards with two rods trolling their respective lure/baits.

a release mechanism to the tow line. Slip your fishing line into the release mechanism and adjust the release for desired tension—for soft-biting fish, for example, you'll want it to free from the line easily. Now, with your line in the release mechanism, begin freespooling or backcranking your reel and the release will side on out the board tow line. You can stop it at any point along the tow line. The first release is usually sent out almost to the board. You can then space one or more other releases as you desire along the tow line so you're covering quite a large water area with your lures.

When a fish strikes, the line pops free from the release mechanism and the release slides down to the board (or next release) where you leave it until bringing the board back in. On a productive day, you might have quite a few releases out there at the board before retrieving it.

Once you become skilled at the basic operation, you'll want to experiment. Although boards have been used primarily for near-surface trolling, creative anglers now sometimes add sinkers to their fishing lines three or four feet from the lures to bring their offerings deeper. You can fish as much as 40 to 50 feet deep using a heavy enough weight and a release mechanism that will withstand the resistance from a pound of pulling

Joe Prince, maker of Super Ski boards, sends out one of his units. He's inserting his fishing line into a release which will be clipped to the tow line, then sent out to be trolled behind the boards.

Prince watches as his boards, trolled by towing line on reel at his left, keeps his lure and line (right) running far from boatside.

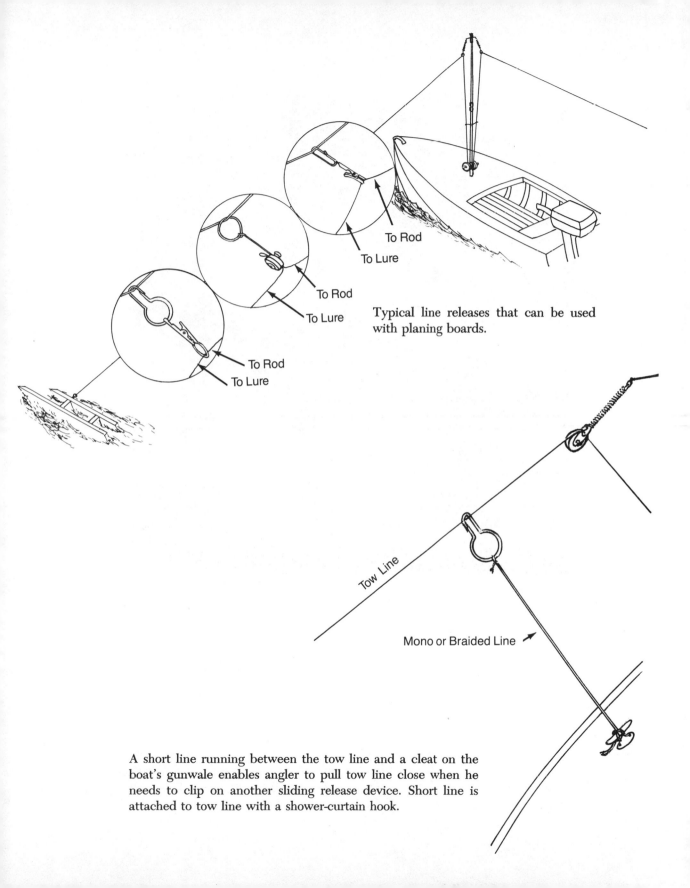

To Rod

To Lure

To Rod

To Lure

To Rod

To Lure

Typical line releases that can be used with planing boards.

Tow Line

Mono or Braided Line

A short line running between the tow line and a cleat on the boat's gunwale enables angler to pull tow line close when he needs to clip on another sliding release device. Short line is attached to tow line with a shower-curtain hook.

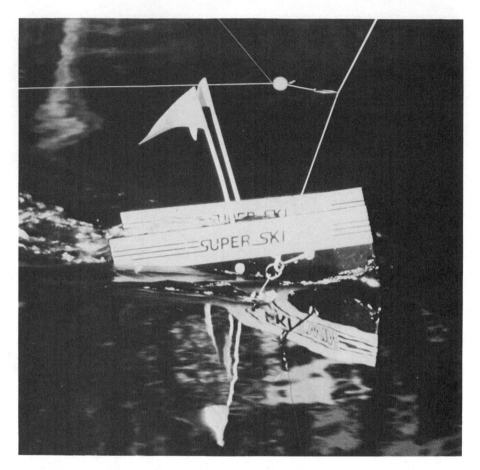

Speeding silently through the water, a pair of Super Ski planing boards tows a fishing line attached to the tow line with a Jolly release.

force. I'd rather play with light weights, however, leaving the deeper trolling for downriggers. Using a variety of weight sizes on different lines, you can have lures riding at different depths all along one tow line.

Side Planing From Shore

Earlier I mentioned the Hot Shot Side Planer designed for shore-bound anglers. Made by the Luhr-Jensen Company, this device was so named because its original purpose was to allow bank fishermen to get Hot Shot plugs out into a river. These diving lures are all-time favorites among steelhead and salmon anglers who stream them from drift boats as they slowly slip downstream. The plugs, thus worked, swim and vibrate into key salmonid-holding areas. Boat-riding anglers have the advantage of being able to hold lures in those areas as long as they desire.

The HS Planer is just 5 inches long, buoyant, and will pull a lure or bait 100 feet or more away from the bank out into the current of a river. Not only does it give the shore-bound angler some of the advantages of a drift boat, but it also allows a bank fisherman to work rivers that boats cannot run, for reasons of regulations or rough water. In the latter case, there may be good drift stretches between areas that are impossible to run with a boat. A fisherman with a HS Planer can easily work these in-between and unpressured fish-holding stretches.

To use the HS planer, set your lure to run 15 to 30 feet behind the unit, depending on water depth and lure diving characteristics. Specific directions with the planer explain how to fasten the unit to your line. Once this is accomplished, you slowly let out a little line at a time, and the planer will pull your offering out into the river. Now begin at the head of a run. With the lure in position, you can let it work there in the current for awhile, then take a couple steps downstream similar to a driftboat slipping downcurrent. By letting out more line or bringing some in, you can make the planer move back and forth across the run. You'll effectively cover every inch of potential fish-holding water.

It's important to keep your rod up while working the HS Planer so as much line as possible will be held from the water. Doing so enables the planer to move out well and eliminates some strain from the line. When a fish strikes, the planer slides down toward your bait or lure, stopping at the barrel swivel you'll have tied at the end of your line. Most anglers tie on a 36-inch length of lighter leader to the end of this barrel swivel stop. Bait or lure is tied to the end of this lighter leader. Although the HS Planer is, in effect, an on-line board, its small size produces only minimal resistance when a fish is fighting—about the same as a medium-size cork float.

The river planers are easily used, even by less-experienced fishermen. They can be set for either right or left-hand running, depending on which side of the river you're on. They come with a large rudder for use in slow water, and a smaller rudder to take them out in faster currents. They break down for easy storage and are excellent rigs to pack along on wilderness river adventures, just for prospecting those huge expanses you cannot cover entirely by casting.

It's obvious that the side-planing devices should increase your success; just how much is up for debate. Mark Wille, the maker of Sea Skee and Delux Sea Skee boards, has an understandable interest in that subject:

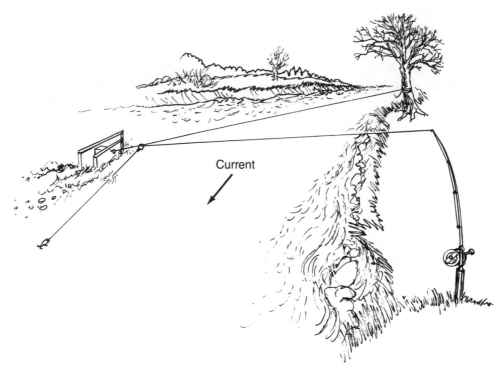

Here's how planing boards can be used to troll a plug in a river. Tow line is anchored to a tree on shore; rod is implanted in a holder, with fishing line attached to tow line with a sliding release device. Current carries boards—and lure/bait—downstream far from shore.

The Hot Shot Side Planer is made especially for rivers and is worked off the rod line alone. The lure/bait is attached to line at the rear of the planer.

"Our field studies show that, assuming a fisherman is using a board for the same amount of time he's using other trolling equipment, he can add 30 percent more fish to his catch."

That figure assumes the angler is trolling deep, with weighted lines coming from the boards, in addition to the shallow lines. Wille pointed out that his board will allow a lake trout fisherman to use a weight of up to *3 pounds* beneath a planing board to reach depths of 120 feet if desired. In my opinion, such deep fishing better fits into the realm of downriggers.

Surface Trolling

Surface or near-surface fishing is still the primary function of planer boards for most anglers. Fish in extreme shallows, or those 8 feet or less beneath the surface but suspended over deeper water, react much more to boat-related noise than that of a streamlined planer board slipping overhead.

Joe Prince, the maker of the Super Ski boards, angler friend Lloyd Perkins, and I were aboard Perkins' boat one day on Lake Ontario. We were experimenting to see just how much high-wave action Joe's big double boards could take. It was substantial. The conversation eventually moved to calmer days and spooky fish. Lloyd brought up a fascinating experience he had.

"I know many surface fish move aside when a good-size boat passes," he said, "even when the fish are over deeper water. I proved that by trolling Joe's boards to the sides of their other boats' wakes and catching the fish they had moved. The guys aboard were going crazy trying to figure out why I was catching fish and they weren't."

Although Steve Halvorsen of Minnesota created the Rover Board system to avoid bothering with retrieval systems, it was his fishing partner Gary Gehrman who really developed the use of the Rovers to a fine degree. A Wisconsin native, Gehrman experimented to develop better control of the movement of his trolling boards, and thus the lures behind them. He learned that when fish were aggressive, he could run lures or baits as close as 10 feet behind the Rovers, instead of the usual 50 feet. This short lure-to-board distance enables precise maneuvering of the planers.

Gary found that if he turned his boat sharply and added a short burst of acceleration, he could run one board around obstacles or into coves and little weedbed pockets. He also learned how effective it was to troll the boards in figure-eight patterns around prime fish-holding areas. This maneuver causes the board on the outside of the turn to speed up and, simultaneously, the board on the inside of the turn to slow down. The lures swimming behind behave correspondingly, rushing ahead as though trying to escape, or fluttering down like injured baitfish as they slow. The weaving action also causes the boards, lures, or baits to bob as though they were being worked on a rod by a fisherman.

"Many anglers have come to think of board trolling as an early-spring

Joe Prince, left, and Lloyd Perkins with a hefty king salmon taken from Lake Ontario, with the aid of planing boards.

affair," Joe Prince told me. "But that's not correct. The equipment can be used all year, depending on the species and where you're fishing. For instance, one day in fall a friend of mine caught and released 22 steelhead near Lake Ontario rivermouths using my boards."

Spring is the time when many anglers concentrate their board trolling, and for good reason. This is a peak period to find big brown trout up tight to shorelines—especially rocky, jagged-faced shores. They'll be seeking a variety of baitfish there, and are likely to be holding shallow. There's no way you can troll close enough with a boat to get your lures over them, you'd drive them out anyway if you could. But the boards produce in summer as well. I've successfully pulled largemouth bass off long stretches of riprap using the rigs. With the techniques Gehrman perfected, I've been able to steer my boards around points, little weedline projections, docks, jetties, and boathouses. Consider what you could do by sending your boards into a school of feeding freshwater stripers, hybrids, or white bass, as well as largemouths or smallmouths.

Night Trolling

Night trolling with boards offers new potential. You can keep track of their position by taping a 4 or 6-inch Cyalume chemical lightstick (See Chapter 15) on top of each. Use a red lightstick on the port board and a green one on starboard. Then send your boards in toward the rocks where you wouldn't want to head your boat—particularly in the dark.

There are some safety factors to consider when using the planing boards. Although all are equipped with bright marker flags, sometimes non-fishing boats either don't see the side planers or don't know what they are, and run between them and the tow boat. All that usually occurs is a cutoff. If you're in a small boat, however, and using a retrieval system with high-strength tow line, there's the potential for tipping or swamping if a larger craft hits the heavy tow line and keeps running. If the retrieval reel has a drag, you at least have some time to cut the tow line as it's running out. But if the tow line is stopped on the boom with a cleat, you'd better be able to react quickly. Some fishermen have taken to attaching the end of their tow line to the retrieval reels with something on the order of 15-pound-test mono or Dacron, which will break instead of taking you for an unplanned-for ride. This eliminates your having to cut the tow line as it goes out off the reel. You may be able to collect all your equipment from the water afterwards.

You'll have to consider boat traffic when deciding just how far out to send your planers. The same holds for anglers working the small on-line planer in rivers. Courtesy dictates that you don't run your lure or bait into water that another angler is working.

The benefits far outweigh the little caution areas, however. Trolling boards will surely enjoy increased growth. You can learn to use them easily, you'll locate fish faster, and you'll be able to work those fish that you couldn't reach or deceive otherwise. Looking back to the days of Tommy Gifford and his early outriggers, I believe the bombastic skipper would have approved. In fact, I'll bet he would have been at the forefront of side-planer board development all along.

Troll Speed Chart for Various Depths Using Rover Boards

(Courtesy Troll Sports, Inc.)

Desired Depth (feet)	Weight Required (ounces)	Dropper Line Length Behind Board (feet)	Lure	Boat Speed
4–5	0–1/4	6–10	Rapala (floater-diver)	4
4–5	0	8	1/2 oz spoon	4
10	1/4–1/2	15–22	Rapala	4–5
10	1/4	20	1/2 oz spoon	4–5
15	1	45	Rapala	4
20	1 1/2–1 3/4	55	Rapala	5
22–25	2–2 1/2	60	Rapala	5
30–40	3–4	60	Rapala	5

Board Manufacturers

Company	*Product*
Prince Mastercraft, Inc. 400 Brown Avenue Syracuse, NY 13208	Super Ski and Super Ski Twin.
Troll Sports Company Box 3 Deronda, WI 54008	Rover Boards: Great Lakes model for weights to 8 ounces. Salt Water Model with brass and stainless hardware for weights to 8 ounces. Regular Model (smaller) for weights to 4 ounces.
Wille Products Box 532 Brookfield, WI 53005	Sea Skee and Delux Sea Skee. Mate Sea Skee to turn Delux model into double board.
Yellow Bird, Inc. 2611 Terrace Circle Sheboygan, WI 53081	Yellow Bird on-line boards.

Retrieval System Manufacturers

Big Jon, Inc. 14939 Peninsula Drive Traverse City, MI 49684	Ski Board Rigger with spool.
Cannon/S&K Products, Inc. 1732 Glade Street Muskegon, MI 49441	Plane-R-Reel Boom, Plane-R-Reel, Plane-R-Reel Elite (with clutch).
Prince Mastercraft, Inc. 400 Brown Avenue Syracuse, NY 12308	Standpole with single or double reel.
Wille Products Box 532 Brookfield, WI 53005	Ski Mast System I, Ski Mast System II (26-inch extensions for pole available).

Release Mechanism Suppliers

Company	*Product*
Action Anglers Box 80 Hilton, NY 14468	Clipper Downrigger Release
Big Jon 14393 Peninsula Drive Traverse City, MI 49684	Bead Release (for Yellow Birds)
Cannon/S&K Products, Inc. 1732 Glade Street Muskegon, MI 49441	Quick Release
Jolly Products 640 Holt Road Webster, NY 14580	Wire hoop Jolly Release with foam pads
Laurvick Release Company 1411 N. 58th Street Superior, WI 54880	TBR-2 Trolling Board Release
Mac-Jac Company 1590 Creston Muskegon, MI 49443	No, 450 Plastic Button Release (for Yellow Birds)
Prince Mastercraft, Inc. 400 Brown Avenue Syracuse, NY 13208	Clothespin Release

chapter 13

New Tactics with Downriggers and Divers

Caller: "They're netting the lake—
I can see them out the window
with big winches on their boat!"
Warden: "Don't worry, they're just downriggers."
Caller: "Thought they were for fishing deep."
Warden: "Using them all year—even spring, now."
Caller: "They catch fish good then?"
Warden: "Pretty darned well."
Caller: "Sure they're legal?"
Warden: "Yep."
Caller: "Where can I get some?"

Trolling fishermen have been fussing after the perfect way to locate and catch down-deep fish for a long time. For years, salmon fishermen on the Pacific coast cannonballed kings and silvers with huge round weights attached to a variety of quick-release mechanisms. On the strike, the cannonball broke free and was forever lost. Ocean fishermen on the East Coast practiced a similar system that eventually gave way to a system called the Chesapeake Underwater Outrigger, which saved the sinker for re-use. The increasing cost of lead had a lot to do with its institution. In the beginning, the set-up consisted of a 5-pound window sash weight, later, a gooseneck trolling drail. This weight was lowered on a stout hand line affixed to a gunwale cleat. Attached to the line that held the weight was a jawed clothespin. Later, more reliable outrigger clothespins were used. The pin released the fishing line on the strike, just like modern downrigger releases do.

Eventually, a firm in Brooklyn, New York, introduced a more modern wishbone-shaped, adjustable release called the Fire Island Drop Back that worked a lot better than the barely-adjustable (with rubberbands) clothespin, but the hassle of having to haul up the heavy drail and its line hand-over-hand still existed. It took the landmark trout-salmon restoration in the Great Lakes during the late 1960's to launch the modern downrigger industry, which today consists of many firms producing a variety of units ranging from quite basic to those incorporating state-of-the-art microchip technology.

Contemporary downriggers are really a natural step up in efficiency and convenience from the Chesapeake Underwater Outrigger.

A basic downrigger unit consists of a large spool from which the heavy trolling weight is lowered. Fine-diameter, braided wire cable with far less water resistance replaced the hand line. To keep the weight from knocking against the boat and the wire from carving into the transom, a short steel arm that extends from the frame and holds the retrieval spool soon evolved. The cable passes over a pully at the end of the arm. Units with longer arms became standard for use on the sides of a boat, while the shorter arm versions continue to be used on the transom. Sophisticated line releases can be placed anywhere along the cable that holds the weight, so you can have one or several lines trolling from one downrigger. As the weight is raised, the releases fixed along the cable break their hold on the line and slide on down toward the weight.

Today, downriggers are standard deep-trolling equipment, even on small boats. Most anglers, however, consider downriggers appropriate for only specific types of fishing. True, downriggers work admirably for catching fish such as lake trout, which are typically caught so deep that you have to learn how to deflate their swim bladders once they are boated if you intend to release them. Downriggers continue to do a yeoman's service of getting spoons and plugs to big steelhead, chinook, and coho, whether in their native Pacific saltwater environment or lurking in the frigid depths of our Great Lakes. They do these jobs with no need to hang huge amounts of lead weight to your fishing lines, which effectively reduces the fighting ability of most of these fish to that of a limp gym towel. (King salmon can be an exception—I've seen these aquatic rhinoceri break water with 8 to 10 ounces of weight flapping from the line. They eventually tore free.)

Ceaseless experimentation by both veteran anglers and downrigger manufacturers have lately proved that the devices are much more than tools for very deep trolling assignments. They are also wonderfully precise line and lure-control mechanisms, at any depth that they're used. They can hold and fish lures or baits from a foot beneath the surface to 1,000 feet down, although the latter is a bit beyond our needs for trout and bass. We're finally coming to understand that downriggers can sometimes be the best way to fish for largemouths, smallmouths, white bass, landlocked stripers, and trout in open water.

Downriggers can be used primarily as trolling locational systems, enabling you to pinpoint groups of fish that can be jigged or cast to if you'd rather fish them that way. As line control devices, they permit you to run two or more lures fairly close together off the stern and still make tight loops and turns without tangling. They effectively replace weighted or unweighted flat lines trolled directly behind your boat. You can use downriggers along with outriggers or side-planer boards. The combination gives you coverage at various depths near the boat as well as away from it. Downriggers enable you to fish in rough, windy weather, until it reaches the point of questionable safety.

I well remember a trip when my inshore bass hotspots had cooled off, to say the least, as far as fishing productivity was concerned. I finally got the message and was exploring deeper water with my graph when I stumbled on a reef I'd never known about. It was in the open lake, quite a ways from a rocky shore, and it came up out of 40-foot water to 28 feet, covering quite an area. I knew it just had to hold some fish. Normally I would begin working it over with my electric motor, but a stiff wind had suddenly come booming out of the south. It was far too strong for boat control with the electric motors, and anchoring was out of the question. The waves had not had time to build, and I hated to leave without giving the place a try before conditions grew worse.

If it weren't for the wind I would have slowly jigged the reef while making a controlled drift, but I was alone and had to tend to steering. I still had my downriggers in place from an earlier landlocked salmon fishing trip. The proverbial mental light bulb went on in my head. I circled wide, using my main engine, to the upwind side of the reef. I rigged up two floating balsa Rapalas. With the boat pointed into the wind and drifting backwards, I stripped out enough line so the plugs were about 20 feet beyond the bow. I clipped the lines into the downrigger releases, then lowered the weights so the lures were just off the bottom. Now in low speed, jockeying the engine in and out of gear to slow my drift, I was able to make accurate controlled passes over the reef, letting the wind push me backwards.

I was achieving an effective backtroll with the engine slowing my stern-first progress. The downriggers had freed my hands for steering. To top it all off, I nailed two big smallmouths and lost a third before the building wind and waves forced me to haul up for the long, rough ride back in. Just think what you could do in good weather.

Think how tightly you can troll around points from shore, or the oddly shaped contours extending from those points in *good* weather. The straight tracking given your lures by the heavy downrigger weights makes it possible. Besides shoals, reefs, and their edges, downriggers let you follow the dips of underwater saddle formations. Channels or slots between islands can be worked with one lure in the deeper cut and another higher up on the channel bank. The old river channels of big reservoirs can be effectively followed this way, too. If you're fishing rocky smallmouth environments, it's best to have another angler aboard standing by to quickly raise the weights as you pass over boulders and shoals. Not only will this keep the cannonball weight from hanging up, but it also keeps your lures tracing near the bottom—vital when smallies are holding deep.

Fishing for Largemouths

Downriggers excel in locating and fishing largemouths in a variety of situations. Consider suspended fish. When largemouths move off points or over major dropoffs, they often either maintain the same depth as the land off which they moved, or they descend slightly. Lures trolled from downriggers remain in the precise zone of the fish. Another suspended bass situation occurs along steep banks, across or near dam faces, and just off the riprap near a dam. In cold weather, troll with downriggers close to these steep areas.

The potential is great for using downriggers on schooling bass—smallmouths, largemouths, white bass, and stripers. Every angler who has enjoyed the thrill of casting into a melee of wildly feeding surface bass knows that he must fish fast and furiously, for the action never lasts long. The fish tear viciously into the bait, then suddenly descend. They remain below for a bit, then resurface somewhere else. White bass and stripers are very prone to this behavior. With your downriggers at the ready, you can switch into a searching pattern as soon as the fish sound. Troll interlocking loops or ever-widening circles using the lures that were successful while you were casting—that is, if the lures lend themselves to being trolled. You'll frequently relocate the school before it resurfaces, and take more fish. If the school does not come up again, this may be the only way to take more fish.

Downriggers are naturals in flooded canyons that have become our desert lakes. Here, largemouths are often found on pinnacles of rock that thrust up from the bottom. Adjust your lures to run close behind the cannonball, then begin trolling around these structures at ever-increasing depths until you find fish.

Another key holding spot in the desert lakes is any rockslide area. Rubble builds up in the water where it falls from the cliffs. Bass hold just over it, at the end of the slide, or just below the end of the slide if it tails out near a major dropoff. By using your downriggers in conjunction with a good depth sounder, you can precisely work the slide and surrounding areas without hanging up.

Even classic largemouth cover in natural lakes is not out-of-bounds for downrigger fishing. The technique is especially valuable on a lake or reservoir that you're visiting for the first time. I've used downriggers to swim my lures and locate fish along edges of flooded timber and around standing trees. I've used them to troll the mouths of bays, beaches, bridge supports, and piers.

Weedlines may be the best of all places to find fish. Troll the inside and outside weedlines and the turns as well, if there is room. When bass are in an aggressive state they'll charge right on out to gobble your offerings. However, after the passage of a front, the fish tend to sink deeply in the weeds and will not leave them to take a swipe at a passing lure.

If most of your downrigger fishing for bass is to be done in fairly shallow to medium depths, you often can get by quite nicely with one of the mini-riggers such as those made by Big Jon and the Wille Company. The little manual downriggers can be clamped to the gunwale of a small utility fishing boat. They come with a small cannonball so, unless you replace it with a heavier weight, they don't perform well at faster trolling speeds. A 50 to 70-foot length of cannonball cable is usually plenty. The little downriggers are handy around much of the heavier cover in natural lakes, and their compactness and portability makes them well worth considering on trips—even to remote fly-in lakes. Here, trout will more likely be the target, and the mini-riggers will certainly come in handy. They'll eliminate the need for wire line or on-line sinkers, letting the fish give maximum account of themselves—which is what you traveled all that way for in the first place.

Landlocked Stripers

When bright sun and warming water push landlocked striped bass down 50 or 60 feet (oxygen levels permitting), more successful anglers are fishing for them with downriggers. Typical among these specialists is Dave O'Keefe, who guides on Lake Amistad on the Texas/Mexico border. O'Keefe finds his deep stripers in or near the old flooded river channel. Especially productive spots are those areas where the old channel comes close to canyon mouths.

The Texas guide trolls jigs with 6-inch plastic curly tails 5 feet above the suspended fish he locates using his graph. He likes white jigs with pearl tails when the bass are eating shad, and green-white jigs when the fish are after any other small forage species.

Action can become frantic when you troll through a school of stripers that are just beginning to feed aggressively. With a couple of downriggers in use and two to four lures down, multiple strikes regularly occur. Clearing rigs and getting the weights up while fighting fish can result in a rather wild time, to say the least.

Trout and Salmon

In spring, when rainbows, various salmon—and even lake trout, if you're early enough—are holding not far from the surface, downriggers can be extremely productive. At times during the early period, a depth variance of just a couple of feet can make the difference between hitting fish or getting skunked. Sure, you can use sinkers, wire line, or a combination of both, but you won't be as precisely accurate as you will with the downriggers, and you won't be able to troll as many lures close together.

When using downriggers for this early spring fishing, I work depths from just beneath the surface down to 10 feet. You can even use two lines on each of two downriggers. Stagger the depth fairly close behind the boat to "strain" the water in what should be the prime fishing zone at this time of year. Because the lures aren't far behind your boat, you can still make the zig-zag turns that often bring strikes. Depending on how many lines are legal where you fish, and how many anglers are aboard your boat, you might also run planer boards to the side and probably catch brown trout as well—if they happen to be in the lake. Browns can also be taken on the downriggers, but usually only when your lure is back a good distance behind the boat.

Downriggers permit extreme accuracy in selecting and maintaining depth, unless you rely solely on the counter mechanism attached to your units. The counter tells you how many feet of cable holding the cannonball are out, but don't forget to consider the "carryback on deflection" effect. Unless your boat is not moving or you are trolling *very* slowly, the downrigger weight angles back as well as down while you motor ahead. Even if your depth sounder indicates the weight is at a given depth, it might not be. What the depth sounder measures is the cannonball's distance *away* from the boat. The faster you move through the water, the greater the weight will angle back behind the boat.

You can use two methods to determine the precise depth at which your cannonball is running. The first consists of simple calculating devices that measure cable angle and tell you how much cable is needed to reach the desired depth. Jawbreaker Tackle Company and Osprey make such devices. The second method is to motor over an even bottom, measure its depth with your sounder, then let out cable until the cannonball strikes bottom. Check the counter to see how many feet of cable are out for the particular speed that you're running. Repeat the operation several times at different speeds, writing down the amount of cable needed to reach specific depths at various speeds. This reference system depends upon your having some means to measure your actual speed through the water. Most trollers use a simple instrument to do so. Usually it's built around a fishing sinker dragging in the water. The weight moves an indicator that points to numerals or color-coded graduations on a read-out face. Using such a device, you'll know just how much cable to let out for a particular speed.

When trolling for fish that are holding tight on a fairly smooth bottom, you can use the bottom-bouncing method favored by many lake trout specialists. To make sure their cannonballs were riding near the bottom where the fish normally held, laker fishermen occasionally lower the weight until it bounces once on the bottom. Then they quickly raise it just a couple of feet. Though the original intent was precise depth control, it was found that the action often triggered lakers to strike. As the cannonball hits, the lure evidently dances around and excites the fish. Today, some sophisticated downriggers have electronic timers that periodically lower and raise the balls to make them bounce. Turning the boat and putting the engine in and out of gear results in similar lure action. Another trick is to wait for a hooked fish, then snap the lure being trolled closest to the fish from its release, and crank it up quickly. This gives an illusion of a fleeing baitfish, often resulting in a strike from a nearby fish already intrigued by his hooked and struggling schoolmate. All these methods were developed for lake trout but should be explored for other trout, as well as salmon and bass.

Another technique should prove extremely effective, even though it was developed seemingly far from our sphere of focus. Fishermen working reefs 600 to 1,000 feet down off the Hawaiian Islands traditionally just lowered their baits on heavily weighted lines. They've now found downriggers—for all the reasons they're popular elsewhere—to be ideal for streaming baits in deep underwater currents at these extreme depths. Some mainland saltwater anglers have keyed on the success of the islanders and now use the same method around wrecks and over reefs. Why can't freshwater anglers? No reason.

The method is very effective for live or non-active natural baits—dead forage fish, night crawlers, or cut bait—in areas where underwater currents exist. If you use the method to stillfish where there are no currents, live bait could tangle around the downrigger cable. Should you elect to try a slow controlled drift using an electric motor, live bait will work. The method is successful on the trout and all the bass we've discussed. It's also good to try on fairly inactive landlocked stripers in summer, when low oxygen levels confine them to springholes.

Downriggers are even finding their way into rivers, especially the bigger ones, for use in steelhead and Pacific salmon fishing.

Drift boaters use the effective technique of pointing their craft upriver, then either anchor upstream of good holes or slowly backslip their way downcurrent while they stream natural spawn bait, vibrating Hot Shots, or Tadpolly plugs off the stern. The lures or baits can be manipulated by careful boat placement so they drop back virtually in front of the fish. With downriggers, you don't need to rely on the built-in depth capability of a plug or weight attached to your line. You raise and lower the cannonball as you move downcurrent from one river holding spot to another.

Diving Planers

The most sophisticated of today's downriggers can be programmed to automatically lower the weight to one pre-selected depth, raise it to another, as well as perform the previously-discussed bottom bouncing function. On the other end of the spectrum are far less-sophisticated devices that can also take your lures deep. These are the diving planers.

Today's diving planers are made of plastic. Most have weights built into their bodies. They come in various designs that can somewhat resemble a paper airplane, a delta-winged space craft, or our popular conception of a flying saucer. They are normally tied to the end of your fishing line, usually via a snap or clip that fastens to various positions at the nose of the diver. At the diver's tail end is a connection to which is tied a leader of varying length. Your lure is attached to the end of the leader. As your boat is trolled, the angle of pull at the front of the diving planer causes the wing or planing surface of the device to dig into the water and descend to various depths, taking your lure with it.

Names like the Pink Lady, Big Dipper, and Deep Six are familiar to long-time trollers. Planers have been termed the working-man's downrigger, because they're inexpensive and have been around a long time. They cannot approach the depths you can achieve with downriggers, although

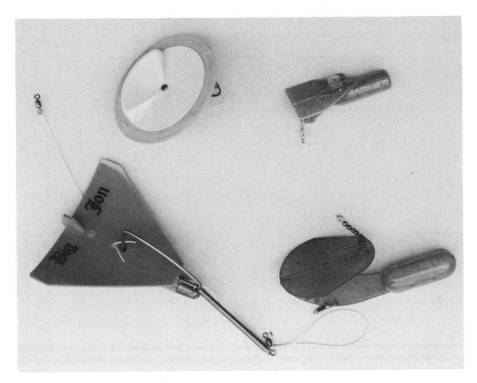

Four popular downrigger-planers (clockwise from upper left): the Dipsy Diver, Jet Planer, Lady Go Diver, and Jons Diver. These devices will get lures deep without the expense of downriggers.

some of them will bring lures 50 or 70 feet down and, as we've seen, lure control at lesser depths is an equally vital function.

One disadvantage of planers is that they are normally attached to your fishing line, which necessitates the use of a rather stout rod and line because of the great drag caused as the planer digs down—especially with the larger units. Modern diving planers trip and change their angle when a fish hits, making it easier to crank the rig and fish back in. Still, there is some resistance, which hampers the fish's fight. Some anglers have found that the planers can be trolled on a separate, heavier line and rod, with a downrigger release placed at the rear of the device so the fishing line will snap free when a fish hits.

A few planers have special functions, and I feel that they have a valid place in the modern troller's collection of equipment. One of them is the Jet Planer from Luhr Jensen. This small diving planer is ideal for use on steelhead or salmon in rivers. It allows you to present natural baits like egg clusters, cut bait, crawlers and shrimp with the back-slipping method, getting the bait down to 20 feet without any extra weight. A key advantage of the Jet Planer is that, unlike other planers, it is buoyant. You can use it to slowly work your baits around logs, boulders, ledges, or other snags. If it hangs up, giving some slack line normally allows it to float free. Slacking off when the unit is not snagged allows the planer to rise, so you can effectively fish shallower spots as you reach them.

Most anglers use 15 to 20-pound-test line and a medium-action rod with the Jet Planer. A 40-inch leader is tied to one end of the planer, and your main line is directly fastened to the rig's front. Sometimes a bit of plastic foam or cork is fixed to the leader so your baits will float and keep them from snagging the bottom.

To use this rig, strip out about 50 feet of line. Now, using motor or oars, hold your boat bow into the current so the planer digs down. After working each hole, you slowly slip downriver.

For trout in smaller rivers, you can use a floating-diving plug with the hooks removed as your diving-planer. Many anglers like the Hot Shot plug, also made by Luhr Jensen. In fact, the company supplies this plug already rigged for use as a planer.

Another interesting unit is the Jons Diver from Big Jon Company. This planer comes in two sizes and is best suited for lake fishing. The unique feature of the Jons Diver is that it can be tripped and reset without taking the rig from the water, so you can work your lures up and down at different levels while trolling. There is also a small tab on these planers that can be set to steer the rigs to the left or right. The Jons Divers dig down close to the boat so, if you want to run your lures farther back, you'll have to lengthen your leader. To give you an idea of this unit's diving capabilities, approximately 47 feet of 14-pound-test monofilament must be out in order to obtain 30 feet of depth.

This business of getting a lure both deep and off to the side is further characterized with the Dipsy Diver planing device. Its down-and-sideways feature can be important when you're trolling a ledge or other break where forage fish and/or gamefish are spooked by your boat passing overhead. Clear water, engine noise, or sonar noise can all spook them at times. On those days—even if the fish are 30 feet down—they'll often either go deeper or shallower as you pass by.

The Dipsy Divers come in two sizes. The larger, as with all planers, goes deeper. Three settings on its base plate determine the degree that the rig will run to the side. You normally use a 4 to 7-foot leader behind the planer. If you plan to use a dodger and a lure, use a 48-inch leader from the planer to the dodger, then a 12 to 30-inch leader section between dodger and lure. A 00 size dodger is best, and the shorter leader should be used when you're trolling a fly or plastic squid-type lure. The longer leader is right for a plug.

The greater the planer's side-running angle, the more line you'll need out to reach the desired depth. For example, on a setting of 3—the maximum side setting—you'll need about 125 feet of line out to reach 40 feet of depth. You'll have to experiment trolling at different speeds over clean bottom (as recommended with downriggers) to determine just how much line you'll need to reach specific depths at different settings. Make a number of runs, record the information when the planer bumps bottom, and you'll be able to make up a chart for your particular needs.

For big fish, it's best to use a surgical rubber snubber attached to the planer ahead of the leader to your lure. These are available from many downrigger and planer suppliers.

Diving planer depth is never as exact as it is with downriggers, especially on turns. And because of the added drag of the planers, you'll need a somewhat stiffer rod than you would when downrigger trolling.

In the final analysis, I'd rather use downriggers whenever possible for their more precise lure control and placement, but will certainly use planers—especially those specialty models just discussed—when appropriate.

The Finer Points

A few other vital elements of downrigger and diver systems should be considered carefully, however, before you consider yourself thoroughly skilled in the use of this equipment. Downrigger weights are one of them.

Weights come in a variety of shapes from the simple round cannonball to torpedo or fish-shaped leads. Some are plastic shells that are filled with lead shot or sand. They're are normally available in weights from 6 pounds through 10 or 12 pounds. For my money, the cannonball with a little keel offers the best tracking, both on straight runs and turns. They are also easiest to handle and store.

Fishermen continue to search for the all-perfect release mechanism. Large manufacturers and basement workshop tinkerers seem to come up with an unending supply of variations. The release holds your fishing line to downrigger cable or planer. It allows you to pop your line free at any time and, of course, releases the line when a fish hits.

I've found several releases that are very effective. The Clipper Release, for example, is a simple unit that offers fine adjustment capabilities. Because you can stack it along the cable, several lines can be fished from one downrigger. Several other releases offer stacking capabilities.

The Big-Jon Jettison Release may be clipped at any position to the cable. The unit is a simple pin that inserts into a socket. It telegraphs movement to the rod tip if a fish too small to trigger the release is hooked, or if the lure has picked up weed.

The Cannon Quick Release has a swinging cable arrangement for attaching to the downrigger weight. This too imparts movement when a small fish is hooked. There is a stacker version, as well, which clips directly to the cable. The Cannon release has two soft vinyl disks to hold your line, so it doesn't have to be twisted as it does with some other mechanisms. Very light lines can be used with this release, and fine settings can be achieved.

The Wille Tattle-Tail uses two hubs to hold the fishing line. These disks are attached to an 11½-inch length of stiff wire. It telegraphs movement

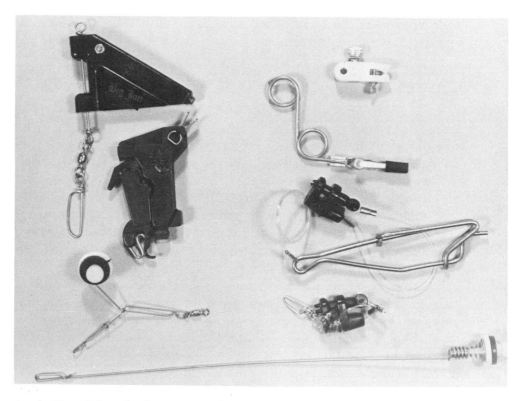

A selection of favorite downrigger releases (clockwise from upper left): Free 'N Easy, Clipper, Laurvick, Jettisons (2), Wille Tattle Tail, Wille A-Tension-Getter, Roemer.

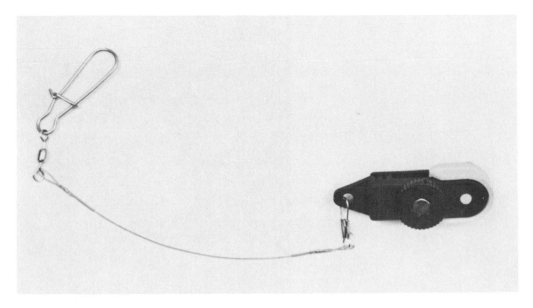

One of the best new releases for downriggers is Cannon's Quick Release. It may also be used as a side planer board release.

when a fish bites but before the line is released. It also lets you know, again through rod movement, if a small fish is on or weed has been picked up.

The Sportsman release is a totally different concept. When a fish hits, it does not have to trigger the release at all. It encounters only the resistance of your reel drag or reel click mechanism. Then you manualy trigger the release. This is done by releasing a second weight called the messenger, which runs down the cable and triggers the release.

For trolling with ultralight lines (see Chapter 14) a homemade rubber-band-paperclip has been employed. As of this writing, the Osprey Company was to introduce a commercial release built around the rubberband system.

For diving planer and downrigger fishing, most anglers prefer conventional reels because of their inherent strength along with smooth, powerful, and widely adjustable drags. The rods for downrigger and planer assignments are somewhat different. Downrigger rods can range from eight to nine feet. They tend to have a strong butt, plus a somewhat flexible tip that may be bent over and held in that position by the release

This is the Sportsman remote-control downrigger release setup. When fish hits, it takes out line freely. Line slips through white release mechanism and fish feels little resistance. Angler frees upper messenger weight, allows it to run down cable to wire arm, which triggers release free.

during trolling. The tip also provides a certain degree of cushion when a fish strikes.

Rods in the 9-foot length are best for diving planers. Remember, unless you use a release mechanism, the planer attaches directly to your line. The planer can only be reeled up to your rod tip. With a short rod you won't be able to get very close to your fish. Because of the strain from the planer, you'll want a somewhat stiffer rod than you'd choose for downrigger fishing.

Most of the standard plugs and spoons you'd use for stripers, largemouths, and smallmouths can be used on downriggers or planers. Lakers

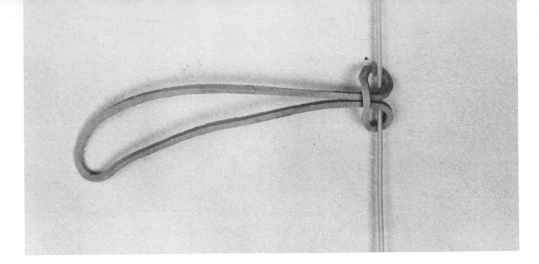

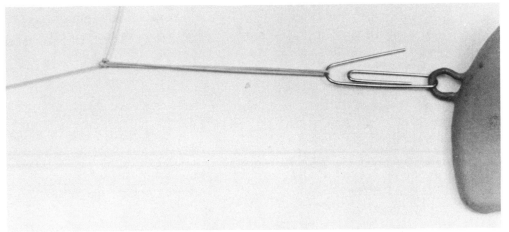

Rubberband release is ideal for trolling with light lines, but also works with heavy ones. Band is attached around fishing line (top) after lure is let out. Loop of rubberband is then slipped over a paperclip attached to downrigger weight (bottom). Weight is lowered to desired depth as angler gives line. Once weight is at proper depth, angler tightens up on line until rod tip bends into an arc.

and brown trout usually find light flutter spoons and some slow-swimming plugs to their liking. Steelhead attack a variety of plugs, plus the higher-speed spoons used for salmon—but often in smaller sizes. King salmon go for J-plugs, and high-speed spoons like the Westport Wobbler and Flutter Chuck. Coho will also respond to these lures, plus fly-and-dodger combinations. Still, you should experiment.

Downriggers and diving planers are wonderfully versatile tools. The more we fish them—whether for deep trolling or line control at lesser depths—the more uses we find for them. I'm willing to bet that as you read this, some angler, somewhere, has just come up with something else.

Manufacturers

Company	*Product*
Action Anglers Box 80 Hilton, NY 14468	Clipper Trolling Release.
Big Jon, Inc. 14393 Peninsula Drive Traverse city, MI 49684	Full line of downriggers, releases, accessories, and planers.
Ed Bohme Enterprises 5759 Larson Place West Vancouver, B.C. Canada V7W 1S5	Sportsman remote-control downrigger release and stacker version.
Bullet Weights, Inc. Box 1186 Grand Island, NE 68802	Downrigger weights.
Cannon S&K Products, Inc. 1732 Glade Street Muskegon, MI 49441	Full line of downriggers, releases, and accessories.
Jawbreaker Tackle Company 16604 Port Sheldon Road West Olive, MI 49460	Depth Calculator for figuring carryback effect.
Laurvick Release & Weight Co. 1411 N. 58th Street Superior, WI 54880	Laurvick downrigger and stacker release.
Li'l Mac Sinker Molds Metalcrafts, Inc. 27770 S.W. Parkway Avenue Wilsonville, OR 9707	Downrigger cannonball molds.
Luhr-Jensen Box 297 Hood River, OR 97031	Jet Planer, Dipsy Diver planer, Pink Lady planer, downriggers, accessories, and lures.
Mac-Jac Manufacturing Co., Inc. Box 821 Muskegon, MI 49443	Downriggers and accessories.

Company	*Product*
Osprey Box 87 Sterling, OH 44276	Computrac Downrigger Guide for calculating cable carryback effect, downrigger releases incorporating rubberbands.
Pacific Atlantic Products, Ltd. 895 South Pitcher Street Kalamazoo, MI 49007	Downriggers, releases, and accessories.
Penn Fishing Tackle Mfg. Co. 3028 W. Hunting Park Avenue Philadelphia, PA 19132	Fathom Master downriggers, releases.
Proos Manufacturing Company 1037 Michigan Street, N.E. Grand Rapids, MI 49503	Downriggers and accessories.
Wille Products Box 532 Brookfield, WI 53005	Downriggers, Tattle-Tail release and accessories.

chapter 14

\\\\\\\\\\\\\\\\\\\\\\\\\\\\\\\\\\

Trolling With Noodles

"If I can do something a different way, I'll do it—especially if it's more effective."

—DICK SWAN, *developer of the noodle rod.*

The scene was madcap. Behind my back it sounded as though an old-time vaudeville routine was in progress. Chicago Captain Dave Arff and Lake Michigan Captain Dick Swan were alternately clapping their hands and stomping the deck of Swan's fishing cruiser the *Light Liner*. They were also accompanying their rhythm by chanting "Do it now; do it to it. . ." over and over again.

Their encouragement was truly from the heart, but I wasn't quite sure it was coming at the right time. A very big chinook salmon at the end of my line was shooting for the horizon off the boat's port side, and the only thing I could do was hold the rod with two hands and blink away the pearls of perspiration that were pollywogging down my forehead and into my eyes. I pretended to snarl at my pals, but it was all I could do to choke back laughter.

The time was spring. The place was not very far out on Lake Michigan, and I had become involved in this hatter's convention of a fishing trip in order to see if Swan's newly developed technique for ultralight trolling worked as he insisted it did. If so, it would offer some very interesting possibilities for trout fishermen across the nation. It would also prove effective for both largemouth and smallmouth bass away from heavy cover, on dropoffs, near rip-rap, over rock rubble, and similar areas. In fact, it might prove to be *the* method for those times when fish shy away from all but the lightest line, a situation that occurs regularly throughout the year in both deep and shallow, clear water. Few species are immune to such periods of fussiness.

If the system worked on the fish Swan was chasing, it would certainly work on the lighter fish. Dick said he was catching big steelhead, big salmon in the 20-pound class on 4 and 2-pound-test line! To boot, he insisted you could use any lure normally successful for trolling, even the hard-digging Luhr-Jensen J-Plugs favored by many Great Lakes salmon trollers. How, I wondered, could the cobweb monofilament stand up to the strain of dragging those lures to say nothing of the smashing strike of such large, strong fish? The answer was in what Swan had done to his so-called noodle rods, and in the simple, inexpensive release device he had taken to using. To understand the theory and principal we have to back-track a little.

A big man with steel-gray hair, Swan is a former high school teacher, coach, and principal who, in the mid-seventies, became heavily involved in river fishing for salmon and steelhead. He figured there had to be a way to cut down the long waits between bites in the cold, clear Michigan rivers he regularly fishes. Logically, he figured the way to go was to use lighter lines. Not only would they be less visible, they would also drift lures or baits more naturally. His first experiments using lighter line on stout rods failed when the rugged lake-run rainbows and salmon that grabbed his offerings began running and leaping. Sometimes the shock of the strike was enough to part the line. It didn't take Swan long to realize what had to be done. Again, logical reasoning dictated a rod that would provide enough cushioning to absorb the shock when a strong fish hit. One of his first experiments involved affixing a handle and spinning reel seat onto one of those fiberglass whips used for bicycle safety flags. The 7-foot Bike Rod was born.

Next, the inventive angler asked himself what might be gained by lengthening his rods. A longer rod, he figured, would enable him to hold more line from the water during hard maneuvers by a hooked fish. He eventually talked a few manufacturers into supplying him with longer, ultraflexible blanks, and soon came up with a series of thin-walled, two-handed spinning rods that could do what he wanted. The rods ranged from seven to fifteen feet, with 10½ to 12½ seeming to be most popular. These rods were made of fiberglass, because no one then manufactured graphite blanks in the length and flex that he needed. Today they do.

The early river rods came with a fixed reel seat and the option of either a three or four-inch fighting butt below the seat. These rods accepted open-face spinning reels but, in the early days, Swan and many of the river fishermen who used his wands liked the old Shakespeare 1810 closed-face, below-the-blank spinning reels. They liked the smooth drag and the ability to instantly free-spool line by backcranking the handle 1/4-inch. With total release from pressure, a fish about to hang up in cover often changes its mind. Even fish that are hung up will often free themselves if you use this tactic.

Today, Dick favors Zebco's Omega CFS series reels. These are closed-face models that also hang below the rod blank like an open-face spinning model. The CFS reels have a trigger-activated casting system, plus many other features including selective anti-reverse, smooth drag, and an over-size line guide that make them an ideal match with Swan's river rods.

To fight fish with these rods and light lines, you set the drag to whisper-light. When a fish stops running and you need to pump it in, you perform the maneuver common to any light tackle: clamping the line against the rod handle. Swan's rods are designed to nearly double over against the pull of the line for which they are designed, without breaking that line. When the fish begins to run again, you release the line you were clamping against the handle so the mechanical drag can take over. The full power of the rod is brought into play by pushing the handle and butt section outward toward the fish and keeping the rod in this position. The blank will describe a curve that Swan and fellow noodlers refer to as the Big C.

Naturally, snag-filled water isn't the place to use such light tackle. You just don't horse a fish on this kind of equipment. Dick and the Michigan noodlers use the gear in rivers with slow to medium currents and gravel bottoms such as the Au Sable near Oscoda, the Platte, the Tippy Dam section of the Manistee, and the Betsie. They are also seeing increased use on New York's Salmon River and some waters in the Northwest.

Drift fishing with bottom-bumping rigs is the technique employed by most steelhead and salmon river fishermen, and it's the method Swan uses with his noodle rods. Imitation or natural eggs will work; so can standard steelhead flies or natural nymphs. With light line, smaller, thin-wire hooks like an Eagle Claw No. 12 and 14 must be used. "There's no chance of straightening these hooks, as a lot of uninitiated anglers think," says Swan. "My light leader would break first." But also, there's no need to really set these light, sharp hooks. The force of the current, plus a steady tightening of line once the fish takes, will sink the barb.

The terminal tackle consists of a three-way swivel. A 3-inch piece of mono hangs from one eye, onto which split shot are pinched. The main line is tied to a second eye, and the leader with lure, bait, or fly comes from the third eye. Leaders are normally about six feet. If Swan is not looking for a record, he'll use the 2 or 4-pound-test line just for the leader, and slightly heavier line (often 8-pound-test) on the spool. If he breaks off,

Dick Swann displays a big silver chinook salmon taken on one of his noodle rods rigged with 2-pound-test line.

as happens with this light mono, just a section of leader or sinker strand will remain in the river. (For record qualification, however, IGFA rules state that the entire line on the spool determines the line class category. It's not hard to understand why spinning enthusiasts disagree with the regulation. A fly angler's equipment qualifies in the various recognized classes with only a 15-inch section of class leader tippet.)

Dick and the noodlers took the tackle and techniques to the West Coast, successfully competing against local steelheaders. As usual, the lightliners had more hookups, just as they do in Michigan water. Compared to heavier gear, the average of landed fish per hookup goes down—at least in rivers. You do have more action, and will probably take more fish at day's end. On the days when the fish are shy, you'll definitely catch more. In lakes, the ratio of hooked fish to landed fish goes up for simple reasons. Because you won't be fishing near cover, there's less chance that the hooked fish will hang up. Besides you can easily follow the fish wherever it runs.

Noodles for Salmon and Trout

Dick's next frontier with the noodles was the Lake Michigan surf. In the spring and fall, salmon and trout move close to shore along the sand beaches and rock jetties of the Great Lakes. During the fall, they seek tributaries to run. In spring, warmer water and baitfish are the attraction. Dick and his pals waded in among the heavy-line anglers along the sand beaches, and had a marvelous time beating them with the noodle rods.

They used the same three-way swivel terminal rigging but, on the leader that held bait and hook, they affixed a tiny marshmallow. The confection acted as a float that held the bait just above bottom when the surf was low and there was no real current to keep it from sinking. They found that the fish liked to eat the marshmallows, too, whether used alone or in combination with other baits. They caught all kinds fish: chinooks, cohos, brookies, splake, rainbows, and even lake trout. The lakers, despite their normal deep water preference, move inshore in fall and even run up a few Lake Michigan rivers.

"Sometimes, when the surf was low, the fishermen using heavier line would be wading far out," Dick remembers. "We'd wade shallow and take fish behind their backs. One evening on Michigan's Upper Peninsula I helped my daughter string five fish. Each time she got a strike, she'd shout and the boys with the heavy lines out in deeper water would turn around and look. You should have seen their faces after awhile. Finally they got the message and waded closer to shore."

Dick and the noodlers proved their point beyond a doubt by setting a number of records for steelhead, brown trout, chinooks, cohos, and Atlantic salmon. It was only natural that they would begin to experiment with the tackle in a trolling situation farther offshore—hence the scenario with captains Swan and Arff clapping and shouting encouragement while the chinook at the end of my 2-pound-test line continued to make for the horizon off Swan's boat. The big fish finally stalled, so I began working on it by pumping line and bending the big graphite noodle into the traditional C, pointing the butt at the fish. The king responded to the pressure, even though it was below the 2-pound breaking strength of the line. The tension nagged and worried the fish, and it finally turned and started in the direction of the continued pressure, toward the boat. And then it stopped. I was unable to get any more line.

Swan started a maneuver used by offshore big-game fishermen, no matter what weight tackle may be involved. He turned the boat and began a slow, wide circle around the fish. At some point, the angle of pull will become just annoying enough so that most fish will again begin yielding to the pressure and you can start pumping line in once again. If the fish sounds, you can relax the pressure and move the boat away so the line angles out rather than down. Then reapply the pressure. Usually, the change in angle is enough to start the fish up. If not, again slack off, turn the boat one hundred and eighty degrees, move off on the new angle, tighten up, and start pumping again fast. That will usually get the fish coming.

In this case, the fish had stalled without sounding. At one point in the wide circle that Dick was making, my salmon started coming again. It made several more fast runs before it was through, and we were able to put the net under it. The fish gleamed like a silvery set of proof coins in the sun. It weighed just under twenty pounds. If this was to be the only fish we took I would not have been convinced of the system, but it was not. Both kings and cohos fell that day, just as had the record-size Skamania steelhead from the Indiana waters of Lake Michigan the summer before.

Trolling with Noodles

Although you can take good fish by surface trolling in the spring and often again in fall, at other times you must run your lures deeper. Using heavy sinkers obviously won't work here. Heavy surges or leaps by a fish against a heavy sinker will only cause the ultralight lines to part. These lines aren't up to the constant strain and fish-fighting surges of a fish against a

Trolling noodles in place in Swann's downrigger holders. Spiral guide arrangement (see text) is visible.

diving planing device, either. It would seem that downriggers are the answer. However, early tests showed that 6-pound-test line was the minimum that stood up to the shock when a fish yanked the line from a standard downrigger release mechanism. To boot, many of the release mechanisms began to quickly fray the 6-pound line, and it was continually necessary to check and cut back the monofilament. Four and 2-pound line seemed hopeless. Then another problem quickly became evident.

Because of its inherent strength, and normally very smooth and strong drag mechanism, Swan wanted to use a levelwind, revolving-spool reel. The placement of guides on a rod designed for a conventional reel is, of course, along the top of the blank. When an ultraflexible rod is bent over while trolling or fighting a fish, the reel and guides stay on top but, as more rod pressure is applied and the blank bends or even twists as it goes over, the line will touch the blank between the guides. When you're using 2 and 4-pound-test line, the resulting abrasion cannot be tolerated.

To solve the latter problem, Swan came up with a guide arrangement that, at first, leaves you shaking your head. Try it once, however, and you'll be sold. The butt guide is placed on top of the blank in conventional fashion. The next guide down the rod is six inches away, but cocked sixty degrees over on the side of the blank. The final guide is placed directly on the underside of the blank. All the guides on the rod tip section are on the downside of the blank, just as they are in a fly or spinning rod. Dick calls it the Swan Twist. Even when his noodle rods are bent over in the classic C configuration, the line remains clear of the blank and runs smoothly through the guides.

To incorporate his guide-twist noodle rods with downriggers, Dick utilizes a do-it-yourself release available from your nearest office supply store. It consists of large paper clips and No. 16 rubber bands. The rubber band is simply looped through itself around the monofilament, then snugged up tightly at the position you want to attach the line to the downrigger cannonball. The paper clip is opened slightly, so one arm sticks out at a small angle. The clip hooks into the eye on the cannonball, and the rubber band just slips over the arm of the paper clip. The downrigger cannonball is lowered as line goes out from the reel.

When a fish strikes, the monofilament—even the light stuff—cuts through the rubber band to release the line. You cannot free the line by snapping the rod up, as with a regular release. Instead, you must raise the cannonball to reach the rubberband. New design releases, such as Cannon's Quick Release with its two soft vinyl pads, may offer potential for the ultralight lines, too.

If you look at most of the boats trolling with downriggers these days, they seem to resemble a porcupine because of the number of rods bristling up like quills. A large number of rods is not recommended when trolling with noodles, however. After a hookup, you cannot simply keep trolling as when using heavier lines. A big chinook can tear fifty to seventy yards of line from your reel very quickly. Even less powerful species will be able to rip off plenty of line when only 2-pound-test is being used. As soon as a hookup occurs on a noodle rod, the boat is thrown into neutral, the other lines are quickly taken in, and the lucky angler gets to enjoy the action unencumbered and without worry that he's going to foul with some other equipment. This is all easier done if only two or three lines are out.

A problem can sometimes develop when other boats are in the area. Occasionally, anglers unfamiliar with the light-line techniques have no idea how far out a fish can run when hooked on the fine monofilament. They may begin cutting between you and your fish. Normally, they can be steered off if you wave at them and use sign language to indicate what is happening. You may encounter a wooden head, but that's rare.

The reels you use must have super-smooth drags with fine adjustment capability at the low end. For his personal fishing, Swan uses Shimano Bantam 500 models. Other good-quality mills are on the market. The

After salmon hit trolled lure from downrigger, Swan plays fish on noodle rod.

drags, of course, must be set extremely light. To get line back you'll need to utilize hand drag, clamp the line to spool and/or blank as earlier described, and the noodle rod must be bent over all the way in order to use all its power.

Although the noodle trolling system can be used with hard-pulling J-plugs with downriggers in 90-foot depths, the method is extremely effective for trolling near the surface—with or without downriggers. A great way to take spooky brown trout is to use the rubber-band release or gentle rubber-pad release on side planer boards to carry the lure away from the boat. And, as earlier suggested, the system offers real potential for small-mouths and largemouths away from snaggy cover.

At this writing, Swan's noodle trolling has accounted for a 23-pound king salmon caught on 2-pound-test, plus an 18-pound steelhead and a 30-pound king on 4-pound-test. Bigger fish will no doubt come.

Noodle-rod Makers

Those who cannot locate these special rods through local dealers should contact the following makers of noodle blanks or finished rods. Availability is subject to change without notice.

Lamiglas, Inc., Box U., Woodland, WA 98674.
Loomis Composites, Inc., Box 907, Woodland, WA 98674.
Gary Loomis, Inc., Box E, Woodland, WA 98674.
Daiwa Corp., 7421 Chapman Ave., Garden Grove, CA 92641.
    This firm has a finished noodle rod in the Regal Strike
    series without the spiral guide arrangement.
Swan's Custom Rods, 3230 Oakland, Clare, MI 48617.
Swan supplies both fiberglass and graphite trolling noodles
    with the spiral guide arrangement.

chapter 15

‖‖‖‖‖‖‖‖‖‖‖‖‖‖‖‖‖‖‖‖‖‖‖‖‖‖‖‖‖‖‖‖‖

Olfaction and Luminescence

". . .There was an old river-keeper on the Stryn in Norway who used to touch his flies with cod-liver oil to mask odors of his fingers. . .I fished with a group of remarkably skilled fly fishermen for steelheads and chinooks in the headwaters of the Sacramento, and their lexicon of tricks included a paste of sardines to dress their flies and kill the odor of their hands. . .the old ghillie who taught me nymph fishing on the Lauterach in Bavaria believed that a particularly selective fish could probably smell his fingers on his flies. His secret was a leader soak box—its thick felt pads saturated in trout slime—for his nymphs."

—ERNEST SCHWEIBERT, from *Trout.*

The quest for the infallible lure has never been abandoned. Today's trend has been to make the best man-made baits even more effective through various enhancers. The first of these are the so-called scent attractants. A variety of such concoctions have been around at least as long as America's traveling medicine men who peddled human health elixirs from their wagons. It would not surprise me to learn if some hard-digging historian has unearthed conclusive evidence that Dame Juliana touted a home-brewed fish aphrodisiac along with her hand-tied flies. I'm willing to bet that, like me, you've slapped down hard-earned bucks for some fail-safe, fish-calling mixture so wildly advertised that P. T. Barnum's work resembles that of a mountain-sequestered monk by comparison. But wait. Although scent potions have the heady aroma of scam about them, some are based upon hard scientific research. The entire concept rests upon the valid hypothesis that, in order to survive, fish rely upon olfaction—the sense of smell—and also upon the sense of taste, which is often inseparable among some species. If you ignore this fact, you could be making a mistake that costs you fish.

The Sense of Smell

Most thinking anglers have always been wary of foreign odors on their lures. But there was heightened interest in the effect of offending odors soon after the classic salmon study back in the middle 1950's in British Columbia. The research isolated the most repelling substance to migrating Pacific salmon. The repellent is an amino acid called L-serine, which is found on the skin of natural salmonid predators—especially sea lions, bears, and man. Biologists rinsing their hands in the water upstream of migrating fish caused the salmon to cease migration or even flee from the area. So powerful is the substance, or so sensitive the olfactory ability of salmonids, that the fish can detect the equivalent of one drop of the L-serine in an Olympic-size swimming pool. Women and children normally exude less L-serine than men, and some men produce low levels of the substance. Some of today's scent attractants attempt to camouflage the effects of L-serine by rendering it less prominent. This is done through the addition of other attracting and neutral amino acids that are highly noticeable to fish. More on that later.

Olfaction affects the entire lifestyle of many fish. It helps them recognize forage, migration routes, and can govern their entire social interaction with members of the same species. The research of Dr. John Todd at the University of Michigan, San Diego State College, and Woods Hole Oceanographic Institute is an example. In one experiment, Dr. Todd placed several small bullheads in a tank. A larger bullhead jumped into the tank from an adjoining aquarium. The big fish began mauling the smaller ones, so that all but two of the little bullheads leaped out and died. The larger fish was removed and the two surviving small fish set up territories at opposite ends of their tank. Some time later, Todd introduced a little water from the tank of the former attacker. The two small fish fled their established territories and hid together. Only when the water from the larger fish's tank had been shut off did the smaller individuals return to their separate territories. Four months later, the smaller fish were still terrified when tank water from the one-time attacker was introduced into their tank. They had not forgotten.

It was discovered in another experiment that scent from a tank in which a large peaceful community of bullheads lived could calm two bullheads that were hostile to one another. Todd refers to the scent from the peaceful tank as a love-in substance. He also showed how, after being beaten in a fight, a once-dominant bullhead's fallen social status could instantly be recognized—through olfaction—by other bullheads.

Dr. Greg Bambenek, a practicing psychologist and anthropologist from Duluth, Minnesota, also happens to be an ardent fisherman. He studied native fishermen in various countries applying various scent substances to the baits they used. He became totally intrigued by the subject and has some salient points on communication through olfaction.

"When you smell," says Bambenek, "you're contacting a substance from another organism or source. Specific shape molecules that make up the scent actually penetrate your olfactory receptor cells like a key fits a lock. The resulting impulse shoots directly like a hot line to your brain. Our other senses are much slower. Even vision. Smell becomes encoded in the brain. It forms the longest term kind of memory. Remember how the odor of something that once made you sick, still can? It's not really the smell, it's the association."

Bambenek eventually devised his own formula, called the Dr. Juice Elixir for his nickname. It camouflages human L-serine via pheromones, and stimulates eating behavior with kairomones.

Pheromones are mainly hormonal substances that are secreted by virtually every living thing. They stimulate behavioral or physiological responses—fear, sex, and anger in individuals of the same species. Humans can't consciously smell them. They make all living organisms react.

Three types of pheromones are in this Juice. There is the pheromone that common baitfish use to keep their schools together. When gamefish feed on forage fish, the minnows give off a fear pheromone. That, too, is included. The third type pheromone is a species-specific sex pheromone. It can cause sexual excitement, attraction, or vicious territorial defense behavior. Even when fish are not in a spawning period, the pheromone will alert them. This last point is especially important when fish are inactive.

While working on his formula, Dr. Bambenek and his wife Pattie took a variety of concoctions to Alaska on their honeymoon. They applied substances to lures while float-camping a river in which chinook salmon were spawning. The kings, like most fish, are reluctant to hit during the actual spawn, but one of the mixtures triggered strikes consistently. Bambenek tried to see how long he could keep a fish interested and began taking a hookless, Juice-annointed lure away from salmon that were attracted to it.

"One fish came up three times," he reports. "I pulled the lure away each time, then suddenly he came up fast, right next to the lure, and started vibrating against it, trying to spawn with it beside my inflatable craft. Despite what his eyesight told him, the fish's nose said, 'do it.' I knew that mixture was a little strong. You want a fish to bite, not try to mate with your lure."

The kairomones in the formula are probably the strangest of all the substances. They are amino acids or organic scents produced by lower organisms, such as plants. They reduce fear, causing a predator to eat or try to.

"We're not at the stage yet to say a kairomone simulates some specific food, "says Bambenek." A fish would probably never eat a plant from which a kairomone is derived. The substances are for attraction. You might compare them to, well, maybe a girl or boyfriend from a long time ago wore a special perfume or cologne. If today you smell it, it probably causes a positive reaction recalling past pleasurable times."

Bambenek fine-tuned his Juice through two lab experiments on various fish species. In one, an anesthetized fish is placed in a pan, the skin over its olfactory organ peeled back so the organ is exposed, and bathed gently in saline solution to prevent it from withering. A tube from an intravenous bag is located over the scent organ. Various test substances are inserted with hypodermic needles into the bag to which the tube is attached. The solution drips onto the fish's olfactory organ. Any response in the fish's brain is registered, because the fish is wired through electrodes to an oscilloscope.

In another experiment, big clay flowerpots line the sides of a large holding tank. Tubes end at the flowerpot holes, and scents come through the tubes. If a particular scent appeals, a test fish in the tank will go to the particular flower pot from which the odor emanates.

With substances narrowed down, Bambenek experimented further in streams and lakes. His early test formulas were aimed at rainbows and steelhead. He would locate fish visually, then place a few drops of formula upstream and observe any reactions by the fish. In the first successful tests, fish that had been in prime holding water would move farther upstream and actually start mouthing objects that floated by, such as little pinecones or grass bits. In holding water farther downstream, where no fish had been, new fish would sometimes appear.

Logic seems to indicate that fish will rely on their sense of smell primarily in low-visibility environments, but discounting olfaction in clear water may be a mistake. A bass or trout chasing a lure in clear water, for example, may follow it and not strike. The scent of plastic, metal, wood, or that of L-serine (for those fish most sensitive to it) on a lure can result in a fish breaking off its pursuit. Perhaps even no odor at all could be off-putting. Because odors are so quickly registered on the brain, fish can make a last-second decision—even after a high-speed chase.

Even the obviously visual situation of a trout rising to a hatching fly can be affected by odor. Insects exude powerful pheromones. For example, pheromones are the bait that attracts male gypsy moths to their demise in traps. An imitation fly with at least some positive odor may encourage a trout to hold it a moment longer, despite its bristly tastelessness—obviously an aid when our reactions are slow.

Then there is the question of a so-called "fright substance," labeled such by German researcher Von Frisch in 1939. Greg Bambenek labels it a fear pheromone. Though Von Frisch established that schooling forage species definitely exude such a substance, there has yet to be confirmation, as of this writing, that predator fish give off such a pheromone. Yet many anglers have learned that releasing a bass, for example, back into a school of feeding fish often causes the remaining school members to cease feeding—or even vacate the area. Of course this could be a response to a released fish acting strangely, darting in terror through the school. Veteran fishermen who are still not so sure do things like cleansing their hands after handling a dehooked fish, and keeping fish to be released in livewells until they've finished working an area. The use of de-scent soaps and pleasant-smelling formula for hand cleaning is becoming increasingly common.

Research has shown that some species of fish have better-developed olfactory organs than others. Salmonids, for example, rely on their sense of smell for migration and preservation against sea lions, bears, and other natural enemies as we've seen earlier. All bottom-dwelling species have highly developed olfactory organs. A bass's sense of smell, like man's, is not as highly-developed when compared to those of other creatures. But bass, just as humans, rely on olfaction in day-to-day living. Bass in the dingiest environments no doubt rely on the sense even more, as would a blind person.

Never tell someone who earns his living by bass fishing that the olfactory ability of a largemouth or smallmouth does not matter all that much. I talked at length with some of the nation's top tournament bass fishermen on the subject, and their comments are intriguing.

The subject of fear pheromones interests Bo Dowden of Natchitoches, Louisiana. Dowden is the winner of the 1981 B.A.S.S. Masters Classic.

"I don't know if it's sound, motion, scent, or taste, but if I'm into bass and catch one that's undersize, I chuck it away as far as I can. If he runs back, he'll lead the whole herd off. Something else, too. After I unhook a fish, I make sure there's not a piece of skin left on any of my hooks. I think there's something there that'll put the others off."

Greg Hines, of Needles, California, is a tournament bass fisherman who took the 1981 U.S. Open. He also does a lot of underwater observation of bass. He believes there's a small percentage of bass that are not caught, but could be by anglers using scent attractants. He does not feel that bass are put off by L-serine on human hands, as are other species.

"Scents aren't really too important in warm water," said Hines. "The fish need to eat, and will, because their metabolism is high. In colder water, scents can help. They're best on slow-moving baits like a jig-'n-eel. Still, the fish are not going to be pulled in from fifteen or twenty feet away because of the odor. You've got to fish in the right places."

Young, up-and-coming bass tournament angler Rick Butler of Ventura, California has done some interesting experiments on scents.

"I've put everything you could imagine on plastic worms to make them smell good to bass," he told me. "I've tried real crushed night crawlers combined with Crisco, witch hazel, and vanilla, for example. Once I tried mackerel oil. It smelled so bad my fishing partner almost left the boat. Then the bees attacked us because of the smell. In my aquarium I tried food with different odors. Are you ready for this? What those bass liked best was bologna."

Butler strongly believes that bass will avoid any man-made odor that indicates danger. He bases this on an incident that, in retrospect, is funny.

"Once, unknown to me, a friend dunked my plastic worm in the boat gas tank while I was grabbing lunch. We'd been catching bass all morning, but after he doctored my worm I fished for two or three hours without a strike. I finally put on a new worm and started getting strikes. That fellow told what he'd done later."

Interestingly, I've met other anglers who have dunked lures in gasoline. They've reported the bass hit the treated lure three to one *over* the clean lures!

Mann's Bait Company has been selling scented worms and scented Jelly Worm Oil for years as a masking trick and confidence builder for anglers. Few fishermen know one of the product's real secrets. Tomm Mann himself volunteered the information.

"We've done a bunch of testing," said Tom. "We've found that these scents first seem to attract bluegills, then silver and gold shiners. These fish seem to get turned on, and the bass then get excited because of it. The scents start a chain reaction. And a bass that grabs a scented worm won't let go fast, either. Now that's getting into taste, but the two are related closely. Anybody who doesn't believe a bass can taste should drop a toad in the water. We've done that in our big tank. The bass will grab the toad and spit it right out again. He'll swallow a bullfrog, though. One more thing—striped bass or striper-white bass hybrids are more affected by odors than largemouths. Man-made odors are offensive to all of them."

Good commercial scent attractants ought to be most effective on fish that are off their feed, such as those in cold water, as Greg Hines maintains. Spawning periods, or times when forage is overly plentiful, are other examples. Even the lordly Atlantic salmon may be susceptible.

Like Pacific salmon, the Atlantic relies on its sense of smell for the final selection of river during the return from the ocean to spawn. Scientists have long speculated how the fish accurately locates its natal stream. Norwegian scientist Hans Hordeng hypothesizes that the final upriver migration of the Atlantic salmon is initiated and directed "by pheromone trails derived from related smolt descending almost continually from their freshwater localities into the sea. Thus, the descending smolt establish population-specific pheromone trails. . .out to the salmon at sea. The maturing salmon respond. . .and start homeward. . .During the final orientation, the smolt pheromones may be supplemented with pheromones drifting from the populations of young (parr). . .and the resident populations themselves may mark the end of the homeward routes."

The year 1985 may go down as the year of the scents in the U.S. tackle industry. A mind-boggling number of sprays, oils, gels, and pastes with supposed fish allure were introduced. In actual use, most of them need to be reapplied regularly to be effective as attractants, except for the simple masking effect of L-serine. For more long-lasting effect, many anglers are putting the attractants on little snips of felt that they hook to their flies or lures. Some manufacturers sell systems incorporating special synthetic and highly absorbent materials that soak up the potions and release them slowly. Small bits of such material are sometimes built into lures, while larger pieces are saturated in the formulas and attached to downrigger cannonballs, to leave an odor trail while trolling. Some of the formulas—the Dr. Juice Elixir and Berkley Strike, for example—can be applied to bare metal lures because of a special coagulant in the mixture. Lures must be dry, however.

Testimonials continue to come in from satisfied customers who have caught more or bigger fish by using attractants. The taking of larger fish seems consistent. Dr. Greg Bambenek feels this is so because large fish have more folds in their olfactory organ, hence are simply more sensitive to smell.

None of these formulas are some kind of miracle drug, guaranteed to take fish every time out. That kind of thing would ruin what sportfishing is all about. We're dealing here with something that should give you an edge—especially when working on inactive or heavily pressured fish. Sometimes, we need all the help we can get.

Light

They called it fire in the water. It can flood the ocean surface in sparkling light. Scientifically, it is known as bioluminescence, caused by the flagellate *Nocticula*. Although the individual organisms may reach just $1/25$ of an inch, their effect when massed is disproportionately greater. It can stop fishing—dead.

When the moon is dark, everything that swims through the fire appears to glow. Fish do. So do fishing lines, leaders, sinkers, snaps, and swivels. All illusion of bait or lure is destroyed. When the fire is present, fishermen usually pick nights of the quarter moon, or twenty-four hours on either side of the full moon on which to fish. The light of the moon somewhat lessens the glowing effect. Yet sometimes, on dark nights when the fire is present and the water is warm, the fish eat. No one knows why.

This is saltwater stuff, you say. How does it relate to trout or bass? Low-level natural light can be a fish attractant, too. It is found in nature as luminescence—the light without fire or heat—which is a velvet-soft glow produced by chemical reaction, friction, or slow discharges of electricity. Lightning bugs create it with the pigment luciferin. Old salts quieted in fear when another form lit up ship masts or yardarms as summer night storms thundered close. It was called St. Elmo's fire, and today is sometimes just as frightening to modern travelers who see the wings of their storm-bound aircraft glow in Elmo's light.

At great depths in the ocean, lantern, headlight, and one form of angler fish have organs or appendages that glow and flicker for communication or attracting prey. A boat that cuts through a dark ocean swell sometimes sparks a sudden flash of light. It's caused by schools of the little sea walnut jellyfish, far more subtle than the *Nocticula* invertebrate that causes fire in the water.

Low-level luminescence can be fascinating to fish. Intense, sudden light flashed on the water can terrify them. As far back as 1859, the Pflueger Company patented phosphorescent lures. Fishermen and tackle makers have been experimenting a long time with phosphorescence, which is luminescence from substances that absorb radiation and continue to glow even after those radiatons have stopped. Glow paints, tape, and built-in phosphorescent finishes are available. Can they really help catch fish?

Divers report that, below forty feet throughout much of Lake Champlain, sunlight quickly fades and all becomes twilight. Keying on their observations, charter captain Bill Lowell began putting phosphorescent tape on the trolling flashers (cowbells) he uses ahead of lures to attract lake trout at 120-foot depths. Lowell is one of the area's more successful lake trout fishermen.

Great Lakes' anglers casting from rock jetties or the surf will not be without glow-tape on their spoons when they fish at night. Chicago captain Dave Arff is an experienced Lake Michigan pro who is in full agreement with the tactic. When trolling, he uses high-vibration plugs like the Tadpolly or Hot 'N Tot in phosphorescent finishes, and puts phosphorescent tape strips on slower vibrating plugs like the Flatfish. The tape also goes on Little Cleo spoons, which are cast and allowed to flutter down. The big chinook salmon can see these lures longer, he insists, and therefore strike them more often. The technique works both from boats or wading the Lake Michigan surf.

Striped bass specialists also feel that phosphorescence helps. Ron Grass of Novato, California, may be the originator of a fly tied with phosphorescent tape, and Jody Kilbourne of Midland, Michigan, ties a white-winged streamer fly with a chenille body that's coated with phosphorescent paint. When fished very slowly, such flies take stripers (and salmon, too) in still waters and slow river sections. The only trouble with phosphorescent items is that they need to be recharged from time to time with a flashlight, lantern, or even electronic photographic strobes.

Back in 1970, the American Cyanamid Company of Wayne, New Jersey, created the chemical Cyalume Lightstick for camping or emergency use. The original was a 6-inch tube of tough plastic with a pale liquid inside it. In the liquid was another small glass vial containing another chemical. You bent the outer plastic tube to break the inner vial, mix the two chemicals, and cause an intense, green light to occur. This chemical luminescence lasted up to twelve hours.

Around 1976, innovative swordfish anglers began using the sticks ahead of their baits as attractors while night fishing. A fishery in south Florida built around the technique boomed for a few years, until commercial fishermen got in on the act. The Lightsticks began to be used successfully on long lines, in gill nets, in crab traps, and by Japanese jig fishermen.

When a smaller, 4-inch Lightstick was introduced by Cyanamid, freshwater anglers became interested. In 1982, Bob Scriver of Lansing, Michigan, came up with a J-Plug look-alike (a lure that has accounted for some excellent catches of steelhead and salmon on the Great Lakes). Scriver's lure had a hollow core, which would hold one of the chemical sticks.

Called the Dandy-Glo, the lure began to catch fish when trolled deep on downriggers, and when trolled shallower at night, dusk, or dawn. Brown trout and lake trout were taken on the plug as well. As anglers experimented, it became evident that the Lightstick was too bright when first activated. In shallow water or in pitch darkness, it seemed to put fish off. Fishermen began activating the sticks a couple of hours before going out, or they used black electrician tape as a mask on the Dandy-Glo to allow just a little light to come through. Fast-trolling the subdued Dandy-Glo in calm water between midnight and 4 A.M. produced trout and salmon best.

Striped-bass fisherman Ron Gardner uses the smaller 4-inch Lightsticks close behind his downrigger cannonballs, with a plug running five or ten feet back where it darts in the edge of the light field. The photosensitive stripers responded, as they did to deep stillfishing using Lightsticks with bait or in combination with jigs.

Black bass anglers were not about to be left out of the developments. Private bass researcher Doug Hannon of Odessa, Florida, felt there had to be some way to use the Lightsticks on largemouths. He came up with a method of utilizing the glowing chemicals to make his soft plastic baits glow. Using a heated length of $1/32$-inch wire, he melted a thin channel down the length of plastic worms. Then he cut open a Lightstick and, using a worm blower or hypodermic syringe, he injected some of the chemical into the channels in the worms. Without the chambers in the soft plastic lures the liquid would spurt out. He created glowing cross-ribs or spot patterns this way, as well as the long stripe down the length of the worms. The lures began to catch bass well at night and in some murky water. According to Hannon, the bass hit the worms out of curiosity. At least that's his theory. He also plans to try injecting the chemicals in the tail section of crayfish and perhaps other natural baits.

My experiments with the method brought success on smallmouths in thirty feet of water, as well. Besides the hot-wire channel, I found that you could inject tiny amounts of the chemicals in the body of soft plastic crayfish lures like Knight's Lit'l Critter. If you inject enough areas, the result will be a lure that glows entirely. Try to inject more than a miniscule amount in any one spot, however, and the liquid will squirt out. The liquid in the Lightsticks is fairly thick so, if you try the injection technique, you should use a large-hole hypodermic needle.

Note that American Cyanamid does not recommend cutting open their sticks. The chemicals are solvents, can sting open cuts or your eyes, and stain clothes and furniture. If you get it on your skin it will continue to glow wildly until you wash it off with water.

Doug Hannon thought that the chemicals might work when injected in hollow bass plugs as well. I followed up on that and drilled a little hole in the side of a red-and-white Cordell spot, then sealed the hole with a little fly-tying beeswax, softened from hand warmth. It was greatly successful on both smallmouth and largemouth bass—especially in a competitive situation when numbers of fish were present. There was no doubt in my mind that the fish could more easily see and track the plug, at greater distances, especially in deep or dingy water.

Even more successful—especially for the big rainbow trout I regularly fish in my home lake—were hollow J-Plugs injected with the Lightstick chemical. I used a clear model that originally had silver foil inside of it. I drilled a little hole in the plug at the rear underside, removed the foil with tweezers, inserted the chemicals, and sealed the hole with wax. I trolled the plugs on downriggers and side-planer boards from the surface to just a little below it.

Now there's a way to achieve the same effect without having to cut open the Lightsticks. American Cyanamid has come out with mini-sticks, first used in Japan inside slim stick bobbers. Its purpose was to act as a signal when a fish hit. The lighted end flipped up on the strike. It was found the glowing bobbers attract microscopic and insect life, which attracts minnows and, in turn, larger fish. The mini sticks are $1\frac{1}{4}$-inch long and $\frac{1}{8}$-inch in diameter. Cyanamid began marketing the mini-sticks under the name Lunker Lights. They have just about the same intensity as the small amount of chemical you would inject in a plug. You can use the Lunker Lights inside lures like the J-Plug. You need to drill a hole large enough to insert the little sticks, then seal the hole over with removable wax or light putty.

After considerable trolling with the plugs so equipped, certain patterns began to emerge. I was catching trout best with the glowing plugs at light turnover periods—at dusk and very early in the morning. They also produced more fish on overcast days or when there was a chop on the water.

The mini-sticks can be inserted into a variety of soft plastic baits and soft, hollow-core vinyl lures. There should be some more experimentation with the Lunker Lights inserted in round and stick-type floats at night. I envision use not only in lakes, but also in river drift-fishing where current allows. Aside from any fish attraction, the chemical luminescence will surely be a big help in keeping visual contact with your float, and whatever offering is below it.

Innovative fishermen will continue to come up with new ways to use the light sticks as well as the rechargeable phosphorescent paints, tapes, and lures. Although excessive fire in the water can put fish off, small directed amounts of gentle luminescence shows consistent promise of producing more fish. Like scents, it's one more area in the world of sportfishing for trout and bass that you simply can't afford to ignore.

Index